The Final Emotional Intelligence Bible:

3 Books in 1 :

*Everything You Should Know About EQ,
Cognitive Behavioral Therapy, and
Psychology 101 to Increase Your Social and
Leadership Skills*

By

Daniel Anderson

Introducing
EMOTIONAL
INTELLIGENCE

MASTERY THE MODERN PSYCHOLOGY TO CONTROL

EMOTIONS, IMPROVE COMMUNICATION AND

BOOST YOUR LEADERSHIP SKILLS

By

Daniel Anderson

TABLE OF CONTENTS

INTRODUCTION

Emotional intelligence has a lot to do with being intelligent, and intelligence is a skill that can be developed upon, man is an emotional being and emotional beings are individuals with feelings, complex feelings as a result of the many happenings that occur on day to day basis can create various issues for humans and how they relate with people, emotional intelligence helps individuals come to grip with this inborn ability that we have been created with and helps us to understand humans around us. Through empathy people can place themselves in the experiences of others and understand how they are feeling. Using skills like self-awareness, self-motivation individuals can improve on their emotional illiteracy and be more aware of themselves, to attain mastery of emotions you would need to take cognizance of your character. Emotional intelligent people are great masters of emotions, they are individuals who are masters at communication, leading teams and learning from mistakes, they are not selfish and through the course of this book we would take time to explain how to achieve emotional intelligence for leaders, at the workplace and at the home how parents can raise emotional children. We would come to understand that lack of adequate emotional intelligence can be a barrier to growth and the attainment of success.

We use our emotions to control how we react to situations and is therefore a major factor in determining our personality, who we are. The number of definitions as to what emotional intelligence really is are, of course, far too many and complex for this short article however, what we can confirm is that there are two constants in all this. Firstly, the concept of what emotions are and secondly, understanding the context of emotions.

Today we can clearly see that being only "book smart" and having a high intelligence quotient or IQ does not guarantee a successful, happy and fulfilled life. There are many people in all parts of the world who are very brilliant academically but are inept at dealing with people and successful at work or in their personal relationships. Academic intelligence is not enough on its own to be successful in life. IQ can help you get a job and earn a living, but it does not show you how to live a life. When it comes to happiness and success in life, emotional intelligence helps you build stronger relationships, succeed at work, and achieve your career and personal goals.

Emotionally intelligent people are able to recognize their own emotional state and the emotional states of others and as a result they connect more easily with people. They therefore communicate better, form stronger relationships, achieve greater success at work, and lead a more fulfilling life. John Gottman was right when he said "In the last decade or so, science has discovered a tremendous amount about the role emotions play in our lives. Researchers have found that even more than IQ, your emotional awareness and abilities to handle feelings will determine your success and happiness in all walks of life, including family relationships."

Our natural state of being, as one with Soul, is a harmonious state of Love, in which the only feelings are of continuous peace and bliss. Therefore if we are feeling any feeling other than peace and bliss, we have got out of balance somewhere. This is due to our conditioned and faulty thinking, which emerges as tolerations, needs and limiting beliefs. Using our Emotional Intelligence equips us to identify the message that Soul is sending us through these feelings, so we can rectify our thinking and thus move always towards Love.

Being Emotionally Intelligent is my ability to consciously comprehend my own emotional States of Being. Being 'Emotional' means that I am aware of the feeling that is my emotional state of being. Being 'Intelligent' means I have a rational knowledge or logical understanding of the situation, occurrence and circumstances that I am currently experiencing. I am Intelligent when I can consciously rationalize what is happening in my reality. I am Emotional when I can feel the awareness of my energetic state of being - my emotional energy.

Emotional Intelligence loses clarity when I confuse 'being emotional' with 'being irrational'. When I am studying negative states of being that cause me to sub-consciously react, I am learning about my own irrational behavior that is without emotional intelligence. I am studying 'irrational intelligence'.

Being emotional is not reacting irrationally; it is being consciously-aware of my emotional state of being. I never react emotionally because with emotional intelligence I am always able to respond intelligently. Negative emotional states of being are irrational because a rationally intelligent person who is emotionally aware (intelligent) would never choose to experience them. Understanding irrational behavior does require emotional intelligence but it is not the definition of Emotional Intelligence. The true test of my Emotional Intelligence is whether I can be Happy & Well as a result of my conscious choice to be so. It is only my emotional ignorance that is depriving me of the happiness and well-being that is my true nature.

Happiness is an emotional feeling. How can a rational man be happy in a state of being disconnected and unemotional? Well-being is an emotional feeling. How can I feel well in a society that medicates physical and mental illness without one iota of emotional intelligence?

Having sympathy for other people doesn't mean anything unless I have defined the compassion that I am feeling. Defining compassion as: "Wanting to relieve the suffering of others", is a rationally intelligent definition of a physical desire not the explanation of an emotional feeling.

It is my lack of emotional intelligence that disconnects me from my true emotional nature. A analytical world has become a world that is devoid of lasting and Happiness, and a world filled with sadness and sickness. We seem to have lost our connection to our true Wealth and our true Health when, as a society, we are divided from our Emotional Intelligence.

Emotional States Of Being

Professional on the study of emotions have claimed that about 90% of emotional information that we feel is transmitted through non verbal means, by tone, gesture and glance and that we are rarely consciously awake of how much we are transmitting or reading from others.

To have to deny, to lie about, to suppress feelings, or to be blind to the feelings of others causes tensions and anxieties that limit us in our ability to connect to and live with others. It is needful that we develop emotional intelligence because the ability to move easily and interact freely in the emotional world is a very important part of what it requires to live an true and happy life on earth.

Emotional 'States of Being' require definition before I can understand them intelligently. When I define an emotional state of being, I give it definition, it becomes a definite emotion, and I become consciously-aware of its existence.

It is my conscious-awareness of the definite nature of my emotions that allows me to be emotionally intelligent.

An 'Emotional' person is aware of their feelings as different emotions.

An 'Emotionally Intelligent' person is a person who is able to consciously define their emotional state of being and create it at will, if and when they so choose. By intelligently defining an emotion, I become both emotionally aware of the feeling and rationally conscious of its definition. I cannot experience a definite emotion unless I am able to define it accurately. In the absence of naming an emotion, it will remain either a positive or a negative experience, dependent on the beliefs that I hold in my sub-conscious.

I have defined emotion (emotional state of being) with an adjective, which is a describing word. Any adjective that describes my feelings or my emotional state of being is an emotion. Without an adjective to describe it and name the expression, an emotion is just a feeling that is really hard to understand. One should not feel that Being emotional is reacting irrationally; it is being mentally-aware of my emotional state of being. I never react emotionally because with emotional intelligence I know how to respond intelligently during situations that call for response. Negative emotional states of being are irrational because a rationally intelligent person who is emotionally conscious (intelligent) would not choose to experience them, they are just not good for you. Understanding irrational behaviour does require emotional intelligence but it is not the definition of Emotional Intelligence.

The Potential Of My Emotional Energy

Emotion is an energetic state of being that I am experiencing. All forms of energy have a force, a magnitude and a potential. Emotions are no different. The potential of any energy is realized when the force and magnitude of that energy unite.

Electrical energy has a force called 'volts', a magnitude called 'amps' and a potential called 'watts'. They are all named after the person who first defined them. Emotional energy is more complicated because not only is its potential divided by force and magnitude but its force is divided by polarity and its magnitude is divided by gender.

The polarity of my emotions is either positive or negative and the gender of my energy is either male or female. (Anger & pride are male whereas meekness & humility are female. However, Impatience and intolerance are usually seen as negative and patience and tolerance as positive).

The degree, to which my emotional energy is unbalanced, by being divided by either polarity or gender or both, determines the intensity of the emotion that I am feeling. The greater is the imbalance the greater is the intensity of the emotional feeling. The intensity of my emotional state of being is the product of both the gender and the polarity of the emotional energy.

Emotional Intelligence requires not only the definition of my emotional state of being but the understanding of its potential for my Life.

Understanding the potential of my emotional energy requires me to be consciously-aware of:

✓ Its force and magnitude

✓ Its gender, polarity and intensity

✓ Its definition or Adjectivity

✓ The sponsoring thought or thoughts that are creating the emotion.

The Ultimate Potential of my Emotional Energy is the Pure Feeling of Love that emanates from my Soul.

Life is an emotional experience.

My Emotional Intelligence requires more than my ability to manage my irrational behavior. It requires the ability to understand my emotional experiences intelligently. The cause of my irrational behavior is my lack of emotional intelligence. I react irrationally with what is sometimes confusingly called an emotional reaction.

I respond with positive emotion once I attain the intelligence and understanding to do so. My symptoms of irrational behavior are created by my lack of rational intelligence. Extreme irrational behavior caused by a lack of rational ability may be diagnosed as a mental illness by a rational person who has no emotional intelligence.

Diagnosing emotional disorder or disease requires emotional intelligence not rational intelligence, which is probably why illness is usually diagnosed as either physical or mental and not emotional. In the absence of emotional intelligence, my life became an unemotional experience as a rationally intelligent man.

In a dualistic world, the more rationally intelligent I become the more contained, disconnected and emotionally unintelligent I am. It is my experience that the more I rationalize my world with tolerance and patience the less I react with the frustration of my anger and intolerance. However, with emotional intelligence I consciously choose to be 'Accepting' instead of tolerant and I choose to be 'Allowing' instead of patient. I no longer choose to be a tolerant patient who is patiently tolerating Life.

I have decided to accept that Life as an emotional experience because I am learning to be emotionally intelligent enough to see it that way.

EMOTIONAL INTELLIGENCE

Emotional intelligence which stands for EI, is the unlearned attribute humans have to detect, assess, and affect their own emotion and the emotions of other people in their immediate environment. This concept of emotional intelligence itself started with Dr. Wayne Payne in the year 1985, but emotional intelligence became popular when the author Daniel Goldman came up with a book on Emotional Intelligence , EI also refers to the an individual's ability to identify and manage one's own emotions, as well as the emotions of others. Though there is some disagreement within the circle of psychologists as to what constitutes true emotional intelligence, it is generally said to include at least three skills: emotional awareness, or the ability to identify and name one's own emotions; the ability to harness those emotions and apply them to tasks like thinking and problem solving; and the ability to manage emotions, which includes both regulating one's own emotions when necessary and cheering up or calming down other people.

Emotional intelligence can also be defined as that in born natural ability to recognize and understand emotions in yourself and others, and your ability to use this knowledge to manage your person, relationships and relationships around you. Emotional intelligence is the "something" in each of us that is a bit abstract. It affects how we manage behavior, how we meander through social complexities, and make individual decisions in one's life so as to achieve positive results in life's endeavors. This ability called emotional intelligence taps into a key element of human behavior that is distinct from your intellect. There is no known connection between IQ and EQ; you simply can't predict EQ based on how smart someone is. Cognitive intelligence, or IQ, is not flexible. Your IQ except in the case of traumatic event such as a brain injury remains the same from birth. You don' t get smarter by learning new facts or information. Intelligence is your ability to learn, and it's the same at age 10 as it is at age 40. EQ, on the other hand, is a flexible skill that can be groomed. While it is true that some people are naturally more emotionally intelligent than others, a high EQ can be improved upon even if you aren't born with it.

There is currently no validated measurement or scale for emotional intelligence as there is for "g," the general intelligence factor, a fact that has led some critics to claim the concept is either a myth or entirely non-existent. Despite this criticism, however, emotional intelligence (or "emotional quotient," as its sometimes known) has wide appeal among the general public, as well as in certain industries. In recent years, some employers have even incorporated "emotional intelligence tests" into their application or interview processes, on the theory that someone high in emotional intelligence would make a better leader or coworker. But while some studies have found a link between emotional intelligence and job performance, others have shown no correlation, and the lack of a scientifically valid scale makes it difficult to truly measure or predict someone's emotional intelligence on the job.

Identifying individuals who have high EQ is usually very easy. They are very self-aware people and they take their time to reflect on their actions and emotions. They recognize what triggers certain emotions and how to handle them even under desperate circumstances. They also know when they may have reached a "boiling point" and need to cool down or take some steam off the situation for a while; they evaluate the situation of things and come up a solution. It is like hitting the pause button on a remote control.

Studies in the early 1990's by John Mayer and Peter Salovey came up with a working model of emotional intelligence that defined it as the capacity to understand and to reason with emotions. In their analysis, Mayer and Salovey, broke emotional intelligence down into four parts:

Self-Awareness: this is the ability and need to understand your own emotions, knowing what those emotions are, and acknowledging those feelings. Self-empathy is the act of giving ourselves empathy, listening to our own feelings and unmet needs with compassion and understanding. This does not make the problems go away, or magically make all our needs met. But it does help us to feel connected and centered within ourselves. It can also be a tool to express ourselves with more honesty. Though it doesn't make problems go away, it makes it easier to endure them. It is that natural ability to know which emotions you are experiencing and the reason why you feel that way. When you understand your emotions, it is easier for you to understand, accept and control your emotions and avoid your feelings from controling you. You also become more confident, and bold as you do not let your emotions get out of control. Being self-aware also enables you to take an sincere stance at yourself, be honest with yourself so you can improve on your strengths and know what your weaknesses are, and work on these areas to achieve better outcomes for yourself and others.

You can start to look at Self-Awareness as setting the starting point for your life. For that reason, it is as an essential starting place from which you build the other important aspects of your life. Although Self-Awareness embraces many things, being concious of your own emotions and feelings should be the first and most vital step to take to becoming Emotionally Intelligent. We undergo many different feelings and emotions on a daily basis. These two words (feelings and emotions) are sometimes used interchangeably, but they have different meanings. If we understand the differences, it can greatly shape us into becoming more self-aware about ourselves.

Self-awareness is the foundational competency of the Emotional Intelligence (EI) model and I have made researches and worked on this topic for more than a decade now. This competency provides a solid base upon which to build and enhance Emotional Intelligence competencies including emotional self-management, emotional self-motivation, and empathy and nurturing relationships. Yet many of us go through our day unaware and very accepting of the emotional roller coaster daily events evoke. Without recognizing where we are expanding our emotional energy, it has now become very hard to progress to developing other EI abilities.

Self-Motivation: this is the ability to remain focused on a goal despite your level of self-doubt and impulsiveness. It means feeling physically along with the other person as though their emotions are contagious. It makes one well-attuned to another's emotional world, which is a plus in any of the wide range of callings. There is a downside attached to emotional empathy that occurs, when people lack the ability to manage their own emotions. This can be seen as psychological exhaustion leading to a burnout as commonly seen in professionals. The purposeful detachment cultivated by those in medical profession is a way to void burnout. But when the detachment leads to indifference, it can seriously hamper the professional care.

Individuals who are self-motivated are always eager to take on difficult tasks and challenges, they are self-assured people and are very energetic internally, they are also very good at raising thier voice towards unpopular opinions, they are decisive and resilient.

Empathy: the ability to tune into the feelings of others and effectively understanding them pretty much the same way as they understand themselves. A type of empathy called Cognitive empathy that is the ability to handle emotions in a mature way that is relevant to the present situation. It means knowing how the other person feels and what they might be thinking. It is very helpful in negotiations or motivating people. It has been found that people who possess good cognitive empathy (also called perspective taking) make good leaders or managers because they are able to move people to give their best efforts. But there can be a downside to this type of empathy. If people, falling within the "Dark Triad" - narcissists, Machiavellians and psychopaths - possess ample ability of cognitive empathy, they can exploit others to the extent of torturing them. Such people have no sympathy for their victims and expertly use their ability to carry out their cruelty.

Empathy is very present in humans to many degrees of extents and, therefore, we are affected by the other person's predicament in a different way. In fact, it is one of the first traits of humans so much so that any individual lacking of this ability is seen as not ok, seen as mentally ill or dangerous. From tests carried out and observation Females most times score higher on standard tests of empathy, social sensitivity, and emotion recognition than do males. Its inherence in humans can be proven by the fact that young children respond to the emotions of family members even from that early age, this is proof that its an innate ability. Besides kids, Some domestic animals have also express their worry, when the family members are in distress. There has been reports of dogs rescuing injured persons from fire or detecting sadness. Some pets would stay around and place their heads in their owners' laps , making sounds, and this shows that even animals have empathy. Besides humans, many other species exhibit presence of empathy to a varying extent. Like dolphins who have rescued people on countless occasions and saved people from shark attacks.

A good case scenario for validating the presence of empathy in animals came from these research. The researchers reported in 1964 in the American Journal of Psychiatry that Rhesus monkeys refused to pull a chain that dispatched food to themselves if doing so gave a shock to a companion.one of the monkies stopped pulling the chain for 12 days after witnessing another monkey receive a shock. These primates were literally starving themselves in order to avoid causing harm to one another. We can express empathy through statements such as, "I can see you not very comfortable with this and it doesnt sit well with you," and "I can see why you are very upset about this issue." We can show empathy through a hug, a pat on the back, body contact, a touch, and even through a "high five to boost morale" when our empathy relates to someone's success. Empathy is not the same emotion as sympathy. Where empathy allows us to vicariously experience and identify with other's feelings, sympathy is a feeling of pity or sorrow for the feelings of others. With empathy we feel with someone else, with sympathy we feel for someone else.

There are many theories concerning the nature versus nurture aspect of empathic development. Are some people born virtuous and some people born evil? Dr. Paul Zak has studied the biological basis of good versus evil behavior over a number of years and has made a very interesting discovery. He found that when people feel for other people, the stress triggers the brain to release a chemical called oxytocin. Likewise, a study at Berkely concluded that a particular variant of the oxytocin receptor gene is associated with the trait of human empathy. In the study, those who had this gene variant were found to have a more empathic nature. Dr.

Zak says that this study demonstrates that some people, about five percent of our population, may have a gene variant that makes them less empathic. In other words, he says, some people are more or less immune to oxytocin.

So there is scientific evidence that the goodness trait is encoded in our genes. But nature is not the only influencing factor. We may be born with the capacity to have empathy, but our ability to apply it, to care and understand, is a learned behavior.

Social psychologists say that empathetic behavior is built from the secure attachment babies develop with their parents or primary caregivers, and by modeling their parents' empathetic behavior towards them and others. Sincere empathetic behavior develops in children whose parents constantly show, teach, and reinforce it. It is a gradual emergence that occurs with the consistency and caring shown to them during the formative years of their social and emotional development. In many cases, but not all, adults who lack empathy have been victims of childhood abuse or neglect.

Those who have had extremely painful childhoods, ones that have involved emotional, sexual, or physical abuse, often lose touch with their own feelings while shutting themselves off from the pain. Their underdeveloped coping skills leave them saddled with distress, whether their own or others, and their lack of ability to experience their own pain prevents them from feeling the pain of others. As adults their elaborately built defense mechanisms block guilt and shame while also blocking their conscience. They live life through fear, threats, punishment, and isolation rather than empathy and kindness.

In many cases the opposite is true-the person over-identifies with others' pain, is overwhelmed by it, and becomes overly empathetic to the point that they absorb the feelings of everyone around them. Their internal pain and suffering is triggered when they see others in pain and suffering, therefore become preoccupied with everyone else's pain and make it their own. I did that for most of my life. Often it was to deflect my own pain but ironically it caused me to suffer more. I had very poor coping skills and my boundaries were out of whack if existent at all. I also modeled the behavior I observed as a child.

I do think that overall, my generation, a generation that relied on human interaction, a generation where families visited relatives and friends every Sunday because there was nothing else to do, is more empathetic than the generations that have followed.

In fact, an eye opening new study presented by University of Michigan researchers at an Association for psychological science annual meeting claims that college students who started school after the year 2000 have empathy levels that are 40% lower than students thirty years prior. The sharpest drop occurred in the last nine years. The study includes data from over 14,000 students.

One reason that this is happening is because students are becoming more self-oriented as their world becomes increasingly more competitive. Some say that social networking is creating a more narcissistic generation. According to lead researchers, it is harder for today's college student to empathize with others because so much of their social interactions are done through a computer or cell phone and not through real life interaction. With their friends online they can pick and choose who they will respond to and who they will tune out. That is more than likely to carry over into real life.

This is also a generation that grew up playing video games. Much of their formative years development has been influenced by input from computer generated images and violent cyber-interactions. There has to be a connection. This may partly explain the numbing of this generation. Another point of view was presented by Christopher Lasch, a renowned and popular American historian, moralist, and social critic, in a book he published in 1979 called, The Culture of Narcissism: American Life in an Age of Diminishing Expectations. Lasch links the prevalence of narcissism in our society to the decline of the family unit, loss of core values, and long-term social disintegration in the twentieth century.

He believed that the liberal, utopian lifestyle of the 60's gave way to a search for personal growth in the 70's. But people were unsuccessful in their attempts to find their selves. So a movement began to build a society that celebrated self-expression, self-esteem, and self-love. That's all well and good, or so it seems, but as a result of the "me" focus, more narcissism was inadvertently created. It all backfired-aggression, materialism, lack of caring for others, and shallow values have been the result.

There are certainly many of us who have not become this way-studies speak for society in general. Today we live with constant internal and external pressures of life. On a daily basis our society faces terrorism, crime, economic crises, widespread job insecurity, war, political corruption. We see the disintegration of morality wherever we look.

As a writer, author, and inspirer I was greatly disturbed by the overwhelming success of a book (I will not promote the name except to say that it has the word "gray" in the title) based on pornography and smut. It astounds me that millions of people have read it. If I were the publisher I would have instantly rejected a manuscript of such low moral content and offensive subject matter. Where has our appreciation for quality literature as a society gone to? And what has happened to our legal system? It has been demonstrated time and time again that the rights of the innocent take a back seat to the rights of the offender. Our laws do very little to control criminals. In fact, it seems as if criminals control the law. If ever an empathy disorder could spur unthinkable violence to erupt in a seemingly normal person, now is the time.

Emotional intelligence is learned through experience, reflection and modeling over a long period of time. Time must be set aside with someone you trust and respect that will allow you to experiment with and practice new behaviors, thoughts and feelings to the point of mastery. The environment needs to be supportive, emotionally engaging and offer time for practice.

If you are really interested in increasing your Self-Awareness, the following steps are necessary:

1. Acknowledge the fact that self-improvement is very vital.

2. Know the kind of person you want to be.

3. Realize your strengths, weakness and limitations as well as your values. Know what you stand for.

4. Find out about what people think of you, get feedback from people - who do people say you are ,

how you are perceived by others can be used to determine the gap between who you want to be and who you are presently.

5. Work with a supportive groups, encouraging people you trust (a coach is ideal) who can guide, teaches you and hold you accountable as you experiment with new thoughts, feelings and behavior in order to build on your strengths.

6. Put them into pracice , try out the new behaviors over time until your ideal self is realized. Increasing the three areas of Self-Awareness is worth the effort. It establishes the foundation upon which to build relationships and handle the challenges in your personal and professional life.

EMOTION AND INTELLIGENCE

Emotions and intelligence are indispensable terms and would be discussed throughout the length of this book. An understanding of these terms is important for an ensuing comprehension of EI (Alston, 2009). The Oxford English Dictionary defined emotion as "any agitation or disturbance of mind, feeling, passion; any vehement or excited mental state". Emotion is a neutral way to look at feelings, on the surface we can call emotions feeling. Among the circle of psychologists the definitions of emotions hardly varies as they all seem to agree. So, although you may feel "repelling" or weird, this is the part where a psychologist tries to detect if an emotion represents sadness, nervousness, irritability, anxiety or anger.

It is very easy to remember the difference between emotions and feelings with this idea: Emotions are the objective state of feelings. Emotions are clear, well-defined, and experienced by all people. Over the year Psychologists have identified several types of emotions that that has been expressed by humans. What they discovered is that you can also have a variety of emotions. A very good example to understanding what I mean by various types of emotions is when you think of mixing various ingredients or condiments together in the kitchen, when you combine flour, milk, vinegar and eggs, and then heat the mixture to make a pie. Now this is how two expressions of emotions can combine together, sometimes it might get a little complicated .Like how annoyance and irritation can combine to create rage if you don't check those emotions. Joy and excitement can lead to optimism. Feelings are the more prejudiced aspects of emotions, feelings can be hard to interprete. Some people are better at identifying their feelings than others are. You may find feelings less clear than emotions. For example, Julia overhears a co-worker telling someone that

Ted just got the job promotion Julia had applied for. She had been so sure that she was next in line for the job. As soon as she hears the news, Julia has a queasy, upset feeling in her stomach. She says she feels bloated, probably from something she ate. Although she believes she's feeling queasy — at least, that's her subjective experience — an outside observer could probably figure out that she really feels a bit traumatized and depressed. Now thats a narraive , another angle to look at it is that sometimes emotions overpower us because we draw them out of proportion we, make it seem bigger than usual. And this is what pessimistic thinkers do. They extend the negative emotion into broad areas of their lives. This is the quintessential "bring the office home" individual. I knew one executive who allowed anger at work to pervade all areas of his life.

Life happens. Events take place that are beyond our control, and some of them can be extremely upsetting and all-consuming. We can't avoid negative situations, nor can we change the behavior or opinions of other people involved. We can only look honestly at our own reactions and try to channel our responses into a positive direction.

Emotional balance is achieved through identifying, feeling and processing our emotional reactions in appropriate and healthy ways.

Here are some strategies to re-shape your reactions and find relief.

1. Briefly summarize the situation. Try to state what's happened as simply and unemotionally as possible, using concise and neutral language. Reducing your problem to its simplest form is a great way of making it seem smaller and more manageable.

For example, your mind may be screaming: "I can't believe she betrayed my trust! Why would she blab something I told her in strict confidence? She promised she wouldn't tell anyone. Now everyone is going to know! I'll never trust her again.

A simpler, calmer description would be: "I shared a secret with a friend who told it to someone else."

Restating the problem succinctly and neutrally takes away a lot of its drama and power. It also makes the situation seem less personal and unique. Lots of people fail to keep secrets and the world keeps turning. You can survive this.

2. Describe your current reaction to your challenge. How do you truly feel at this moment? Don't hold back. Are you angry, fearful, regretful, anxious, overwhelmed, defeated, resentful, or agitated? Get in touch with your true feelings. Acknowledge them; they belong to you and they are real.

3. Create a rating system (numbers, stars, plus signs, exclamation marks, etc.) and evaluate the intensity of your reaction. This is a form of validation and a way to judge where you are along the path of emotional healing.

4. Envision your desired emotional reaction. What's your concept of a healthy and appropriate response? How do you want to handle this situation? What kind of genuine reaction would make you feel like you handled yourself with dignity, fairness and grace?

5. Think about actions you can take to move closer to your desired reaction. For example, you may think you owe someone an apology, even though you might not be ready to make it at this time.

Look at what role you played in creating the current situation. Do you need to change your attitude or perspective? Make the situation less personal or important? Or do you need to simply do nothing until a desirable course of action becomes clearer?

You may need to repeat these steps a number of times before you experience a calmer, more serene response. Keeping a journal may help you gain insight and see progress. Hopefully, with repetition and persistence you will streamline your path towards peace and emotional balance.

CRUSHING STRESS WITH EMOTIONAL INTELLIGENCE

Work stress is as old as work itself and so are the ways we respond. You can just imagine the first cave-clan's leader spending sleepless nights counting stalactites, worried about how he was going to break the news to UG and the other hunters that the decreasing wild beast population meant they were going to have less to eat.

Stress always has, and probably always will, go hand-in-hand with work.

Unfortunately, stress appears to be on the rise. In a study conducted earlier this year at the University of Rochester Medical Center in New York, Dr. Diana Fernandez, MD, found that job stress not only makes workers unhappier but also harms their health. In her study of 2,782 employees at a large manufacturing facility, Fernandez and her team found strong links between job stress and cardiovascular disease, depression, exhaustion, and weight gain. After a tense day of pink slips circulating around the office, many workers told Fernandez's team that they looked forward to going home and "vegging out" in front of the TV. In the American Psychological Association's 2009 Stress in America Survey, 42% of Americans said their stress levels had increased since the previous year. A lukewarm economy and high unemployment suggest that 2011's numbers aren't going to improve.

But what if you could reduce stress without having to wait for the economy to improve? A promising stream of research linking emotional intelligence (EQ) to stress-reduction offers exciting new clues about how to beat stress in spite of economic woes.

A team of Belgian researchers led by Dr. Moira Mikolajczak found that levels of emotional intelligence-a person's ability to understand and manage his or her own emotions and those of other people-determine how effectively people cope with stress. Mikolajczak found that people with high emotional intelligence report better moods, less anxiety, and less worry during times of tension and stress than those with less ability to identify and manage their emotions.

But emotional intelligence is not just about naïve optimism or disguising negative emotions by forcing yourself to put on a happy face. Emotionally intelligent people actually feel less stress. Emotionally intelligent people have improved their ability to engage their emotions and rational thinking simultaneously. This results in a more contained, comfortable reaction to stressful circumstances. As your EQ increases, you actually feel less stress. Without consciously trying to control their reactions to stress, high EQ individuals show fewer physical signs of stress reactions, such as sweaty palms, elevated heart rate, and increased secretion of certain hormones and brain chemicals. When facing a situation that sends most people climbing up the walls, a high-EQ person approaches the stressor with the same calm composure that most people demonstrate only in the most trivial of circumstances.

In other words, emotionally intelligent people not only claim to experience less stress, they also physically and mentally experience less stress.

Why Emotional Intelligence Matters:

The Belgian researcher's uncovered two primary reasons for emotional intelligence limiting stress. First, they found that emotionally intelligent people evaluate their environment differently. In the words of Dr. Mikolajczak, they "are particularly inclined to look for the silver lining, invoke pleasant thoughts or memories in order to counter their current emotional state, think about what steps to take in order to handle the problem, and put it into perspective. In contrast, they seem less likely to catastrophize or to blame themselves for the occurrence of the problem and/or for their incapacity to solve it."

Second, and perhaps most important, people who are good with emotions are more likely to choose a "problem-focused" coping strategy. Each problem we encounter presents us with two choices: address the problem head-on or bury our heads in the sand, hoping that the issue will resolve itself. People who employ a problem-focused coping strategy devote their attention to solving the problem, rather than ignoring it. This adaptive approach to solving problems works to squash the cause of the stress and lessens the amount of stress experienced because the mere act of devising a plan makes you feel more relaxed and in control. People enjoy challenging jobs, crossword puzzles, and Sudoku for the same reason-solving problems is mentally stimulating.

In contrast, less emotionally intelligent people let their fear and anxiety drive them toward a "problem-avoidance" coping strategy, which only prolongs the tension. As you might guess, these two strategies become a self-fulfilling prophecy-confirming the belief that led the individual to think that way in the first place and furthering his or her conviction that the problem is too much to handle. The habit of avoiding problems doesn't make you forget them. Instead, it keeps you wallowing in the negative emotions that accompany a burdensome challenge. The problem itself remains a perpetual source of stress, amplifying the bad feelings that make stress hard to deal with.

In theory, it would seem that you could take a shortcut by skipping the emotional intelligence piece and just learning the adaptive coping strategies. The only problem is that people who aren't good with emotions are also poor at using a problem-focused strategy. Only the emotionally intelligent bunch-who know how to fend off the distractions created by fear, sadness, anger, jealousy, shame, and the like-are able to effectively implement a problem-focused approach.

EQ Training: The Gift That Keeps On Giving:

Fortunately, virtually anyone can develop emotional intelligence with training. The Belgian team proved that emotional intelligence could be significantly improved with only a handful of short training sessions. In a series of four 150-minute trainings spread out over a month, participants significantly increased their ability to identify and manage emotions. The trainings included such basic training elements as short lectures, role-playing, group discussions, reading assignments, and a daily journal entry about one emotional experience.

Most amazing, however, is that the people who received emotional intelligence training not only maintained their new emotional intelligence skills six months after the training ended but also showed a slight improvement in their EQ at the six-month follow-up. We can only imagine how much they would have improved had they received even a brief reminder to practice their emotional intelligence skills every few days.

How To Beat Your Stress:

To start reducing your stress by improving your own emotional intelligence, there are two basic steps.

1. Get an EQ education. The best way to educate yourself is with the help of a reputable, certified emotional intelligence trainer or coach. If you check with your training department, you might already have access to such a professional within your organization.

2. Practice. After you have developed the right foundation of emotional intelligence knowledge, you must practice using it. You can do this with the old-fashioned system of sticky notes on your nightstand and bathroom mirror, or you can get a little more precise with an automated reminder system.

In sum, the research you've just explored means that people-all people-are very capable of eradicating stress with a relatively small amount of emotional intelligence training. A little emotional intelligence training goes a very long way in helping you to reduce stress and handle the obstacles that life inevitable throws your way.

ROLE OF EMPATHY IN LIFE

Empathy plays great role in our life in almost every sphere. The skill of empathy, though we inherit it, can be cultivated, which plays a significant role in making us successful in those spheres. Role of empathy in the life of an individual is actually dependent on its conceptualization by the individual, which varies widely. Nevertheless, empathy acts to reflect what has been perceived and creates a supportive or confirming atmosphere. Empathy is a powerful communication skill that is actually underused by many. It allows one to understand thoughts and resultant feelings created by them in others. Empathy also makes one to respond to other's feelings sympathetically so that they can win their trust, which promotes communication further. Our fear of failure, anger, and frustration suddenly drop away, allowing for a more meaningful dialogue and a deepening of relationships.

Empathy is more than simple sympathy, which makes the individual understand others with compassion and sensitivity. That is why it is plays an important role in the workplace, where many people work together to achieve something of significance. It helps create deep respect for the co-workers, thereby fostering a harmonious atmosphere in the workplace. Similarly, empathy is helpful in our professional life because, besides facilitating communication, it makes us a sympathetic listener to our clients, whereby we are able to understand them better. Because empathy makes us able to communicate effectively and listen empathetically, we stand a better chance of making our personal and social relationships successful. In fact, empathy is capable of nurturing every kind of relationship we enter into or are in. As it is clear that empathy affects our life with far reaching ramifications, we should help our children to develop this inborn trait so that they can become better human beings for themselves and for the world. Since empathy promotes pro-social behavior, it will help our children develop close relationships, maintain friendships and develop better communities. Emotional intelligence has assumed great importance over the past twenty years as an instrument in developing an ability to work with our own and other's emotions. One of the most important components of emotional intelligence skills is empathy.

Undoubtedly, empathy immensely affects our everyday life. This trait will come in handy in situations, where we find ourselves trapped, because it will make us understand other's perspectives. While it's true that we are born with this trait and it's in unnaturally, it happens to be underused by many. As empathy is one of the most important skills to be practiced for success in everyday life, we should encourage our children to cultivate it.

Empathy is an inherent trait in humans but it is present in changeable extent in us. That is why everyone doesn't empathize to others to the same extent and in the same way. Nevertheless, it plays a significant role in our day-to-day life, contributing extensively to our personal, professional and social success.

EMOTIONAL MATURITY AND EMOTIONAL INTELLIGENCE

Emotional maturity moves beyond "intelligence" to a higher state of consciousness, guided by what one senses, feels and intuits, and one's heart.

Five principles underlie emotional maturity:

1 - Every negative emotion we experience right here and right now is actually a childhood reaction applied to a current person, circumstance or event.

2 - Most adult's are 3-4-5-year-olds in adult bodies wearing adult clothes.

3 - No one can make you feel a way you don't want to feel. You hold the power to how you want to feel.

4 - An adult can be emotionally mature and child-like or immature and child-ish.

5 - Mindfulness, focus and presence are the keys to emotional maturity.

First, emotional maturity begins with an exploration of how emotional make-up forms early on in life, based on interactions with our primary caregivers, then with extended family, teachers, friends, clergy, etc. Around seven, our psychological and emotional "programming" is set. Our reactivity (e.g., anger, sadness, fear, shame, hurt, guilt and loneliness, etc.) to people, events and circumstances that triggered us early in life is stored in our cells, and arises when "related" triggers appear later in life.

The emotionally mature adult identifies and experiences emotions without acting out, or stuffing or suppressing them. Some emotionally intelligent, but "immature," adults," knowing about emotions, are often unable to appropriately identify or manage emotions. Rather, they resort to "defended" reactivity, sidestepping their emotions: intellectualizing, explaining, analyzing, disagreeing, attacking, flattering, joking, apologizing, evading, going silent, becoming aloof or suspicious, rejecting, criticizing, judging, etc. These emotionally intelligent, but immature, folks come across as: superior, arrogant, stubborn, defiant, hostile, people-pleasing, wishy-washy, phony, resentful, intolerant, self-pitying or victimized, etc. Not mature behavior. When we explore the nature of our emotions, we move towards a "that was then; this is now" perspective, becoming less triggered by current events and circumstances. We don't "futurize" our past.

Secondly, not exploring the developmental nature of emotions, many aren't aware that childhood emotions play out in "adult" life - that we bring our "family" to our adult interactions - at work, at home, at play and in relationship. Our adult reactivity to people, places, circumstances and events that push our buttons is actually an "unconscious" reminder of childhood people, places, circumstances and events. For the emotionally immature individual their paradigm is "that was then; this is still then." Their past leaks out on to current situations.

Third. When we "work" to understand the nature of our emotions, we "get" that, as a child, we reacted the way we reacted to either feel safe and secure, or to receive acknowledgment, approval and love. The emotionally mature adult is not a child in an adult body, wearing adult clothes and does not react as a child. The emotionally mature adult understands "my emotions are not me, but mine; I'm in control, not my emotions." In this place of non-judgment, we experience an event with greater objectively, optimally with no emotional charge or at least with less emotional charge. Emotional maturity teaches us how to detach from a person, place, and event or circumstance that would normally trigger reactivity. Here, we can remain in a state of equanimity or manageable or aware arousal. In this place, we don't choose to blame a person or thing for "making me feel" a certain way.

Fourth. Our behavior is always vacillating between the ends of two continua: (1) the child-like, emotionally mature adult and (2) the child-ish, emotionally immature adult. What do these look like? The "child-like" qualities of an emotionally-mature adult include: lively, excited, alive, juicy, adventurous, joyful, happy, open etc. The "adult" qualities of an emotionally-mature adult include: nurturing/supportive, firm/fair, helpful, respectful, self-responsible, non-judgmental, heart-felt, honest, sincere, allowing, accepting, focused on well-be-ing; one serves, coaches or mentors. On the other hand, the "child-ish" qualities of an emotionally immature adult include: reactive, acting out, throwing tantrums, fearful, scared, needy, angry, resentful, pushy, bullying, jealous, envious, shut down, quiet, withdrawn, defensive, argumentative and grandiose, etc. The "adult" qualities of an emotionally immature adult include: non-loving, overbearing, micromanaging, controlling, disrespectful, fearful, angry, negative, judgmental, critical, abusive (mentally, emotionally, psychologically, physically), dishonest, insincere, narcissistic and focused on the self and the ego. The question, "How old do I feel right now?" can support one to experience where they are on the continua in any given moment.

Fifth, The most visible and effective outcome of emotional maturity is our ability to be in the moment, in our body and present (non-reactive, non-judgmental). We track our emotions in our body. We don't "do" anything, "fix" anything, or change anything as we witness and observe our emotions rise and fall. Being present to our emotions allows our True Self (not our mind) to drive as our Heart and Soul inform us of "right knowing," "right understanding" and "right action." We have the emotion without "becoming" the emotion. We understand the "trigger" for my reactivity may be "outside" me, but the "cause" of my emotions is within. So, we watch, witness and observe as we're triggered and allow our True Self to support our inner journey and exploration, with curiosity, not efforting or mentally changing our experience. Mindfulness, presence, focus, trust and surrender to our emotional experience bring about whatever is needed in the moment. Our Heart and Soul never call for negativity or reactivity, but a considered, emotionally mature response.

In our never-ending journey of unfolding our infinite potential, emotional maturity can be thought of as a next step in the evolution of our humanity and the opening of greater, conscious awareness to our self and to others.

FUNDAMENTALS OF EMOTIONAL INTELLIGENCE

Those fundamentals include: self-awareness, self-regulation, motivation, empathy and social skills. We can spend our lives accumulating degrees, job experiences and the many certifications that we seem to need more of, but in reality, long lasting success comes from within us. Some call it wisdom. You might argue that wisdom is something that cannot be developed, it must come to us. In some cases that may be true. However, EQ or emotional intelligence can be developed and worked upon. This in turn will help us use our best thinking, and come up with the more reasonable decisions, and this in turn will help us be wiser.

Most of us have various strengths and opportunities when it comes to the building blocks of emotional intelligence. If possible, It is advisable that you take an some tests and find out how you fair compared to others. You may be surprised by the results and discover that you have strengths in areas you might not have suspected. And you may also discover that you have weak points and attributes that are holding you back from professional and personal success. However, even if you don't have the opportunity to take an assessment to learn your particularly strengths and opportunities, it can be helpful to get an understanding of the ingredients of emotional intelligence and get some ideas on how they might be strengthened.

Self-awareness as we defined earlier is the ability to recognize and understand your moods, emotions, and drives as well as understanding their effect on others. You're able to understand your limitations, strengths and emotions and then self-manage. With self-awareness, you can reduce negative leadership traits and express yourself better. You're also more likely to have higher stress tolerance and restraint. You're less likely to lose control and cause workers distress when you're frustrated or dealing with stress and/or change. This means you know how you are feeling and why. It also involves having a sense of your self-worth and your strengths. Suggestions for improving your self-awareness include. Pay serious attention to your behaviors and see if you recognize patterns throughout the day, reflect on the connection between your emotions and your behavior. Write in a journal about your emotional responses to situations that were significant. Share your introspective discoveries with a family member or trusted friend. Make a list of your strengths and areas for improvement. Look at it on a daily basis.

Self-regulation is defined as the ability to control or redirect disruptive impulses and moods and the propensity to suspend judgment and think before acting. This involves keeping your disruptive emotions and impulses in check. It involves taking personal accountability for your actions. And, it is the ability to be comfortable with new ideas, approaches, and ways of doing things. Suggestions to improving your ability to self-regulate include:

Practice self-restraint by listening first, pausing and then responding. When becoming frustrated, identify what brought on that emotion. Create effective responses to stressful situations by finding strategies for altering a negative mood. Discuss ways of dealing with change and stress with family members, friends or a trusted advisor. Focus on events that provide a sense of calm or positive emotions. Motivation as it relates to EQ is defined as a passion to work for reasons that go beyond money or status and a propensity to pursue goals with energy and persistence. This involves a readiness to act on opportunities. It also means that you are persistent in pursuing your goals despite encountering many obstacles. Ways to improve your EQ motivation include the following practices:

Set specific goals with dates for achievement. Clarify why these goals are important to you. Ask yourself not only, "What are my goals?" but also, "Why are they my goals?"

Work with a peer or trusted advisor to create detailed action items to work toward your overall goals. Set aside time to work on your goals each day, even if it is just five minutes at a time. List your goals and post them where you can see them every day.

Empathy is defined as the ability to understand the emotional make up of other people. This is your ability to sense others' feelings and perspectives and taking an active interest in their concerns. It is also the ability to cultivate opportunities through different kinds of people. It helps you anticipate, recognize and meet the needs of others. You can learn to practice more empathy by doing some of the following:

Attempt to understand others before communicating your point of view.

Observe nonverbal behavior to evaluate the negative or positive emotions of others.

Watch interactions of other people that you determine to be empathetic. What can you do to model that behavior?

Break bad interpersonal habits, such as interrupting others. Observe body language for nonverbal messages being expressed. Seek clarification from others when attempting to read emotional responses. Be nonjudgmental in your interactions with others. Social skills are a proficiency in managing relationships and building networks. These skills help you work with others toward shared goals and create group synergy in pursuing collective goals. They help you listen openly and send convincing messages, while negotiating and dissolving disagreements. You can improve your social skills by:

✓ Being aware of the message your body language is communicating.

✓ Asking those you admire to describe their experience when socializing with you.

Remembering people's names. Everyone has a hard time with it. Use memory techniques and be known as the one that remembers! After making a mistake, take accountability quickly and find ways to make amends. Taking notice when emotions are taking over an interaction and then find ways to remove yourself from the situation. Showing a genuine curiosity for others' well-being

EMPATHY VS EMOTIONAL INTELLIGENCE

Empathy is the ability to feel what the other person is feeling. It is to experience their emotions. It is the ability to put yourself in the other person's shoes in a big and meaningful way. Emotional intelligence is the ability to manage your own emotions, as well as the emotions of others. This is a skill that all great communicators possess (more about this tomorrow).Empathy and emotional intelligence work together in sales, enabled by caring, to produce long-lasting relationships. Together they are the foundation of trust.

Empathy in general would mean feeling what the other person is feeling and 'being in the shoes of the other'. Empathy creates emotional link and involvement and could be between lovers, family members, friends, or even strangers. Empathy relates to contentedness and a sense of just knowing what another person is feeling. Some individuals are simply more empathetic than others whereas some individuals could find it hard to relate. Some questions that psychology would deal with are what creates empathy and why are some individuals more empathetic than others.

Empathy or a feeling of contentedness and being in the shoes of others is closely related to intuition as intuition helps in the understanding and recognition of emotions in others. Even if emotions are covert and not manifested, empathy helps in identifying these emotions through intuition. Empathy is thus described as recognizing other people's emotions through intuition and is marked by a feeling of connecting to the other person.

In any leadership situation such as in political leadership and social leadership, it is necessary for leaders to feel certain degree of empathy with the other members of the group as the leaders have to feel connected to the followers to make an impact in their opinions and decisions. Teachers also have to feel empathy with the students as this creates a contentedness without which the teaching experience is meaningless both for the teachers and the students. Empathy is about motivating or influencing the other person by tapping in on his or her emotions. It is easier to influence or change people if you are keenly aware of what they are thinking or feeling as this helps to predict the possible responses. Finally we have understanding of other people only when we are able to predict their responses and empathy adds a predictive quality to the interaction.

Stages Of Empathy

We can say that empathy starts with intuition and ends with prediction, and prediction is when one person is able to foretell the emotional responses of the other. The stages of empathy are thus given as:

1. Intuition

2. Connection

3. Consideration

4. Prediction

5. Motivation

The first stage of intuition involves one person naturally intuitive towards the other as with intuition of the other person's emotions and feelings or thought processes; the next stage of empathy or a feeling of connection is created. The connection between two people naturally leads to a feeling of mutual consideration and the next stage of predicting each other's responses to situation. In some cases empathy could be mutual although in many cases as in a relationship between a therapist and her patient, the empathy could be one sided. After the connection is established and there is a deep sense of consideration for the others feelings, and an understanding as to why the person is feeling in a particular way, one person who empathizes with the other is able to move to the next stage of predicting the emotional responses. Understanding the response patterns in other people is an essential part of connecting and relating to them closely and would definitely suggest the ability of being in the shoes of the other. The last stage of empathy deals with the more directional aspect as in the case of teacher or therapist there is a need to motivate or influence the other person following an empathetic connection. In fact the empathy may have been established to influence the other person to attain some goals or reach some targets. So influencing and motivating the other person is an integral part of empathy and is a tacit goal of empathetic relations.

Apart from the five stages of empathy discussed, empathy could involve subsequent feelings of friendship, love, rapport, admiration, dependence and this would depend on whether the empathy is between a teacher and a student, a therapist and a patient, a leader and his followers or between lovers or friends. From a psychological point of view, empathy would involve fulfilling the safety and security needs of other individuals and also their love and a sense of belonging. Our need for Empathy are thus somewhere in between the love-attachment-belongingness (psychological) needs of individuals and the safety-security needs of individuals and the need for empathy exists in every individual and is manifested in both the forms of giving and receiving empathy.

Individuals fulfill their love and find a sense of belonging, needs created by relating to others and empathy uses love and belongingness to provide safety and security. Thus the purpose of empathy as explained with Maslow's hierarchy of needs theory is to make the other person happy by providing a sense of security and lending support as is the goal of empathy could mean a positive influence of one person on the other. Empathy highly enhances social interaction as it adds elements of familiarity, connectedness and consideration between people and help to instill and maintain human values.

WHY IS EMOTIONAL INTELLIGENCE IMPORTANT?

An emotionally intelligent individual is both highly conscious of his or her own emotional states, even negativity—frustration, sadness, or something more subtle—and able to identify and manage them. These people are also especially tuned in to the emotions others experience. It's easy to see how a sensitivity to emotional signals from within and from the social environment could make one a better friend, parent, leader, or romantic partner. Fortunately, these skills can be honed.

Many people are not completely aware how important emotional intelligence is in their lives. We attempt to read many books and articles about this matter just for the knowledge, but we ignore the fact that if we apply emotional intelligence in our daily life and work, it could lead us to somewhere else that we never expected.

The key skills of emotional intelligence could be learned by anyone, at any time. Imagine if you are able to overcome, control and get over your daily life stress with just being emotionally aware of everything that goes right there around you.

Emotional intelligence could be summarized in the ability to express your emotions and to control them at the same time, understand and interpret to others feelings.

There are four easy steps that can lead you to the emotional intelligence you always wished to have;

The first one is sensing the emotions: you should concentrate and accurately perceive the message someone tries to tell you, this actually involves not only understanding the person's intended words but also watching the non-verbal signs, body language and facial expressions.

The second one is reasoning with emotions: we should use our emotions to promote thinking. Emotions help in prioritizing what we pay attention and react to. This means that emotions play a very big part in guiding our minds to believing things that might or might not happen. We naturally react to things that attract our minds.

The third one is understanding emotions: emotions may carry whole different meanings at many times, some people can express their anger in an indirect way, this can actually be very obvious in the example of the angry boss; he can scream, shout and give you a very hard time just because he has an issue related to your work, or he experienced a bad morning with his wife. We should never get confused in understanding the reasons behind people's reactions and that's why training yourself to have emotional intelligence can help you in this matter.

The fourth and last one is managing emotions (the ability to manage your emotions): Emotions are valuable, and offer a bounty of benefits. Once we're able to process and cope with them effectively, we can then learn a lot about ourselves and our needs. If you feel something, let it out, do not engage yourself in another action hoping you can distract your feelings, this can lead you to many problems.

Managing and controlling your emotions and feelings are very important; it is a step towards reaching the emotional intelligence of knowing how to perfectly understand people around you with the least words and actions they make.

Despite the fact that emotional intelligence lacks the volume of quantitative empirical cognitive research that IQ has, the research in the field of cognitive learning has suggested that emotional intelligence is a key fundamental aspect of learning. According to a report published by the National Center for Clinical Infant Programs, the level of success that a student has learning new material boils down to their individual levels of confidence, self-control, curiosity, their ability to communicate, their cooperativeness, their elatedness and their intentionality. All these traits are aspects of emotional intelligence.

More recently social scientists are beginning to uncover the relationship of emotional intelligence to other organizational psychologies, such as leadership, group performance, individual performance, interpersonal exchange, performance evaluations, and change management. Humans are social beings and as such our level of success when dealing with people is intimately linked with our level of emotional intelligence.

Our Heart and Soul never call for negativity or reactivity, but a considered, emotionally mature response.

In our never-ending journey of unfolding our infinite potential, emotional maturity can be thought of as a next step in the evolution of our humanity and the opening of greater, conscious awareness to our self and to others.

So, some questions for self-reflection are:

Do you ever feel you need to change the way you respond to others?

How do you feel when others challenge or disagree with you?

Do you find yourself feeling fearful, angry or anxious? Do you know why?

How do you respond to others' feedback?

Are you ever taken back by the way you react to others?

Do you ever feel afraid about exploring your emotions? Why?

Do you consider yourself to be emotionally mature? What would others say?

IMPROVING YOUR LEVEL OF EMOTIONAL INTELLIGENCE

Researches and scientists see the intelligence quotient, also known as I.Q., as fixed, meaning that it does not change throughout one's lifetime. E.I. differs greatly from I.Q. in that E.I. can be improved through a combination of life experience, maturity, conscious thought and perseverance. You can improve your level of emotional intelligence by doing the following:

Reflect back to the most recent time you can remember of when you had hurt somebody's feelings when they got close to you and trusted you, study what your reactions were at the time and analyze what you said that inflicted emotional pain on the other person. Try to put yourself in shoes of the other person' and empathize with them, try to feel what they feel like you were in that position. In this drill, you will effectively increase your understanding of empathy thereby increasing your level of emotional intelligence as a result. Rather than you finding fault with others, work on developing a mindset of positive thoughts and try to come up with possible solutions on a given problem. Remember that everyone you deal with is human and as humans we make mistakes.

Also by being human we have the ability to learn from

our mistakes and by creating a positive attitude we can effectively coach other people and ourselves to move forward instead of blaming other people or events for mistakes. Then you should now come to the realization that in order to succeed in this game we call life, it becomes important to have a high level of one to one communication with those the people around you. You are, for the most part, helpless without other people to help you along the way. By better understanding their emotional needs you will be able to communicate with them more effectively and more accurately thus paving the way to your own personal success.

What You Need To Be Emotionally Mature

1. The ability to deal constructively with reality

To deal with reality in a constructive manner, we must face truth, the facts, rather than deny them. Running from problems or hoping they do not exist does not make them go away. Regardless of how unpleasant they may be at times, facing the facts is the first step to dealing with any situation. When people have difficulty facing reality, they resort to all sorts of unhealthy ways to deal with the unpleasant feelings and pain. They try to soothe themselves with alcohol, drugs, or any other way that temporarily masks their reality and pain. There are healthy and constructive ways to cope that lead to greater emotional maturity and growth. It may not be the easiest path to take, but it leads to healing, lasting comfort and hope.

2. The capacity to adapt to change

Change is not always easy. It can turn our world upside down at times and cause a great deal of stress. Whether the change is minor, like having to change our plans for the day, or more significant, such as moving to a new home, changing jobs, getting married or divorced, adapting to change is to make necessary adjustments. Sometimes the most important adjustment is in our attitude. Change can annoy us as it disrupts our routine and expectations, but we can choose to accept it and allow ourselves time to get comfortable with change.

3. A relative freedom from symptoms that are produced by tensions and anxieties

The symptoms produced from tensions and anxieties can include physical distress (headaches, stomach problems, rapid heart rate) and emotional distress (worry, restlessness, panic). Anxiety is a major mental health problem affecting millions of people every day. It negatively affects all levels of people's lives--their mental and physical health, relationships, work. To live free of its destructive symptoms and consequences is to cope with life stress in a healthy manner, learn to relax, release worries, and develop inner peace.

4. The capacity to find more satisfaction in giving than receiving

People who give of themselves--their time, attention, help, finances, or what they are able-- are generally more fulfilled and happy than those who do not. People who are primarily takers are more likely to use others for their own personal gain and are often considered selfish, stingy, and/or greedy. Like the old scrooge, they end up miserable. Givers, on the other hand, want to contribute and make a positive difference in this world. It is healthy to give cheerfully and willingly as it contributes to our sense of purpose and helps us connect with others and our society.

5. The capacity to relate to other people in a consistent manner with mutual satisfaction and helpfulness

Like I always say, life is all about relationships. We relate to others every single day--whether it is a relative, co-worker, neighbor, or stranger, our lives are intertwined with others. Love and respect are two key factors to relating successfully to others. Unlike dysfunctional relationships, healthy relationships are stable and provide deep satisfaction and joy.

6. The capacity to sublimate, to direct one's instinctive hostile energy into creative and constructive outlets

If we were to release all our frustrations and anger on the world, we would have a hostile existence. Instead, we can take that energy and direct it into something good and productive. It has long been said that sports is a great outlet of extra energy. Anything that is positive, constructive and creative can redirect our energies and put them to good use. A basketball player once told me that the court is where all his angry energy was released. He redirected his hostile energy in an acceptable way within specific guidelines and limits. It gave him a constructive outlet and helped him to really enjoy what he was doing without hurting others and/or himself.

7. The capacity to love, Love is the greatest power in the world

There's hardly any exact definition for love, because its that inexplicable beautiful feeling As humans, we are born with the capacity to love. The greatest differences between us are how we communicate our love.

Self-love is not opposed to the love of other people. You cannot really love yourself and do yourself a favor without doing people a favor, and vise versa. ~Karl Menninger

Experience is not what happens to you, it's how you interpret what happens to you. ~Aldous Huxley

Maturity has more to do with what types of experiences you've had, and what you've learned from them, and less to do with how many birthdays you've celebrated. ~unknown

TYPES OF EMOTIONAL INTELLIGENCE

Emotional Intelligence consists of five basic components namely self-awareness, self-regulation, motivation, empathy and social skills. The first three competencies are intra-personal and concern your ability to know and manage yourself. Empathy and social skills are inter-personal competencies and concern your ability to interact and get along with others. The better your intra-personal skills, the easier it becomes to express your inter-personal skills. Mastering these skills will allow you to live a better, happier and more successful and fulfilled life.

Self-awareness is the first component of emotional intelligence. It is the ability to know which emotions you are feeling and why. When you understand your emotions, it is easier for you to acknowledge and control your emotions and prevent your feelings from ruling you. You also become more confident as you do not let your emotions get out of control. Being self-aware also enables you to take an honest look at yourself and better know your strengths and weaknesses, and work on these areas to achieve better outcomes for yourself and others.

Recognizing our own emotions and how they recognize our own thoughts and behavior is what is essential for proper performance in workplace. Knowing our strengths and weakness and developing self-confidence is the prime for success in career.

Self-Regulation is the ability to control your emotions and impulses and choose the emotions that you want to experience instead of being the victim of whatever emotions arise. In self regulation you are a complete master over your emotions and when you are able to manage your emotional state, it becomes easier for you to think before you act and this prevents you from making impulsive and careless decisions. This skill also allows you to transform negative exhausting emotions into more positive and productive ones. Regulating ourselves is an essential component of Emotional intelligence. It is important to manage change that life brings in and for this we require self-regulation. Changes are the one which never change and so regulating ourselves to adapt to the new and different environ is essential.

Motivation :The third component of emotional intelligence is motivation. This is about using your emotions to remain positive, optimistic and persistent rather than negative and pessimistic. When you have a high degree of emotional intelligence you tend to be very motivated, productive and efficient in everything they do. You also use your emotions positively to take the right actions to persist and achieve your goals even in the face of considerable adversity or difficulty. Motivation is the ability to remain optimistic and to keep ourselves going even in case of failures and setbacks is called as motivation. Motivation is that internal power that you find when there is no reason to move foward, its that feeling you have after you have failed that makes you want to keep trying even when it looks stupid. Motivation is the one which makes us move towards our goals and desire. Facing organizational commitments, learning to improve performance, setting up challenging goals and being ready to seize opportunities is the most essential in today's corporate environment. All these can be done only through motivation.

The combination of all these competencies together make up the Emotional Intelligence quotient and possessing these skills are very important to succeed in the highly competitive, fast-moving, hi-tech world.

The corporate industries we have in the world today demands something more than powerful IQ. It sustains and takes hold of any individual with various social and personal competencies that allow them to regulate and manage the emotions of themselves and others around them. This ability to regulate the emotions with respect to the environment is known as Emotional Intelligence

Empathy is the fourth component of emotional intelligence. It is the ability to truly recognize and understand the feelings and point of view of people around you. Empathetic people usually possess the ability to listen effectively and accurately to others and are usually very excellent at managing relationships, improving communication; building trust and relating with others. Empathetic people are people you want to open up to , they have a way of making you talk about deep things you never want to talk about ,they are good listeners and if you are empathetic then it means You're able to understand the needs, wants and feelings of your subordinates and their situational issues. Having empathy, you're more likely to know what motivates workers to be more productive and pleased with their jobs, its like you've studied them and can feel what goes on in their head. You also have more of a team mindset and you , which means you're more open to improving team relationships and environmental issues that affect health and productivity. You can also better recognize desired traits in job candidates.

The fifth component of emotional intelligence are social skills. People with Social skills are the life of a party, emotionally intelligent people have good social skills and are excellent at building and maintaining relationships. When you are highly emotionally intelligent, you no longer focus on your own success first and you always have other's best interests in mind, you are constantly trying to see what you can do for people, what you can contribute. You always promote an environment where people cooperate with each other instead of compete with one another and you always help others develop and grow.

BENEFIT OF EMOTIONAL INTELLIGENCE

Your emotional intelligence (EI) is the ability to control and use your emotions in a constructive and productive manner.Its about making the best use of emotions to your benefit and to the benefit of others. It is very important to leadership and for successful relationships and I would advice anyone planning on taking leadership responsibilities to get trained properly in the use of emotional intelligence. It's your ability to intuitively communicate so effectively that you inspire others while not being derailed by upsetting or extreme circumstances to respond most appropriately as opposed to react in haste. Most times leaders are usually hated by their subordinate because they fail to consider the feelings, they use their powers and authority as superiors to behave irrational towards their staffs and this is because they are not emotionally intelligent, emotional intelligent leaders are loved by the staff because they have a way of correcting their subordinates without ridiculing them. Leaders who are strong in this skill have good emotional self-control, think clearly even when they are experiencing strong emotions, and make decisions using both their heart and their head. This does not mean they don't have sensual feelings. On the other hand they are passionate people just like you and I. However, they understand that a man in passion can sometimes get in the way of their personality, making them tough as a nail and hard to relate to so they need temper their passion immediately.

Along with the general competencies for various job roles, you may want to focus on your company's key competencies and this is where emotional intelligence skills come in again. If your company focuses on great customer service, for example, you may want to focus on customer service-related competencies. Likewise, if your company's progress is centered on fast innovation, this would suggest a greater emphasis on creativity and innovation competencies. Leaders high in emotional intelligence are connected to the people around them. They present as authentic and empathetic, willing to practice expansive thinking, constantly seeking to include and understand rather than exclude and ignore. This means resilient and empowering leadership that isn't afraid of others opinions and doesn't feel the urge to have the final decision or always be proved correct. These leaders are centred and in control of both themselves and the world around them, which inspires confidence and trust, creating an atmosphere where employees energetically collaborate to produce the best possible results for the business.

The question is - who do we think of when we reflect on our own personal experiences of emotionally intelligent leadership? The sad truth is that, for most of us at least, there's a relative paucity of these people in the places we work. The majority of businesses still thinks of emotions and feelings as valueless and reward people not for HOW they get results but WHAT results they deliver. As a result, when we consider our own experiences, we are far more likely to recall distracted and busy leaders that don't have time to listen or who don't really listen even when they're sitting in front of us watching our mouths move.

The good news is emotionally intelligent leaders are not a fictional narrative , they are out there in organizations somewhere; and some companies are even investing and looking to foster and encourage leaders in their organizations. These businesses not exactly doing anything beyond the ordinary but they're simply accepting that there is a better way of doing things. They believe that creating a better place to work is achievable, and that assessing and developing the necessary skills is very much easy and achievable, it's has actually been a tried and tested practice that has been around for years.

These organizations are constantly looking to determine and instil the five components that all emotionally intelligent leaders should have in common; we have discussed these components in previous chapters. They are trying to build leaders who:

1. Understand and read the meaning behind thier own feelings

2. Can effectively express what they feel

3. Can 'Tap into' their feelings and into the emotions of others, especially their subordinates and leaders

4. Manage facts and feelings to yield great results

5. Positively influence their own and the feelings of others

In order to hold effective emotional intelligence you must first be self-aware, we have talked about this component earlier. In a culture focused on quantifiable deliverable, that is making it big with the number of sales, decreased production time, increased cost benefits, etc. Self-reflection isn't a priority. I say make it a priority before it costs you money, your job or valuable relationships.

Why is it important to have emotional intelligence? The first and simplest reason I can give you is that it builds confidence. Self-assurance grows with heightened self-awareness to a life driven by purpose and an ability to execute one's goals for a greater good. Confidence is essential for healthy relationships and communication unhampered by disruptive, self-destructive emotions. So if your behavior in certain situations is predictably ineffective and unfulfilling, improve your emotional intelligence the same way you build other skills, by learning and practicing.

Most of us call it gut feeling, but now psychologists are calling those feelings emotional intelligence or EI. Emotional intelligence is something like your IQ. Your IQ score doesn't tell you how much you know it simply tells you what your capacity to learn and comprehend is. Your EI is a tad trickier to measure and there is a great deal of disagreement on how it should be done. However, scientists can agree that in general, people who have a high EI, meaning they can identify their own emotions and the emotions of others, tend to have certain behaviors. Here's a quick list of some of those behaviors.

1. Adaptability

Developing emotional intelligence allows an individual to understand the emotions or motives of others and as a result they are more willing to adapt to a situation than a person who can only understand what they personally are feeling.

2. Managing emotions in others

As we have mood swings, excessive ego, and emotional breakdown and stress it is best that we keep everything simple. So that we don't flare up and hurt other people, managing emotions is not really about us despite the facts that we have a lot on our plate, its about understanding that the emotions in others is a key leadership trait which allows the person with high EI to influence others. Understanding needs and feelings lends itself to developing courses of action that will fulfill those needs and at the same time accomplish what the leader wants accomplished.

3. Emotional control

Persons who have a high EI understand their own emotions and can analyze them rationally. So when they are faced with frustration or fear or anger, they are less likely to react to them instinctively and are more likely to act in a controlled and informed manner. Emotional control can sometimes be developed with emotional maturity , well there are quite a number of younger individuals who have been able to master emotional control than many adults. Emotional control keeps you in check and discipline you , it takes so much intentional effort to achieve this feat.

4. Less Impulsive

High Emotional Inteligence means bad news for marketers who take opportunity of people's impulse to buy products. People with high EI don't react impulsively but rather look at their feelings and make rational decisions without the interference of overwhelming emotional pull.

5. Strong relationships

Maybe one of the greatest advantages of elevated emotional intelligence is the ability to enter into and sustain strong and fulfilling relationships. Being able to understand and appreciate the emotions of others and not being driven by a "me first" need can result in more satisfying and less conflictive interactions with the people around you.

6. More optimistic face it.

We live in a culture that sees the glass half empty more than we see it half full. High EI develops high self-esteem which in turn gives the person the confidence to see the brighter side even in difficult situations.

7. Better stress management

Precisely because they have more self-esteem, self-confidence and an optimistic viewpoint of life, people with developed EI can handle more stress and pressure than others. Being able to identify stress points not as threats but simply as challenges to be met, changes the nature of the stress to a manageable condition. There are obvious advantages to developing emotional intelligence but there are also arguments over how that can be done. Some say it is simply an innate skill that you are born with. Others say you can improve it through training programs like emotional intelligence workshops. Whatever the answer is, it's obvious that understanding ourselves and the emotions of others has a distinct advantage in communications, relationships and personal behavior.

EMOTIONAL INTELLIGENCE
FOR LEADERS

It is usually easier to identify those who have high EQ. These people are very self-aware and take the time to reflect on their actions and emotions. They recognize what triggers certain emotions and how to handle them even under dire circumstances. They also know when they may have reached a "boiling point" and need to back off from a situation temporarily, review what has happened, and devise a solution. It is like hitting the pause button on a remote control.

In addition, they understand that for one to develop emotionally there are times when they may face criticism from others and they need to see this as an opportunity for growth; in other words it is viewed as a learning lesson. They are also willing to provide feedback to others on their team, but they do it in a manner that is helpful not hurtful. These individuals are also sensitive to others' feelings, so they know when they may have overstepped and need to offer an apology. This does take courage because many would rather avoid a situation versus getting into a conflict with another team member. It is much trickier to figure out those who have low EQ. Some may have excellent technical skills and have been successful in their career so far but when a crisis occurs they fall apart. Others may exhibit chronic emotional distress which includes being negative all the time, inconsistent in their behavior, and/or holds grudges. Unfortunately there is no magic formula or pill for these people to change from low to high EQ.

So what is a leader supposed to do? The first step is to delicately converse with the low EQ person about what is being observed amongst the team members and to collaboratively devise solutions to rectify the situation. It is a good idea to have an objective third person present (human resources, coach, or senior executive) to steer the conversation in a positive manner but also to be a witness to the reactions of the employee. If it is agreed upon that the person needs some assistance, the leader should handle this as quickly as possible. If it gets delayed, the employee could be less trusting of the leader and more problems could occur. If the employee resists taking action, it is then up to the leader to suggest a few alternatives - layoff, reassigning to another department, or suggesting other courses of action outside the workplace i.e. classes or therapy.

EQ is hard to detect during the interview process so leaders should consider different means to identify a candidate's EQ. Reference checks only go so far because the references may be fearful of lawsuits or other means of retaliation. Assessments and testing are helpful but are time-consuming and expensive. Multiple interviews over a period of time are a smart move because the interviewers can see if the candidate demonstrates consistent behavior. Ideally a combination of all of these should ensure that the final candidate has a high EQ.

Leadership involves dealing with people. Some folks are extroverts and some are introverts. The extroverts feel comfortable around social functions and in dealing with groups almost all the time. On the other hand, introverts tend to be shy and to focus more on individual interactions. Yet, being an extrovert is not an indication of emotional intelligence. Introverts can also show emotional intelligence or what has become commonly called as EQ. What exactly is this EQ? It simply means the capacity, skill and ability to manage one's emotions in relation to other people. Have you ever heard of the quote "people won't care about what you know until they know you care"? That is very true. People care less for knowledge than for emotional connection. And if you are able to connect emotionally to more people, you become a more successful salesperson, businessman or a leader.

Adolf Hitler, Winston Churchill and Barack Obama managed to connect emotionally with people and that is why they became very popular in their respective countries. Connecting emotionally is just one side of the coin. The other side is leadership. Emotional intelligence and transformational leadership go together. One of the tenets of transformational leadership is motivation and idealism. When you appeal to the values of people and to what they hold dear, you can easily sway them to your cause and make you popular. When you are able to do that, you can then sell your transformational agenda to them.

This is not an easy path to take. If you fail in engaging people emotionally, you will be exposed as a fraud and you can easily lose your integrity and your ability to influence people. But if you manage to balance them, you will be able to become an effective leader.

How Emotional Intelligence Helps You Become A Flexible Leader

Emotionally intelligent (EQ) leaders are flexible in adapting their leadership style to those they choose to lead. You will influence and engage employees by being socially savvy regarding which leadership style would be the most appropriate with certain personalities and in specific situations.

The Blanchard and Hersey Model of Leadership

As a leadership model, the best known example was developed by Ken Blanchard, the management guru who later became famous for his One Minute Manager series, and Paul Hersey. They created a model of situational leadership in the late 1960s that allows one to analyze the needs of the situation, and then adopt the most appropriate leadership style. The model has two fundamental concepts; leadership style, and development level.

Leadership Styles:

Blanchard and Hersey characterized leadership style in terms of the amount of direction and support that the leader provides to his or her followers. They categorized all leadership styles into four behavior types, which they named S1 to S4:

S1: Directing Leaders define the roles and tasks of the follower, and supervise them closely. Decisions are made by the leader and announced, so communication is largely one-way.

S2: Coaching Leaders still define roles and tasks, but seeks ideas and suggestions from the follower. Decisions remain the prerogative of the leader, but communication is much more two-way.

S3: Supporting Leaders pass day-to-day decisions, such as task allocation and processes, to the follower. The leader facilitates and takes part in decisions, but control is with the follower.

S4: Delegating Leaders are still involved in decisions and problem-solving, but control is with the follower. The follower decides when and how the leader will be involved.

No one style is considered optimal or desired for all leaders to possess. Effective leaders need to be flexible, and must adapt themselves according to the situation. However, each leader tends to have a natural style, and in applying Situational Leadership he/she must know his/her intrinsic style.

Development Levels:

The right leadership style will depend on the person being led - the follower. Blanchard and Hersey extended their model to include the Development Level of the follower. They stated that the chosen style of the leader should be based on the competence and commitment of his/her followers. They categorized the possible development of followers into four levels, which they named D1 to D4:

D1: Low Competence, High Commitment - They generally lack the specific skills required for the job in hand, however, they are eager to learn and willing to take direction.

D2: Some Competence, Low Commitment - They may have some relevant skills, but will not be able to do the job without help. The task or the situation may be new to them.

D3: High Competence, Variable Commitment - They are experienced and capable, but may lack the confidence to go it alone, or the motivation to do it well or quickly.

D4: High Competence, High Commitment - They are experienced at the job, and comfortable with their own ability to do it well. They may even be more skilled than the leader.

Development Levels are also situational. You might be generally skilled, confident and motivated your job, but would still drop into Level D1 when faced with a task requiring skills you do not possess. For example, many managers are D4 when dealing with the day-to-day running of their department, but move to D1 or D2 when dealing with a sensitive employee issue.

Leadership Development Matching:

Blanchard and Hersey indicate that the leadership style (S1 - S4) of the leader must correspond to the development level (D1 - D4) of the follower. In addition, it is the leader who must adapt, not the follower. To get the most of situational leadership, a leader should be trained in how to operate effectively in various leadership styles, and how to determine the development level of others.

What are your ideas and experiences related to situational leadership? You and your company leaders might from working with an executive coach as part of an emotional intelligence-based leadership development program.

Emotional intelligence in work place

Intelligence is the psychological feature or functioning of a human being's mind and it is being measured by IQ (intelligence quotient). But IQ alone is not the only determinant of a person's ability to get used and adapt with the complex situations of life and his work place efficiency. Intelligence based on emotions can be a factor for determining the success of a person at a work place or outside the work environment. Possessing a good IQ can help decide if you get hired, and EQ gets you fired or promoted. These two skills are common traits you'll find in high flying achievers globally and a combination of both determines the professional success. There is a very close linkage between an individual's intrapersonal function and his interpersonal skills. Here are examples called the 3 R's Concept.

1. RECOGNIZE

2. REDIRECT

3. REFLECT

Recognizing one's own feelings and redirecting those feelings (intrapersonal capacity) and reflecting that redirection of feelings in one's behavior for better communication, effectiveness in interactions and exhibiting greater understanding of one's environment. While human beings are able to relate on a more rational and emotional levels, emotions are the center of our energy, they are the power house of our life. An employee's emotional reaction and their work performance the pendulum has now swung towards recognition that employee emotions are unavoidable and they influence their work behavior and outcomes. The notion that emotions influences work performances are not a strange discovery, what is new that we have found a way to linking emotions to efficiency in work performance and its valuable consequences in organizations.

Your organization is made of people, processes, and property. For a long time, "common wisdom" has been that returns come from investing in the latter two. Yet, in the last decades, new research has challenged that assumption and is increasingly proving that a company's people are the differentiating factor.

In fact, for most businesses, products and property yield little competitive advantage. You develop a new process, and in a week your competitor replicates it. You increase efficiency and lower product cost, and next month a better version is being produced more cheaply in another country. You invest in specialized equipment - and so does the guy down the street.

So where can today's businesses find competitive advantage? With a mobile workforce, globalization, and on-demand information, products and property are not enough. Exceptional organizations are investing in their relationships with customers, employees, and leaders - and over the next decades the people side will increasingly become the only meaningful competitive advantage. If emotional intelligence helps build customer and employee loyalty, helps people innovate and perform, helps leaders build value, then these competencies are essential for world-class performance.

Emotional intelligence affects employee performance in multiple avenues. The employee's own EQ, the interaction between the employee, and the emotional tone - or climate - all significantly affect the way employees feel about work, and the effectiveness of the work they do.

Emotionally Attractive Leaders Create Lovable Companies

If you pause to ponder about the best work you've ever delivered, you'll probably realize you didn't do it all for yourself; you did it for that adorable boss or some other endearing leader who has been your hero in all aspects.

Recall the number of times you may have reached home aglow with a feeling of elation, reliving a positive encounter with an upbeat and supportive boss, perhaps savouring a lighter moment with him or a witty remark about your performance. The bounce that you feel, and the eagerness to get back to office to offer your very best, the 'Thank God It's Monday' phenomenon and the Friday Blues; that's the "afterglow" that lingers and gives you renewed energy to be more productive, and to bring your finest talents to work.

Inspiration is at the core of efficiency and employees react and respond best to leaders who exude warmth, and authentically invest time and effort to connect with them.

In today's global market place most powerful way to influence--and lead--is to be lovable.

The leaders control the switch that can alter the intensity of engagement of the employees of their organization. A leader's jaunty disposition allegorically oxygenates the blood of followers - it's a transfusion into the arteries of corporate ecosystem.

Studies indicate that since World War II, the human brain has been changing on the emotional front. The amygdala, which coordinates emotions, has grown 0.5 of one percent-that is "physiologically remarkable."

Emotions are infectious and leaders are the "emotional thermostats" of the groups and organisations they lead. A fine example to consider this would be Military forces. How would an "overwhelmed", "nervous", "irritated", "indecisive" or "inconsistent" commander effect troop morale and vigour? How would he energise and inspire his team to weather all storms and lay down their lives at a single command?

"Indecision," is transmissible." It can become incapacitating and habit-forming in an organization, as people take their cues from the leader's state of mind. We want our leaders to be predictable because there is comfort and safety in consistency. Predictability engenders trust and an impulsive leader elicits anxiety and, in some cases, even fear, both of which negatively affect performance and productivity.

Bosses who are lovable, emotionally attractive and charismatic draw people like a magnet. Their ceaseless energy and eternal optimism, ignites their followers to stretch beyond boundaries and deliver superlative performance. They harbour passion for what they do, and this spills over into their business relationships. They blossom because they love people and people love them. There is an emotional bond between the leader and those led. It is seen that organisations with upbeat, enthusiastic, and cohesive executive team are likely to yield better business results. The study also showed that the longer a company was managed by disjointed executive team that didn't get along well, the poorer its image and market returns.

Among the most admired leaders across the world, the following names have stood out owing to their charisma, ability to build a powerful emotional connection with their followers, and communication that inspired and electrified their audiences.

Winston Churchill, Steve Jobs, Mahatma Gandhi, Nelson Mandela, Jack Welch, Abraham Lincoln, Margaret Thatcher, Ronald Reagan, John F Kenned, Bill Clinton, Napoleon Bonaparte

Those with a strong vision were most admired, but motivational, caring, innovative, persistent and ethical qualities were also held in high regard.

For example, John F. Kennedy personified emotionally attractive leadership even before the concept was popularized. Self-awareness, spirited intelligence, self-will, image discipline, empathy and savvy connection to communication, audiences and relationships made him an adorable public figure.

An inspiring speaker, he related to the masses and connected with them on relevant issues. Genuinely likable, when JFK spoke, audiences wanted to concur with him. His tone, poise and deportment communicated credibility and responsibility. He declared a new re-awakening for America and political Washington... people believed. When he was assassinated, a bit of everyone was extinguished.

For charismatic leadership like his, the right blend of emotional intelligence and magnetic charm causes spectacular upshots. It sets the tone, connection and rapport to energize teams to higher levels of synergy and superior achievement. Organizations that cultivate emotional intelligence at the leadership levels experience high levels of team engagement, support for a wide array of initiatives, and a focus on excellence.

The law of reciprocity states that people will reciprocate emotional experiences. Sometimes they reciprocate in a direct reflection (back at you) and other times they reciprocate in an indirect defection (at the next Customer, a coworker or family member).

Research shows that up to 30% of a company's financial results (as measured by key business performance indicators such as revenue growth, return on sales, efficiency and profitability) are determined by the climate of the organization.

Roughly 50-70% of how employees perceive their organization's climate is attributable to the actions and behaviours of their leader. A leader constructs the ecosystem that determines people's moods at the office and their mood, in turn, affects their productivity and level of engagement.. In an organisation people continuously spread their own moods and are impacted by others' moods. When they work in groups, they literally can catch each others' emotions like viruses, a phenomenon known as emotional contagion.

Because employees pay great attention to their leaders' emotions, leaders can strongly influence the mood, and thus attitudes and performance, of their teams through emotional contagion.

There is significant research showing how emotions influence memory, perception and cognition. These factors influence every aspect of an employee's performance - in fact - what is "performance" other than the combination of thought, feeling and behavior?

The varied moods set off a chain reaction: A cranky and ruthless boss creates a toxic organisation filled with negative dark horses who ignore opportunities; an inspirational, inclusive leader generates acolytes for whom any challenge is surmountable. The final link in the chain is performance: profit or loss.

Good moods fire up good performance. The most effective executives display moods and behaviors that are relevant to the prevailing situation, with a healthy blend of optimism. They not only understand and appreciate how other people are feeling - even if it is blue or overwhelmed; but they also exemplify what it looks like to move ahead with hope and humor." The golden trio here is - 'optimism', 'hope' and 'humor'.

But in today's leadership environment, the stress is ever-present. Therefore if you want to be successful over time while maintaining your equilibrium, you have to develop a new skill... emotional talent." Be emotionally attractive. Your emotional attractiveness is directly proportional to your 'likability factor' and translates into how well you consistently produce "positive emotional experiences" in the lives of others, including your staff, prospects and clients.

A word of caution here - In order to be perceived as upbeat and reliable, the leaders cannot be putting on a game face every day. People are very sensitive and can easily see through strained or fake cheerfulness and inconsistent decisions. Leaders cannot sustain their effectiveness if they cannot sustain themselves.

It is required that an executive ascertains, through reflective analysis, how his emotional leadership drives the moods and actions of the organization, and modifies his conduct correspondingly.

How to elevate your emotional attractiveness quotient:

1. Establish Consistent Friendliness - Friendliness is a communication event. It's important for your people to perceive you as friendly. Over time uniformity in behaviour counts far more than first impressions.

2. Relevance is the extent to which a person is able to connect his or her interests, wants, and needs to

another's "sweet spot." Mutual interests establish a higher level of relevance. You can accomplish more by developing interest in people than you will in trying to get others interested in you.

a. Identify your frequent contact circle

b. Connect with others' interests

c. Connect with others' wants and needs

3. Empathy is the ability to accurately perceive and comprehend another person's internal frame of reference. It is based upon deep listening and the ability to pick up on more than words.

a. Show an interest in how others feel

b. Experience others' feelings

c. Respond to others' feelings

4. Realness is capability to be genuine and true. It is impossible to have a high EAQ without being genuine, true, and authentic. People who are authentic inspire trust and make others feel good about themselves. They have a strong sense of who they and what they value.

With an ever-expanding marketplace and increasing competition, possessing a high EA factor can be the one thing that distinguishes your business organisation from many others in the race, and can spell the difference between success and failure. It is about enhancing relationships at workplace, which will lead to more effective communication, increased cooperation, satisfied employees, and delighted customers and, ultimately, drive success of your teams and organisations.

LEADERSHIP LIFESTYLE TO EMULATE

Many organizations are aware of the value of emotional intelligence to a leader's success, but uncertain about how to apply it. To gain the full benefit of EI in a leadership role, companies needed to better understand how to best grow EI among leaders.

Correlating leadership styles with emotional intelligence strengths makes it easier for organizations to identify different emotional styles among their leaders/managers and as a result place them in roles calling for their strengths. Because emotional intelligence is a skill and it's very easy to learn, companies can provide training and support for leaders who need to modify their leadership style to be more effective.

Leadership styles are often determined by the leader's emotional strengths, often expressed in four or five distinct clusters of emotional strengths: Self-Perception, Self-Expression, Interpersonal, Decision Making and Stress Management.

These 5 clusters also reflect five different leadership styles and much is gained by naming them in more commonly used terms i.e.: The Star, The Coach, The

101

Social Worker, The Engineer, and The Physician makes it easier for everyone to comprehend the differences. The necessary skills among the 5 clusters are the same but the names have changed. A "Star" styled leader, for instance, is likely to call upon his/her self-awareness and self-confidence to lead while a "Physician" style leader is likely to leverage their ability to manage stress and "role with the punches" to manage. A "Coach" styled leader is often engaged in making certain their direct reports understand the rules and strategize for victory, while a "Social Worker" styled leader is always focused on others and attempting to achieve goals through other by better understanding them. Finally, the "Engineer" is all about tasks and problem solving and creating realistic objectives.

Of course, each of these leadership styles is shaped by their understanding and natural abilities but determining the style most needed for the task and finding a leader with the necessary style, has just become a lot easier. Now organizations can ask and scientifically identify the leadership style that matches the needs of the job. For example, what kind of task would likely require a "Star" type leader?

Tasks that require "Star" type leaders are those jobs what have ambitious objectives, requiring a positive attitude and ability to motivate others would be a simple description. What type of leader could best head-up a large public project, for instance? The

"Social Worker" leader might be good fit here since he/she is likely highly skilled at connecting with people and sensitive to the needs of others.

This subject really requires much more space and time than we can give it here, but I am betting that you are beginning to get the picture. The picture of how results can be improved by matching Emotional Leadership Styles with the needs of the job and how many profits can be advanced by doing so.

In organizations the skills needed for SELF can be grouped into self-awareness (emotional awareness, accurate self-assessment, self-confidence) and SELF MANAGEMENT (self-control, transparency, adaptability, achievement, initiative, optimism). Other social awareness skill are social awareness (empathy, organizational awareness) and RELATIONSHIP MANAGEMENT (inspiration, influence, developing others, change catalyst, conflict management, teamwork and collaboration).

In the course of this book we have discussed and talked about self-management, self-awareness and empathy, it would be reasonable that this time we can talk about work place relationship in terms of relationship as a social awareness skill.

Relationship Management

The management of relationship has been a facet of business for as long as business transactions have existed. On the most basic level, Relationship Management is about interaction with customers. From a broader perspective one can consider employees, suppliers and consumers as customers, the employees being the internal customers of the organization. Relationship Management deals with the treatment and management of partnerships, connections, linkages and chains between business entities.

For the purposes of this paper, we view Relationship Management (RM) as a conscious and planned activity. It would be misleading to suggest that there have not been relationships in business or any focus on relationships by companies. However, the thrust of RM, as expounded in recent times, points to a more tactical and strategic approach to focusing on the customer rather than a relentless focus on the competition.

After the economic downturn of the 90s, many companies started to examine the possible benefits to be gained from less negotiation strong-arming, closeness to suppliers and the establishment of constructive relationships with strategic stakeholders. This does not suggest that RM was founded in the US, or has not existed before then; the Japanese had perfected RM and value-concretization into an art form on the basis of social structure and communal creed.

RM itself has not just many types but many levels. The manufacturer has his suppliers and the end users as his customers; the retailer has the manufacturers and the end users as his customers, and manufacturer, the supplier and every organization with a tactical or strategic agenda have internal customers.

Different types of RM have been identified, ranging from the transactional, the collaborative and the formation of alliances, which is also known as partnerships or value-added exchanges. The alliance is a partnership with suppliers that involves a mutual beneficiary arrangement where cost-cutting ventures are jointly addressed by both buyer and seller, the seller being considered an extension of the buyer's organization. The business relationship between Japanese suppliers using JIT is a good example. For example Toyota holds a strong alliance even with its 3rd tier vendors. The result of such partnerships means added value, reduced production and transport costs, a more seamless supply and delivery network, and maintenance of exceptional quality, as per TQM considerations.

Traditionally, companies were preoccupied with rigorous competition, firm-induced and firm-controlled business strategies, focus on short-term profits and strategies and independent decision-making. This transactional existence meant a focus more on the competition than the customer, a concentration on short-term profits rather than long-term strategic gains and likelihood to be blind to opportunities for expansion and change. Today's strategically-minded companies are pre-occupied with partnership with other firms, collaboration and coaction, boundarylessness, joint decision-making and a focus on long term benefits. With today's business climate, one can easily foresee a rapidly changing business environment where manufacturers will have the most fruitful partnerships with every member of the supply chain and the consumers, a scenario where the manufacturer will run a 'virtual factory' with the effective and efficient use of value chain networks unlimited by geographical location or consideration.

RM functions on a strategic, a tactical and an operational level. Businesses that are product-oriented ensure effective performance of their products, in the design, the features and output; the production-oriented business (not to be confused with the product-oriented) believe in mass production at a cheap scale on the notion that the customer uses low-price as a singular consideration; sales-oriented businesses put a lot of stock in advertising, promotions and public relations while the customer-centric enterprise strives to understand its customers preferences and purchasing behavior and models its business activities to suit this. This is considered strategic RM. The operational level deals with automating the customer management process using computer applications and devices across market, sales force and service categories. Tactical RM deals with using the data from customer management computer applications to add value both to the customer and the company.

While it would be immensely useful to run a customer database to keep the organization in sync with full information with its customers, RM especially from a strategic perspective delves deeper than mere software; it deals with a 'pull' strategy, letting the wants and needs of the customer dictate what products and services are offered, rather than the other way round, using a production-oriented strategy to 'push' products and services that the consumers may or may not need, but which does not ultimately satisfy the customer.

Companies generate more revenue when they satisfy - and because of this retain- their customers. It is hereby propounded that the simple economic fact that customer retention is cheaper than customer attraction provides the customer with an intrinsic importance to business performance than anything else.

Relationship management: The final area you need to develop in raising your EQ is that of relationship management. We can look upon this trait in connection with your profession. This is the aspect of your EQ that enables you to succeed in inspiring other people and helping them to reach their full potential. It is also vital in negotiating successfully, resolving conflicts and working with others toward a shared goal. Your success in this final area is directly correlated to your success in the other three areas because management is all about successfully interacting with other people. At the end of the day isn't efficient management all about getting the work done?

LOW EMOTIONAL CAPABILITIES CAN RUIN YOU

Some time ago I observed at the place where I work that employees having low emotional competencies tend to lose their jobs even after being selected from hundreds of applicants who were interviewed. There was this employee joined the organization, during the faculty development programme was called to share her experiences but she refused by saying that she is not prepared, our director took her refusal as her shyness, nervousness to come in front and gave so much motivating examples from his own life and with expressing his disappointment due to her refusal and then again asked her to speak but all in vain because she took that behavior as insult failing to recognize her emotions and emotional responses and those of director's and reacted as a slave of emotions. She could not bear that incidence and never came back.

Emotional intelligence can help explain why employees with strong academic backgrounds or cognitive skills are not always the best team members and leaders. Emotional Intelligence shapes human behavior in diverse realms including workplace, community and schools. On the individual plane, it is found to relate to work performance, our ability to communicate effectively, build meaningful interpersonal relationships, resolve everyday problems, scholastic achievement, and even our potential to make moral decisions. Admitting the possibility of EI to amplify our understanding of how individuals behave and adjust to their social environment, it forms an area of immediate attention to HR managers and practitioners.

Bad emotional experience always takes its toll in terms of thwarted problem-solving ability, innovation, commitment, creativity and productivity. Diversity in appearance, food habits, beliefs, thought patterns, reactions, choices and so on define any and every workplace. Nothing could be easier to handle this except by honoring it. HR people need to ensure that staffers have means to express their varied beliefs and opinions. To encourage and stimulate healthy emotional climate among employees, HR managers should:

1) Promote open communication and honest feedback.

2) Emphasize that speaking about emotion within organization is fine.

3) Specify that loud thinking among team members is okay.

4) Enlighten staffers that it is no sin to admit some of management's ideas may be flawed.

5) Organize standardized training on Emotional Intelligence and competency building.

6) Stress the value of striking emotional bonds with one's allotted task.

7) Highlight the benefits of maintaining informal, cheerful and positive work spaces.

Emotional intelligence is supposed to factor as a crucial recruitment criterion along with other relevant technical skills or business knowledge. It should be considered or should be used for the recruitments of fresh staffs into organsations. In case of promotions and succession planning, EI should figure as a decisive factor, mainly if leadership roles are foreseen. Even while selecting and grooming people with good potential EI should be emphasized. Similarly training and development programs must spotlight EI. Through some emotional release session or team-building exercises, the fact is, today, more and more CEO's are passing on the mantle of responsibility as counselors to their workforce. The biggest imperative before all the leaders and business owners is to make sure that negative emotions do not end up creating negative spaces and negative consequences within organizations. Unleashing a culture of positivity and openness holds the key to effective emotion management in any company.

EI FOR THE SALESMAN

EQ enables you to maximize your own sales potential by firstly understanding yourself and then understanding how other people are made up - enabling you to communicate in a way that they would like, rather than from your point of view.

Emotional Intelligence is known as EQ which for the dyslexic people out there (of which I am one) does cause some confusion but highlights the recognition that EQ and IQ are similar; one is a measure of intelligence and the other a measure of the emotions.

Emotional Intelligence is more important than IQ.

Research shows that EQ in a commercial environment may actually be significantly more important than information processing abilities and technical expertise combined. In fact, some studies indicate that EQ is more than twice as important as standard IQ abilities. Furthermore, evidence increasingly shows that the higher one goes in an organization, the more important EQ can be. For those in leadership positions, Emotional Intelligence skills are believed to account for close to 90 percent of what distinguishes outstanding leaders from those judged as average. IQ gets you hired, but EQ gets you promoted.

So what makes a great sales person and can EQ help?

I am sure you have heard many times people referring to someone as 'a natural'. Or that someone can 'sell fridges to Eskimos'. These sales people have great people skills or EQ; they are in tune with peoples' emotions, body language and can read people. It's a gift. Like playing great golf.

I can remember when I was working in presales on an account. When we finished the presentation the sales guy said to me:

"That went well, don't you think?"

Went well!?! It was terrible, people were looking at their watches, there were no questions, and we really had not understood the client's issues as we spent most of the time telling them how great we were. I could not understand how he could have come away from the same presentation with such a different point of view. We were clearly in trouble, and needed to do some serious rethinking if we were going to win the account.

The difference between the sales guy and me was in gauging how the pitch went. He had not tuned in to the unspoken signals that the people in the room were giving out.

Almost everyone at a pitch will be polite and tell you the meeting was a positive one, and that they can see good things ahead, but is this verbal reassurance backed up by the other signals they give out? If you can't pick up on these signals - you won't win many accounts, and sales will be a short career.

Emotional Intelligence Decreases Workplace Stress

Social Responsibility

At work, as in relationships, you have certain choices you can make. You can act like a mature, thoughtful, empathic, and responsible person or you can indulge what Freud called in his personality theory the id. This nasty little piece of who we are was described by Freud as blind, instinctual, irrational strivings. If you give in to your id responses, you will show very little social responsibility and you will become an aggravating and difficult colleague. Being prepared to give and take, to understand the other person's point of view, to maintain perspective and keep a larger view, and be generous in your relationships with others will increase harmony and decrease workplace stress for you and your colleagues.

Interpersonal Relationships

It's not unrealistic to say that there two types of people in this world - the givers and the takers. When I'm involved in marriage counseling I do a quick assessment to see which end of the spectrum is the chief personal style of each partner. Obviously, if you have two takers and no compromise you will have a marital battleground where each partner slugs away to get as much they can from the other. If you have a giver and taker then you will find one person whose life opportunities are sacrificed to the selfish interests of the other. When you have two givers, you'll probably have a comfortable, generous, caring, reciprocal sharing relationship - you know you are on a winner. In many ways, you can see the same system operating in the workplace with some people fighting tooth and nail to win at every opportunity. Developing collaborative teams requires people to be sensitive and committed to building positive, respectful, sharing relationships. When these relationships are the dominant interpersonal characteristics of work teams everyone's workplace stress is reduced.

Stress Tolerance

Everyone has a different capacity to deal with stress and anxiety. Some people have, as they say, a short fuse and are unable to tolerate even the smallest amount of stress. This is a pain and misery to everyone around them who has to put up with their limited capacity to manage stress. We can improve our capacity to deal proactively and effectively with stress; we can increase our stress tolerance mechanisms. This requires us to be mature and thoughtful and not indulge ourselves in juvenile expressions of frustration and impatience.

Impulse Control

One of my research areas is ADHD and a key characteristic of some people with ADHD is a diminished capacity for impulse control and self-regulatory management. Unfortunately, there are too many people in the workplace who show a reckless disregard for even a small amount of impulse control. They seem to believe that they have an incontestable right to vent their emotional eruptions whenever they feel like it and without regard to others. The converse of this is the responsible person who doesn't elevate other people's stress levels but carefully and effectively deals with the pressures and stress that they are experiencing.

This is probably a little too technical and I certainly have glossed over some of the complexities of each of these personal styles but these are complex matters. I could have given a simple tip checklist to reduce workplace stress based on emotional intelligence but this wouldn't be fair to either the interested reader of this fascinating area of personality and cognitive theory. My message is fairly simple - if you want to manage personal stress and reduce workplace stress you have a responsibility to behave in a mature, emotionally intelligent way. Of course I know the response most people would make - I'm not the problem, it's my colleague who has very low emotional intelligence and creates all the stress in this organization. Well, let's begin as they say - physician heals thyself. Then, after ensuring that you are OK, work to develop behaviors that reflect emotionally intelligent groups. I agree with the Harvard research that highly skilled work teams do reflect high group emotional intelligence and are much more productive. I'm also certain that people lucky enough be working in groups with high emotional intelligence and strong interpersonal responsibility have much lower personal stress levels and cope much more effectively with workplace stress.

Some real life examples of the benefit of developing emotional intelligence in the workplace include:

1. Greater sales

A study of over 40 Fortune 500 companies revealed that sales people with high emotional intelligence out performed those with medium to low EI by 50%.

2. Greater productivity

That same study revealed that technical programmers who were measured in the top 10% of the emotional intelligence competencies were cranking out new software three times faster than those with lower measurements. Even more astounding, a Dallas based company who underwent measuring its entire staff determined that employees with a high EI were 20 times more productive than those with a lower score.

3. Stability of staff

Another Fortune 500 had been using personality assessment for years in an attempt to slow down turn over in its high turnover sales force with little success. By implementing EI assessments, and including EI topics like stress management, self-awareness and social skills, they were able to stop the brain drain and increase retention by 67%. The firm calculated it saved over $30 million by reducing recruiting and training costs and increasing sales through retention.

4. Worker satisfaction

A Midwest community bank was forced to cut staff by 30% due to the tough economic times we have experienced recently. The remaining staff was evaluated for their emotional intelligence which resulted in certain changes in organizational structure. People were assigned positions where there EI was best suited for the task. The result is the bank now produces more with fewer people because the fewer people are now better suited for their positions and find them more fulfilling.

5. Improved risk management

Two studies, one for retail operations and one involving the construction industry determined that there was a correlation between low emotional intelligence and theft or shrinkage. In addition, persons with a low emotional intelligence score were more likely to have accidents on the job.

6. Amazing customer service

A luxury car dealership whose entizre marketing plan was built on customer experience and customer service was expanding and wanted to make sure they hired the best customer oriented employees to staff the new facility. The dealership utilized an EI assessment test and EI interviewing techniques that were designed to uncover a high level of empathy in candidates. This process was used to select everyone from the GM down to the valet. One year after opening, the new dealership was rated in the top 10% of the auto companies 200 plus dealers for both sales and customer satisfaction.

7. Better organizational communication

A Towers Watson study of both U.S. and Canadian firms disclosed that companies who do a better job of communicating with their employees outperform those who do not financially. On average a company with an exceptional communications program delivered a 47% greater return to shareholders than the least communicative firms.

Could your organization benefit from assessing your staff's emotional intelligence? Can you see how including EI in training and personal development programs can help the bottom line? As a professional, you owe it to yourself to at least investigate the possibilities.

8. When a team is created it will create an environment of social interdependence and that can be a good thing or bad depending on how it is managed. If the team leader explains that the group will focus on team goals and requires the input of all team members to be successful, the result is a greater effort to collaborate. However if the team is set up as competitors ie "the first one to sell 100 widgets gets a big bonus' then you have a team that consists of individuals with individual goals.

9. EI and team work

Positive and effective relationships between team members have been demonstrated to be the superior emotional setting to drive results. Members who share a bond both professionally and personally will work harder to achieve success for those for the group than a team where those relationships have not been developed. Developing emotional intelligence through exercises and training can greatly improve the odds of effective team performance.

If you are a team manager you really set the tone. If you want the most out of your team, work to set an environment that develops the relationships not tears them down through competition

12 ELEMENTS OF EMOTIONAL INTELLIGENCE

Intellect can be measured by standardized IQ tests but there is no actual measure of the "EQ," or Emotional Quotient. Even without a test, it's obvious when someone has a high IQ and it's just as obvious when someone has a high EQ. Rather than try to measure it, though, it's more useful to look at the various elements that go into emotional intelligence.

While the IQ remains stable over a person's lifetime, the EQ can be developed. Acquiring and practicing the following elements will enable you to boost your EQ.

The first element of emotional intelligence is empathy. The ability to understand what other people are feeling will make you more sensitive and aware and will result in more meaningful relationships.

The second element is the recognition that your actions have consequences. This understanding will enable you to make conscious choices in your life and to avoid unnecessary difficulties.

Third on the list is good judgment. The gift of making well-thought-out decisions and seeing people for who they really are will maximize the possibilities of success in all areas of your life.

Number four is personal responsibility. When you hold yourself accountable and don't blame anyone else for your mistakes or misfortunes, you are empowered to change things for the better. Other people respect you, because you own up to your part in your relationships.

The fifth element is insight. The ability to see yourself clearly and to understand your own motivations allows for the possibility of personal growth. Insight into others allows you to have a greater impact in your relationships.

Element number six is mental flexibility. Being able to change your mind or to see things from different points of view makes it possible for you to navigate all sorts of relationships and to succeed where other, more rigid thinkers would fail.

The seventh element is compassion. Being honest with yourself can be painful but with a kind and gentle attitude, it's much easier. This type of compassion facilitates personal transformation, while compassion toward others supports deeper, more loving connections.

The eighth element is integrity. Following through on commitments and keeping your promises creates much good-will in personal and professional relationships and promotes success in both arenas.

Ninth on the list is impulse control. Thinking before speaking or acting gives you a chance to make deliberate, even sophisticated choices about how you present yourself to others. Not acting out of primitive impulses, urges or emotions avoids social embarrassment.

The tenth element is the ability to defer gratification. It's one thing to want something but the ability to put off having it is empowering. Mastery of your needs allows you to to prioritize around life goals.

Number eleven on the list is perseverance. Sticking with something, especially when it's challenging, allows you to see it through to completion and demonstrates to others that you are dependable and potentially a high achiever.

The twelfth and final element is courage. Emotional courage (as opposed to the physical variety) is the ability to do the right thing, see the truth, open your heart and trust yourself and others enough to be vulnerable, even if all this is frightening. This causes others to hold you in high regard.

All these elements combine within you to make up your emotional intelligence. With a high EQ, even a simple person is at an advantage in life. Without it, even someone with the most brilliant intellect is at a disadvantage.

EMOTIONAL INTELLIGENCE IN THE HOME: RAISING EMOTIONALLY INTELLIGENT CHILDREN

Parents need to be emotionally intelligent to have any influence on teens which will allow them to become socially conscious while remaining stable and flexible in their emotions.

When a parent interacts with a child, especially a teenager, certain stress levels are brought in. The parent needs to keep this stress under control as this can be easily perceived by the teenager. This stress could lead to the child finding interaction constantly irksome and could cause the child to avoid the situation where he has to talk to people, basically this is why certain kids are extremely shy and avoid social life. Accept the fact that as a parent you are also a human and have your own needs of time and space. Let the teenager know this firmly enough and it is almost sure that the teen will accept the fact and live with it. Be consistent in all your dealings with their problems and even if they find your decisions irksome, they will still respect it for the constancy that you show.

Let not any feeling of guilt come into any dealings with your teenager. Children are always quick to spot such feelings and more than likely to take advantage of it. If

125

you are feeling guilty in any way, better to correct the situation that has caused this guilt. Show your children the respect that his fledgling and developing personality has come to expect. Listen to their problems and the suggestions that they have and never lay down the law. Explain your situation in an adult manner. Teenagers will respond when you put the onus of understanding on them.

Emotional resilience learned early in life assists in recovering from misfortunes and disappointments, thus fostering emotional health. Teaching your child to be emotionally resilient will help him/her be in control and build confidence to work through challenging situations effectively. Becoming emotionally resilient in childhood will provide a basic foundation for your child's emotional health in adolescence and adulthood. Emotions shape your child's interactions with others and affect his or her behaviors resulting from those interactions. In order to avoid conflict, or address situations adequately when it arises, your child should learn to understand his or her feelings, be able to identify them, and regulate them. It is important to teach children there is a whole gamut of emotions that can be expressed in various ways. However, knowing how to express them in a meaningful way will help your child in solving social conflicts and maintaining relationships. One way of promoting development of emotional competence is to help your child develop vocabulary that expresses feelings. Parents can also assist their children in recognizing various emotions and teaching them that emotions can be changed by their thinking.

Emotions are driven by behaviors. However, children must learn that emotions should not take control over their actions. It is crucial for children to know that expressing feelings helps in preventing and resolving problems. They need to be taught that bottled-up feelings lead to misunderstandings, anxiety, anger, and depression.

When your child does not express emotions, he or she is more likely to experience angry outbursts that might come from being sad, embarrassed, or frustrated. Perhaps, your child feels guilty about something he or she did, is afraid, or feels helpless and chooses to express those negative feelings of emotional stress with angry outbursts. This inability to deal with stress in a constructive way most of the time stems from the lack of understanding one's own emotions, emotions of others, and lacking the ability to express feelings effectively.

Signs of Emotional Fragility

✓ Regression of behaviors

✓ Withdrawal

✓   Excessive clinginess

✓   Bedwetting

✓   Nightmares

✓   Aggression

One of the most important things a parent can do to foster a child's healthy emotional development is to promote positive family communication. That includes positive reinforcement, which is praising your child for positive behaviors, giving encouragement, and avoidance of negative criticism when expected outcomes are not achieved. Also, providing consistency is extremely important for a child's emotional health, as it aids in avoiding ambiguity and uncertainty. If a child knows what's expected of him or her, they will most likely comply, thus avoiding frustration, anger, and possibly humiliation.

Younger children might be more open and willing to express their feelings. In adolescence, family communication might become more challenging as the teen tries to suppress their feelings in an attempt to resolve them alone. Parenting teenagers requires patience and the ability to be supportive. Frequently, conversation with your teen at home might be extremely difficult. However, your teen may try to open up while riding with you in a car where there is no eye contact, thus the confrontation seems to be less intimidating. Building a sound foundation of emotional resilience in childhood will help your adolescent achieve emotional health. Should getting through to your child become impossible, or he or she become withdrawn and exhibits signs of emotional instability, don't be afraid to seek help.

UNDERSTANDING THE EMOTIONS OF OTHERS

As hard as you may try to understand other people's situation and suffering, you'll not find it easy to relate with unless you go through the same circumstance. You will find it hard to understand their needs but if you are sensitive enough to feel what they feel, I am sure there is no problem expressing your empathy rather than your sympathy. When you put yourself on other people's shoes, you also feel their emotions like being angry, sad, hurt and left out. The ability to be able to predict how other people might feel is a part of emotional intelligence (EQ), a skill we can all improve on with practice. When we understand how other people are likely to react, it can guide our interactions and dealings with them.

By nature, people are extremely self-centered, always thinking about themselves alone and everyone tries to look at a situation from their own perspective, which is a perspective that reflects from the cumulative experiences of their lives, they hardly empathize any situation and try to look at it from the other side. Sometimes we just fail to comprehend the situation because we make decisions quicker than we thought. Our peripheral vision is blurred due to our easy to judge behavior. When we understand other people's feelings, it actually requires a threshold level of empathy to even be aware of what others feel. Most of us are not able to understand other people's feelings. We are too preoccupied with our own shortcomings that we failed to notice that there are still other beings out there who suffered more than we've been through. Though life is a matter of choice; our willingness to listen and understand others predicament can help boosts their morale. This is easier said than done. In reality, we are quick to make assumptions without digging deeper what makes them act or do such foolish actions that made them suffer than satisfied. I can understand that it is really difficult to feel what other people feel because some people are not willing to listen. We just need to regard people not on what they do but what their situation is because when it comes to understanding others, we seldom use our heart. Most often than not, we use our mouth to speak harsh words to others rather than let our emotions speak the truth.

We are more thoughtful when we listen with our hearts than our ears. We need to learn how to accept our mistakes before we can understand the mistakes of others. Most sensible people understand what they do. But it does not mean that they are mean. It just happened that they focused mostly on themselves rather than on other people you will find out that people who frequently have outbursts of anger, depression or flamboyant enthusiasm are generally disapproved of in the early stage of their childhood. There are some children who suffered emotional trauma in their formative years because of parents' neglect. True, we have to be patient in understanding their situation but it doesn't mean that we are going to tolerate such display of inappropriate behavior. If they are not corrected right now, then they will become liabilities of the society than assets.

But never ever assume everything is fine just because someone isn't having a nervous breakdown. We all have our individual problems, angst and upsets in life. We just have to be sensitive with the underlying currents that made them who they are. It gives us an advantage in trying to help. Emphatic understanding is very important especially if we want to know what others have been through.

Although many people have heard of empathy, (psychics who are able to sense or feel the emotions of others), few people fully understand what it means to possess empathic psychic abilities. People naively assume that this ability is a great and wonderful gift, and that it does not come at a cost to the psychic who possesses it. The truth is, this rare talent can also be a deadly burden to bear.

These psychics come with wide ranges of sensitivity. On one end of the spectrum are the emphatic psychics who can only vaguely recognize other people's feelings, while on the other end there are the powerful psychics who feel people's emotions as though they were their own. People who are able to relate with people on an emotional or empathetic level is called an empath, To be a compassionate person, we have to accept the kind of person we are and embrace our good values. The very essence of being compassionate is the eagerness to show empathy, to feel and help others with their suffering. This feeling helps us to generate more positive thoughts, real emotions and acts as a starting point for developing happiness within ourselves. Admittedly, it can be wonderful to be able to understand another person's feelings, and to be able to understand them and to help them cope with their feelings if they need help; empathic psychics are often skilled at emotional healing therapy. This is a process in which the psychic can share the burden of an extreme emotion, thereby lessening the pain that it is causing the patient. Alternatively, a psychic can guide a patient through difficult emotional distress by using their sensitive, intimate understanding of a patient's emotional state of mind.

How Can We Develop A Kind And Compassionate Mind

To develop a kind and compassionate mind it's going to take a lot of practice, but you will find a way to handle it. You can start by feeling compassionate for yourself every day. It might sound uncomfortable to imagine this. But try and say to yourself loudly so you can hear yourself say at any time of your day, make positive words of declaration every day say to yourself "I am a kind and compassionate person". Make it a priority to stay in conducive environment that is quiet, where you are relaxed, pause, slow down and spend at least three minutes every day to take deep breaths and get your head space. Reflect on all the wonderful qualities you would like to have as a person who is kind, loving, compassionate and someone who is full of life. Now, understand each emotion and find an opportunity to express that emotion. Imagine the kind person you are, feel it and do something as an act of kindness. Imagine the loving and compassionate person you are and feel it. See how your thoughts change, how your body reacts, what sensations you feel, how you see the world around you right when you feel these emotions. Take each quality and imagine being a person who thinks feels and act with this quality.

EMOTIONAL INTELLIGENCE AND SELF-ESTEEM

Emotional intelligence (EQ) is about being aware of your emotions. If you have a high emotional intelligence you know what you are feeling from moment to moment, and in most cases you also know why you are feeling as you do. Furthermore, you know what it is that you need to do in order to change your emotions in situations when you wish to feel differently. Emotional intelligence thus makes you more aware of your personal needs and it increases your ability to take good care of yourself. Having a high emotional intelligence cannot be unaccompanied by high self-awareness. Thus, if you have a high EQ you also know yourself well. It is easier to build a high self-esteem (i.e. to develop a good relationship with yourself) when you know yourself. How can you accept and love someone you don't know? For this reason, self-esteem and emotional intelligence go hand in hand. As you raise your emotional intelligence you also learn to understand yourself better, accept yourself (including both negative and positive emotions), satisfy your personal needs and value yourself more. Everything gets easier when you improve the relationship with yourself.

Emotional intelligence is not only about understanding oneself, but also about understanding other people. With a high EQ you can enter a room full of people and immediately get a sense of how the people in that room are feeling at that moment. You can understand other people's needs better, and this makes it easier for you to help them to satisfy those needs. This makes it easier to handle all different kinds of people because you know how to make them feel good. We all have a social need, and as we raise our emotional intelligence we become better at building and keeping relationships that help us satisfy that need. We make ourselves feel better and we raise our self-esteem by helping others feel good.

To raise your emotional intelligence you simply have to listen to yourself more often. Take a break and ask your body what it is feeling. Do you feel some tension or pain anywhere? Listen to your intuition (your gut feeling). As soon as you open up to the information that is already within you, you will find out that you "know" much more than you were aware of before. Do not ignore or try to push emotions away. They have something important to tell you. Your emotions will help you to raise your self-esteem. Many people with low self-esteem try to ignore their negative emotions. They may have learnt through their childhoods that negative emotions are bad and should not be expressed, or they may simply not know how to handle their emotions. People with low self-esteem often translate having negative emotions into being a bad person. They assume that if they are feeling sad, angry or scared it must be because they are either doing something wrong or they do not deserve to feel differently. People with high self-esteem pay attention and are sensitive to their emotions without ignoring them or sweeping them aside. They do not equate feeling bad with being bad. They handle negative feelings in a positive manner. People with high self-esteem learn from their negative emotions and take active steps to make themselves feel better (for example by making sure that they get their unfulfilled needs met).

To keep your self-esteem high you thus have to accept your emotions. Ask yourself what you need in order to heal your wound or to find better balance. If you need social support, ask for it! If you need to slow down and relax, do it! You may simply need to have a good cry to offload some pressure, and everything will be fine again. Welcome your emotions and listen to what they are trying to tell you!

How to Improve Your Emotional Intelligence

1. Identify your own emotion at the time you are exhibiting it or shortly thereafter and name it. (Anger, frustration, joy, grief, abandonment, fear, love, confusion, etc.)

2. Identify what caused the emotion. (Memory from the past, friction with a disrespected colleague, threat of looking bad.)

3. Accept the emotion and what it has meant to your emotional development. (Is there a pattern? Are you perceived as eruptive, self-centered etc.?)

4. Express the named emotion and the cause to whoever is witnessing it or to someone else appropriate. (This may include an apology, an explanation, a compliment, etc.)

If you feel that others have a pre-conceived negative opinion of you, you may ask them how you are being perceived. If you don't want to do that, build your own self-awareness by quickly naming your emotions as they develop, identify what causes them, accepting them and expressing them to someone. Only then will you be able to catch yourself and project in a calmer more collective manner as opposed to exhibiting predictable negative behavior. Decreasing the negative behavior will help to reform opinions from colleagues.

If you are able to identify and control your own emotions with practice, then you are ready to put those skills to use for your team whenever there is a conflict or need for change. For individuals to work together they must build bridges across perspectives with compassion. Compassion is not agreement. It is a consideration for another person's feelings and is essential on teams before two objecting parties' lapse into defensiveness and a toxic work environment ensues.

Emotional Intelligence With Your Colleagues.

1. Ask yourself what you need to stop doing to make the team work effectively.

2. Be curious and compassionate to the others' perspectives. Learn to view things from their angle too. Be a good listener ask questions. Articulate what you understand their point of view to be. Use "I" statements and not "you" statements.

3. Use the steps above to understand the emotions and behaviors of others.

4. Make a suggestion as to how the conflict may be handled with compassion to all parties.

Identify the ideal self, In a way, this is analogous to imagining the future state of an organization - what it would look like without defects, rework, misalignment of work and requirements, etc. - but the ideal self is much more personal. One person's ideal self, building on his or her core identity and aspirations, will be different from another's ideal self. Personal change starts with envisioning the ideal self - the way one would like to be, to work, and to be perceived, but this is much more personal. This has three elements:

Awareness Of One's Strengths

An image of the desired future and a sense of hope that the desired future is attainable Insight into the ideal self are not always straightforward. One might simply extrapolate a trend of the present instead of envisioning a truly desired future self. Talking about aspirations with trusted friends or mentors can help. But identifying a clear picture of the future self-one wishes to be is a foundational step in Intentional Change Theory.

Identify the real self is not as easy as it sounds. In "Primal Leadership" Goleman, Boyatzis, and McKee report, "We found that an alarming number of leaders do not really know if they have resonance with their organizations. Rather they suffer from CEO disease; it's one unpleasant symptom is the sufferer's near-total ignorance about how his mood and actions appear to the organization. It's not that leaders don't care how they are perceived; most do. But they incorrectly assume that they can decipher this information themselves. Worse, they think that if they are having a negative effect, someone will tell them. They're wrong." The greatest challenge is to see oneself as others do. Using multiple sources of feedback can be very useful. Many organizations use 360 reviews for all individuals in management positions. However, the self-assessments are customarily inflated because it is the start of negotiation position. [Boyatzis uses 360 reviews to measure the correlation between EQ and operating results, but he says they throw away the self-assessments as "they are largely delusional."] Identification of the actual self requires honest and objective feedback. Behavioral feedback (such as video) and psychological tests can also help.

Develop a learning agenda, come up with an agenda and plan in contrast to the stream of to-dos and complying with agendas of others, the learning agenda is development focused. In Leadership Development from a Complexity Perspective, Boyatzis says that "a person often needs a type of permission to let go of old habits and try new ones." A learning agenda provides that type of structure for exploration and learning. The fourth step is Experimentation and Practice, look for feedback, and practice again. A consultant, coach or mentor should help the individual who has embarked on intentional change to find safe settings to practice the characteristics of the effective leader he or she envisions. Finally build Helping relationships, someone whose experience you can learn from. People like Coaches, mentors, guides are very helpful to someone aiming to transition to the ideal self through practicing greater EQ and inspirational leadership.

HOW TO USE THE ABCDE THEORY OF EMOTIONS

The ABCDE model is a model that makes it necessary for each stage be completed before advancing to the next stage. During moments of low emotional intelligence the ABCDE model is a useful tool to help employees reach a resolution. Let us take a closer look at each stage of the ABCDE model and how it's been used by coaches to groom people into becoming better emotional beings.

ABCDE Model

A = Activating event

B = Belief system

C = Emotional Consequences of A and B

D = Disputing irrational thoughts and beliefs.

E = Cognitive and Emotional effects of "updated" beliefs

Activating Event/Situation: The activating stage involves a triggering occurrence or situation and coming to terms with the negative feelings and emotions that are related to the event. It is important to look closely at the automatic thoughts - those thoughts that have an immediate reaction to an experience. It is helpful to put down these thoughts and feelings associated with the event in writing. This stage must be completed before moving on to stage

Belief System: the second stage is the belief stage, in this stage a coach guides the employee to recognize that beliefs trigger negative automatic thoughts. This is significant because thoughts ultimately determine the actions that are taken. Beliefs are formed throughout a person's life, from childhood on, and need to be analyzed in order to change those beliefs that cause negative thoughts and actions.

Emotional Consequences: This stage involves discussing the internal and external trait that followed as a result of an employee's beliefs and situation. The internal consequences are those emotions felt inside such as a change in heart rate or stomach butterflies. External consequences are the behaviors exhibited such as yelling at another person or slamming a door when exiting a room. As in all stages, this must be completed before progressing to the next step.

Dispute: In stage 4 thoughts and beliefs now at a disputed to cross check if they are rational or irrational. If they are worth it or not should and must beliefs that seem concrete and do not allow flexibility need to be disputed for validity. For example, if a belief that all employees must be nice to each other is held, during this stage it will be disputed to determine if this belief is true.

When looking at the Dispute stage there are three key kinds of disputes that can be used:

Scientific dispute – Are there any proof to the claims or basis for the belief, feelings, or thought pattern

Functional dispute – Is the belief supporting some other, potentially unconscious goals?

Logical dispute – Does the belief system make common sense? Is there any generalization or other thought pattern influencing these beliefs?

Example: A person who recognizes the thought pattern and changes and sees they are not based on truth or logic and adapts over the time to a view of believing that they can do a better job at expressing his beliefs.

Exchange: In this final stage, beliefs that have been disputed and determined as irrational are exchanged for beliefs that are rational. Replacing negative beliefs that cause negative thoughts is necessary to reframe an employee's thinking for the future. Changing beliefs, thought patterns and actions does not occur over night. But once the new, positive beliefs and thoughts have been identified, they can be written down and referenced as often as necessary until they become automatic thoughts.

The ABCDE Model of coaching is a great tool that HR managers can use in the workplace to assist developing higher emotional intelligence level in employees. As a result of systematic CBC conferences, employees experiencing instances of low emotional intelligence can be led to have healthy automatic thoughts that will equip them to make wise decisions and produce positive consequences.

Emotional Contagion And Empathy

Emotional contagion in its most positive form is the basis of the human virtue of empathy. We need to be emotionally in tune with others in order to understand them, get along with them and to function effectively in the human social world. Highly sensitive people's finely detailed observational abilities make them more responsive than most to the nuances of other people's feelings. This sometimes leads them to shy away from crowds since the mass of emotional messages is just too confusing. But even one-on-one relating can be emotionally challenging to a person who reads and responds strongly other's subtle emotional cues. Since HSP's own emotional responses are intense, quick to arise and hard to shake off, they often find themselves getting caught up uncomfortably in other people's feelings. Being attuned to the rawness of other people's emotions and even taking them on through emotional contagion can be an unpleasant and aversive experience.

Danger Of Co-Dependency

Since vicariously experiencing others unhappiness, rage or despair are so painful for a highly sensitive individual, it is easy to understand why it would be tempting for them to collude or manage social situations so as to keep others on an emotionally even keel. When the need to ensure that those around them are never angry or upset becomes a preoccupation there is a danger of developing co-dependent relationships.

MASTERY OF EMOTION: A KEY TO A BETTER LIFE

To live a better and happier life, you must take charge of the natural instinctive state of your mind arising from circumstances, moods or relationships with others. Controlling your emotions doesn't mean ignoring them, it means you recognize and take rightful actions on them. You must be in-charge of your emotions day-to-day! If you truly desire unlimited happiness, you must control your emotions. Do you struggle to control your emotions? You have the power to create your state of blissful and favorable emotional circumstances. A clear mind is better and able to control emotions. Un-clutter your mind!

Emotion is the generic term for subjective or conscious experience that is characterized by psycho-physiological expressions, biological reactions and mental states. It is often associated and considered reciprocally influential with temperament, personality, mood, motivation and depression. Emotions can be influenced by hormones and alcohol. It is the force behind human actions and reactions. Emotions can be expressed in the form of fear, joy, envy, excitement, distrust, depression, curiosity, contentment, desire, despair, embarrassment, confidence, gratitude, happiness, shame and shock.

With the harsh weather conditions, the economy in a miserable state, lack of job security, infidel partner, stubborn children, nagging co-workers, and unrest in the society, it can be easy to allow your emotions to run amok. An uncontrolled state of mind can make a bad situation worse. Every emotion begins with a thought. If you learn to control your mind and thoughts, you can rule your emotions. Guard your heart because out of it flows the issues of life. As you think in your heart, so you are. While it does take practice, you can be in firm control of any of the particular feelings that characterize the state of your mind, such as hate, horror, anger, fear, happiness or love.

Learning to control your emotions during challenging times of emotional stress is beneficial to your mental and general health. Emotions play a great role in life, and decisions are often based on feelings. However, problems occur when emotions are out of control. Becoming a master of emotional intelligence which involves emotional literacy, emotional coping and emotional awareness will help improve your emotional sagacity which helps you develop a good emotional freedom technique. To go higher in your career, build good relationships with people and be successful in life, you must keep a tab on your emotional quotient. It is common in day-to-day life to regret those actions we took because of uncontrolled emotion. There are keys that will help you lead a healthy and better emotional state in life.

1. Recognize Your Emotions

Human feelings are expressed in different forms. Take time to understand the nature of your feelings. Some of the most difficult emotions include anger, depression, anxiety and fear; the good News is that they can be subdued.

2. Meditation

The best way to maintain a good emotional health is to focus and dwell on uplifting and empowering thoughts. This will help you harmonize your mind, spirit and body. Meditation helps you to be in-charge of your physical, mental and emotional health. Some people meditate using prayer, yoga, reading a life-enriching book or listening to soul-uplifting music.

3. Affirmation

Affirmation is like confirmation. Through this means you speak faith into your circumstances and gladly expect the best result with cheerful expectancy. Say to yourself, "Am a success." "Am favored beyond measure and things are falling in pleasant places for me." This kind of positive thinking and confessions can change your mood from bad to good.

Over 80% of the things we worry about never happen and 15% out of the other 20% of the time, things don't happen as bad as we thought. Worrying only saps you of energy and vitality. These keys listed above can help you develop your cope capacity, create and be in-charge of your favorable emotional state 24/7. You can handle situations more than you ever thought possible by taking full control of your emotion in your day-to-day life.

GROWING EMOTIONAL INTELLIGENCE

So, what can you do about this? How can you turn this around and begin to grow your Emotional Intelligence?

A first step is to pay more attention to your emotions by noticing their sensations in your body. Before reaching for the TV remote, that sugary snack, caffeine, alcohol, or painkillers, notice the sensations of emotion.

Ask yourself, "If this feeling were located somewhere in my body where that would be?" Then, describe it as a physical sensation. Is it hot, cold? Is there tightness or pressure? Numbness? Tingling? Itching? Nausea? Expansion? Contraction? Rising? Sinking?

While noticing these sensations, especially if they feel uncomfortable, may seem like an odd thing to do to be happier, it's a first step toward connecting with emotional guidance. There's a deeper wisdom nudging you in these sensations. Paying attention to the sensations of emotions is a way to access them, observe them, and allow them to inform you.

Once you are in touch with the sensation, ask yourself, "What is the message in this emotion?" Just notice what comes to mind.

If you're hesitant to engage with emotions, it's

important to keep in mind that emotions are transient. No feeling lasts forever. They arise with a purpose. While present, an emotion gives you information about what is going on inside you, around you, and with others-along with energy to do something about it. Once emotional guidance is heeded, it subsides.

How Does Emotional Intelligence Affect Your Life?

Performance at work - EQ helps you to comfortably handle social complexities of workplace, motivate and guide others and succeed in your career. Now-a-days companies view emotional intelligence as being an important aspect and perform EQ testing before hiring.

Physical well-being - Stress is imminent in today's world no matter which profession you belong to. Stress is a familiar factor leading to serious health issues in most of the people. Uncontrolled stress level is known to increase the risk of heart disease. Our immune system suffers when stress level are high.

Mental well-being - Stress affects mental health negatively. You might have read or heard about stressed people going to the extent of committing suicide. When you cannot manage your emotions you become a victim of mood swings or other mental disorders that can seldom allow you to form or maintain strong relationships in life.

Personal relationships - Understanding your emotions help you to express your feelings to your loved ones. When there is a block in communication your relationships suffer both at work and in your personal life.

Improving Communication

If you want to improve your communication skills, it may be easier than you think! It is generally accepted that communication is the skill of both talking and listening, however, there are other more subtle ways to communicate, which can sometimes let us down. Body language and non-verbal cues such as facial expressions and hand gestures all have their place in good communications.

Most people who want to improve their communication skills do so because of their perception of themselves. They may be shy at parties, unwilling to participate in meetings, or feel they have nothing to say at social gatherings.

Yet those same people can often talk the hind legs off a donkey if they are able to discuss a subject close to them - better still if they are in their own home. This all comes down to confidence.

The simplest way to develop the confidence to talk freely at a social event is to pursue a popular pastime, sport or hobby that involves other people. While stamp collecting is fine, unless you happen to be in the same room at the same time as a fellow enthusiast, you'll struggle to make an impression. However, if you opt for let's say, learning a musical instrument, or playing any sport, you will be able to engage people's interest even if you're playing the guitar and they're playing piano. So making good conversation is not necessarily about having the same passions as everybody else - you just have to have a passion for something.

Being a good communicator can also help advance your working career. If you walk into the boss's office staring at your shoes, and mumbling about the pay rise that you deserve, you won't get far. However, if you enter the office with your head held high and your shoulders back, speaking clearly and decisively, you may actually walk out with a bigger raise than you were hoping to achieve.

Changing Negative Emotions

Negativity exists in our lives. There is no way around it. No matter how hard you try to live in the moment, focus on positivity, or practice being grateful every day, you will still experience times of negative emotions in your life. But this can be a good thing. Negative emotions signal that you need to make a change in your life. Whether it is stress, anger, fear, jealously, resentment, or any other negative emotion, the point of them all is to warn you that something needs to change.

Negative Emotions Are Our Number And To Transfer Negative Emotion We Need To :

1.) Change your energy field. Close your eyes and imagine the emotion as energy around you. What does it look like, what color, shape, form etc. does it take? Now allow it to change and smooth out, becoming transformed, harmonized, peaceful. What does it look and feel like now?

2.) Change your perspective on the situation. Re-frame it in a way that's positive/productive for you. Ask yourself, how this situation can help you. What is good about it? How are you growing from it? A positive attitude about something can help resolve it for you, even if it's a difficult situation. A new mindset can change everything.

3.) Ask self what the lesson you are learning from this situation is. Knowing the lesson helps transform the negative feeling and take on the mastery of the lesson you are in the process of learning.

4.) Put a new and positive picture in your mind about the situation that is causing the hurtful emotion. Instead of dwelling on the painful scenario or the trauma incident or being yelled at or treated disrespectfully, replace it with one of yourself healed, happy, successful, determined to move on etc. Whatever feels great and counters the old feeling. Keep the new picture in place whenever the old feeling comes up. The mind and body respond quickly to pictures, so this will shift you fast.

5.) Inner Listening. Get very quiet and go into the silence within. Allow your inner guide to bring you new insights, wisdom and solutions for healing and transformation.

6.) Forgiveness means letting go. It doesn't condone bad behavior, but lets the pain go. You and others have the right to make mistakes and grow. Forgive self if needed and forgive others. This doesn't mean that you will choose to stay connected with anyone who harms you. It means you let go of the painful movie, get the lesson and move forward. You stop the images and negative emotions from their endless control over you. Restore your self- esteem if you've acted poorly and wish the other person well if they have. To clean yourself completely, do a systematic of forgiveness for everyone in your life. You will be rejuvenated. Forgive; let go and say goodbye to these emotions.

7.) Change a gripe to a goal. If you regularly complain and feel negatively about something or someone, set a goal for yourself and be determined to accomplish it. For example, if you are jealous of someone who has a degree in art; stop it and find a way to get one for yourself. If you are short of money and angry at others who have it, stop it and chart your path, make a plan to increase your income. Things happen first in the mind, so begin to visualize yourself having what you want already now. Feel the joy of it and for 5 minutes several times a day, sit quietly and feel the emotions you would have if it were yours now. Soon you begin to believe you have it. In the Biology of belief, Bruce Lipton offers scientific proof that we get what we believe.

8.) Thoughts and emotions are intimately connected in fact, inseparable. One leads to the other. What repetitive thoughts do you have that are hurting you? Are you taking charge of your negative thoughts and transforming them? Think the opposite of your negative thought as soon as you catch yourself having it. Correct yourself on a daily basis; over and over. Repetition of the new corrected thought forges a new brain pathway and pattern. Strong intention and follow through is necessary.

Don't let your mind wander all day without direction or self-monitoring. You can change your mind at any moment into a more positive state. Letting your thoughts run wild will take away your peace. Take charge of yourself and choose thoughts that will help you.

9.) What belief about yourself do you want to change

Finances, relationships, self-concept, accomplishment of a specific goal; health, personal qualities etc. Beliefs that limit and cause pain keep your emotions at a painful level, and only you can change that.

Taking Positive New Action

1) Set clear boundaries. You decide what you will and won't accept from people and act on it.

2) Practice assertive communication with others. Tell them how you feel without blame or judgment; just how you feel. Stand up for self if needed.

3) Be creative. Create something positive from your experience.

For example, women who have been abused have set up women's shelters around the country. People who grew up hungry have started programs to feed poor children.

All of these techniques work. Practice and practice and you will see yourself and your life become fulfilled and beautiful. Be very patient with yourself, as this is hard work and takes a lot of self- control, intention and discipline. It's a progressive unfolding of the highest part of self. Over time we blossom!

Steps in Review:

1.) Stop and control self.

2.) Release the emotion.

3.) Transform the emotion.

4.) Take positive new action.

5.) Replace negative emotional reactions with spiritual actions and personal spiritual qualities.

Change your life by taking control of your emotions instead of being taken over by them and held in their grip.

Acknowledge That the Negativity Is A Sign

The first thing you need to do is actually sit down and acknowledge that you are in a negative space. Maybe you've just been dumped and are feeling sad, or maybe you are stressed out and resenting your job. It is OK to feel this way. In fact, it's normal!

Sometimes bad things happen that impact our lives in negative ways. The oft-used phrase "shit happens" nails it on the head. Shit really does happen, and it is fine to experience some negative emotions when it does. The important part is what you choose to do next. Once you have accepted your negative emotions you need to acknowledge that they are a sign that something needs to change. Do not ignore them. You are feeling that way for a reason. It is time to make some positive changes!

Figure Out What Action Is Required

Now that you are at one with the idea that some change is required in your life you need to figure out what that actual change is. What are your emotions telling you to do? It's normally pretty obvious. Are you stressed in your job? Find a new one. Hating your relationship? End it. Bored with life? Sell everything and take a holiday. Well it might not be that simple as this but I can assure you that it is pretty simple. You can go a little deeper by assessing exactly what is negative about your current situation. Try to break it down to the smallest possible level.

For example, once you start doing this you might realize that your job really isn't that stressful normally but it is just this one project that is killing you. So now you know that you only need to fix your current workload and you actually don't need to quit your job, sell your things, and go live in a cave as a hermit. Phew.

Take a step

This is the hard part. Acknowledging the negativity and figuring out what action is required is easy most of the time. Actually doing something about it is where most people will encounter trouble. The biggest blocker to taking action is a fear of change. People are often scared of change because they do not know exactly what is going to happen once the change occurs. Well I've got news for you - the future is constantly changing and you will never ever know exactly what is going to happen. Never!

The very definition of the future means that it a step forward in time which means that things have changed. Time has progressed and billions of actions have taken place. And this occurs every second! You cannot stop the change process because but you can make sure that in your life you are the one in control of the changes. Inaction and indecision are common symptoms of a fear of change (and fear of failure/success). By not taking action you let everyone else in the world decide what will happen for your life. You give away your power and become helpless. But if you choose to be decisive and start taking action you begin creating the changes that you want instead of being inundated by the changes that everyone else wants.

Keep Adjusting

You won't get it right first time but you will learn a hell of a lot along the way. Maybe the first change you made was not enough. Maybe you really did hate your job after all and just fixing that one project didn't help. So you readjust. You take stock again, assess the situation, and make another change. Another positive change that is. Or maybe the first change you made was too drastic and you realize that the original situation was better than the one you are in now. That's fine too. Just readjust and try again until you get it right and find a place where you feel happy, excited, and passionate.

Delete Negating Emotions From Your System

There is nothing beautiful about negative emotions; it's an obstacle to living a well-deserved life. despite the fact that life doesn't always turn out the way we expect we must keep a check on our emotions and not allow circumstances decide how we live our life .Negative emotions, across the board, could be reduced and the cumulative effects of the emotions from all spiritual experiences could be deleted-just like you delete things from a computer's hard drive. Essentially, we would then have less negative emotion to ruin us. And when we have one new emotion, it would not trigger all the previous old emotions in combination with each other.

In the case of a mother, for example, worrying about her child's welfare is not going to change anything for the better. In fact, the mother worrying about the child's health will actually make the condition worse for the child, so the worries have to be reduced or pretty much deleted. There should be no worries, no negative thoughts and no negative emotions about a child.

It's not about suppressing, repressing or denying the negative emotions and negative thoughts. Nor does it work to numb yourself out or try to forget about them. These emotions and thoughts should be truthfully deleted, so they can't come back and haunt the situation.

If left undeleted, negative emotions can cause a continuous struggle throughout your entire life-not only your life, but the lives of those around you.

You can learn the skill needed to delete emotions for yourself and others. In order to delete the emotion of sadness, for example, you could just get in touch with one thing in your life that makes you feel the emotion of sadness. This establishes a baseline that you can check into later in order to feel the change.

Essentially, all you do is put some thought energy on your midline while deleting the cumulative effect of all the sadness in your spiritual experiences. There is a three stage deletion process to this protocol, but after you experience the process, it would become more automatic and almost instantaneous. This is a good skill to learn for everyone.

CONCLUSION

Paying attention to your emotion is the first step to becoming a master of emotional intelligence, emotions are inborn and we have seen through the course of this book that emotions can be found in humans as well as in animals in the form of empathy, we see that animals are able to relate with their owners during times of distress, pain sorry, fear we see that some behaviors like adaptability allows an individual to understand the emotions or motives of others and as a result they are more willing to adapt to a situation than a person who can only understand what they personally are feeling. We come to realize that empathy is the highest level of communication skill and it should be put to use more often as it allows one to relate well with peoples unspoken words and the feelings created by them in others. Empathy is also responsible for how we respond to other's feelings sympathetically so that they can win their trust, which promotes communication further. Our fear of failure, anger, and frustration suddenly drop away, allowing for a more meaningful dialogue and a deepening of relationships, we are finally able to feel what others feel and skills like emotional control helps the individual control their emotions when they try to go overboard . During times of stress emotional intelligence plays a great role as they are able to find a way around it, they are optimistic and are good at building strong relationships. We also learnt that being a good communicator can also help advance your working career, improve relationship between employee and boss; EI and EQ are useful for human relations as they help clients decide

Developing these skills takes a lot of time, even years. But a little conscious effort can reduce this time down to a fraction of how long it would ordinarily take. The journey to mastering emotional intelligence is not for individuals who are ready to make a difference in life and make things work out for them as they climb up the ladder of success. You can Change your life by taking charge of your emotions rather of being taken over by them and held in their grip. One must remember that emotions are powerful but we decide what gets to us. Mastery will be within our reach once we are able to acknowledge the benefits of emotional intelligence to our lives. Remember to acknowledge That Negativity Is A Sign , then try to figure Out What Action Is Required to make this problem go away , then take the necessary actions.

INTRODUCING PSYCHOLOGY

HOW TO STOP PROCRASTINATION ANDDISCOVER POSITIVE THINKING, MOTIVATION AND CONFIDENCE

By

Daniel Anderson

COPYRIGHT © 2019.

ALL RIGHTS RESERVED.

TABLE OF CONTENTS

HISTORY OF PHSYCOLOGY

It is always a difficult question to ask, where to begin to tell the story of the history of psychology. Some would start with ancient Greece; others would look to a demarcation in the late 19th century when the science of psychology was formally proposed and instituted. These two perspectives, and all that is in between, are appropriate for describing a history of psychology. The interested student will have no trouble finding an abundance of resources on all of these time frames and perspectives (Goodwin, 2011; Leahey, 2012; Schultz & Schultz, 2007). For the purposes of this module, we will examine the development of psychology in America and use the mid-19th century as our starting point. For the sake of convenience, we refer to this as a history of modern psychology.

Psychology is an exciting field and the history of psychology offers the opportunity to make sense of how it has grown and developed. The history of psychology also provides perspective. Rather than a dry collection of names and dates, the history of psychology tells us about the important intersection of time and place that defines who we are. Consider what happens when you meet someone for the first time. The conversation usually begins with a series of questions such as, "Where did you grow up?" "How long have you lived here?" "Where did you go to school?" The importance of history in defining who we are cannot be overstated. Whether you are seeing a physician, talking with a counselor, or applying for a job, everything begins with a history. The same is true for studying the history of psychology; getting a history of the field helps to make sense of where we are and how we got here.

A Prehistory Of Psychology

Precursors to American psychology can be found in philosophy and physiology. Philosophers such as John Locke (1632–1704) and Thomas Reid (1710–1796) promoted empiricism, the idea that all knowledge comes from experience. The work of Locke, Reid, and others emphasized the role of the human observer and the primacy of the senses in defining how the mind comes to acquire knowledge. In American colleges and universities in the early 1800s, these principles were taught as courses on mental and moral philosophy. Most often these courses taught about the mind based on the faculties of intellect, will, and the senses (Fuchs, 2000).

Physiology And Psychophysics

Philosophical questions about the nature of mind and

knowledge were matched in the 19th century by physiological investigations of the sensory systems of the human observer. German physiologist Hermann von Helmholtz (1821–1894) measured the speed of the neural impulse and explored the physiology of hearing and vision. His work indicated that our senses can deceive us and are not a mirror of the external world. Such work showed that even though the human senses were fallible, the mind could be measured using the methods of science. In all, it suggested that a science of psychology was feasible.

An important implication of Helmholtz's work was that there is a psychological reality and a physical reality and that the two are not identical. This was not a new idea; philosophers like John Locke had written extensively on the topic, and in the 19th century, philosophical speculation about the nature of mind became subject to the rigors of science.

The question of the relationship between the mental (experiences of the senses) and the material (external reality) was investigated by a number of German researchers including Ernst Weber and Gustav Fechner. Their work was called psychophysics, and it introduced methods for measuring the relationship between physical stimuli and human perception that would serve as the basis for the new science of psychology (Fancher & Rutherford, 2011).

Wilhelm Wundt

The formal development of modern psychology is usually credited to the work of German physician, physiologist, and philosopher Wilhelm Wundt (1832–1920). Wundt helped to establish the field of experimental psychology by serving as a strong promoter of the idea that psychology could be an experimental field and by providing classes, textbooks, and a laboratory for training students. In 1875, he joined the faculty at the University of Leipzig and quickly began to make plans for the creation of a program of experimental psychology. In 1879, he complemented his lectures on experimental psychology with a laboratory experience: an event that has served as the popular date for the establishment of the science of psychology.

The response to the new science was immediate and global. Wundt attracted students from around the world to study the new experimental psychology and work in his lab. Students were trained to offer detailed self-reports of their reactions to various stimuli, a procedure known as introspection. The goal was to identify the elements of consciousness. In addition to the study of sensation and perception, research was done on mental chronometry, more commonly known as reaction time. The work of Wundt and his students demonstrated that the mind could be measured and the nature of consciousness could be revealed through scientific means. It was an exciting proposition, and one that found great interest in America. After the opening of Wundt's lab in 1879, it took just four years for the first psychology laboratory to open in the United States (Benjamin, 2007).

Scientific Psychology Comes to the United States

Wundt's version of psychology arrived in America most visibly through the work of Edward Bradford Titchener (1867–1927). A student of Wundt's, Titchener brought to America a brand of experimental psychology referred to as "structuralism." Structuralists were interested in the contents of the mind—what the mind is. For Titchener, the general adult mind was the proper focus for the new psychology, and he excluded from study those with mental deficiencies, children, and animals (Evans, 1972; Titchener, 1909).

Experimental psychology spread rather rapidly throughout North America. By 1900, there were more than 40 laboratories in the United States and Canada (Benjamin, 2000). Psychology in America also organized early with the establishment of the American Psychological Association (APA) in 1892. Titchener felt that this new organization did not adequately represent the interests of experimental psychology, so, in 1904, he organized a group of colleagues to create what is now known as the Society of Experimental Psychologists (Goodwin, 1985). The group met annually to discuss research in experimental psychology. Reflecting the times, women researchers were not invited (or welcome). It is interesting to note that Titchener's first doctoral student was a woman, Margaret Floy Washburn (1871–1939). Despite many barriers, in 1894, Washburn became the first woman in America to earn a Ph.D. in psychology and, in 1921, only the second woman to be elected president of the American Psychological Association (Scarborough & Furumoto, 1987).

Striking a balance between the science and practice of psychology continues to this day. In 1988, the American Psychological Society (now known as the Association for Psychological Science) was founded with the central mission of advancing psychological science.

Toward A Functional Psychology

William James was one of the leading figures in a new perspective on psychology called functionalism.

While Titchener and his followers adhered to a structural psychology, others in America were pursuing different approaches. William James, G.

Stanley Hall, and James McKeen Cattell were among a group that became identified with "functionalism." Influenced by Darwin's evolutionary theory, functionalists were interested in the activities of the mind—what the mind does. An interest in functionalism opened the way for the study of a wide range of approaches, including animal and comparative psychology (Benjamin, 2007).

William James (1842–1910) is regarded as writing perhaps the most influential and important book in the field of psychology, Principles of Psychology, published in 1890. Opposed to the reductionist ideas of Titchener, James proposed that consciousness is ongoing and continuous; it cannot be isolated and reduced to elements. For James, consciousness helped us adapt to our environment in such ways as allowing us to make choices and have personal responsibility over those choices.

At Harvard, James occupied a position of authority and respect in psychology and philosophy. Through his teaching and writing, he influenced psychology for generations. One of his students, Mary Whiton Calkins (1863–1930), faced many of the challenges that confronted Margaret Floy Washburn and other women interested in pursuing graduate education in psychology. With much persistence, Calkins was able to study with James at Harvard. She eventually completed all the requirements for the doctoral degree, but Harvard refused to grant her a diploma because she was a woman. Despite these challenges, Calkins went on to become an accomplished researcher and the first woman elected president of the American Psychological Association in 1905 (Scarborough & Furumoto, 1987).

G. Stanley Hall (1844–1924) made substantial and lasting contributions to the establishment of psychology in the United States. At Johns Hopkins University, he founded the first psychological laboratory in America in 1883. In 1887, he created the first journal of psychology in America, American Journal of Psychology. In 1892, he founded the American Psychological Association (APA); in 1909, he invited and hosted Freud at Clark University (the only time Freud visited America). Influenced by evolutionary theory, Hall was interested in the process of adaptation and human development. Using surveys and questionnaires to study children, Hall wrote extensively on child development and education. While graduate education in psychology was restricted for women in Hall's time, it was all but non-existent for African Americans. In another first, Hall mentored Francis Cecil Sumner (1895–1954) who, in 1920, became the first African American to earn a Ph.D. in psychology in America (Guthrie, 2003).

James McKeen Cattell (1860–1944) received his Ph.D. with Wundt but quickly turned his interests to the assessment of individual differences. Influenced by the work of Darwin's cousin, Frances Galton, Cattell believed that mental abilities such as intelligence were inherited and could be measured using mental tests. Like Galton, he believed society was better served by identifying those with superior intelligence and supported efforts to encourage them to reproduce. Such beliefs were associated with eugenics (the promotion of selective breeding) and fueled early debates about the contributions of heredity and environment in defining who we are. At Columbia University, Cattell developed a department of psychology that became world famous also promoting psychological science through advocacy and as a publisher of scientific journals and reference works (Fancher, 1987; Sokal, 1980).

The Growth Of Psychology

Throughout the first half of the 20th century, psychology continued to grow and flourish in America. It was large enough to accommodate varying points of view on the nature of mind and behavior. Gestalt psychology is a good example. The Gestalt movement began in Germany with the work of Max Wertheimer (1880–1943). Opposed to the reductionist approach of Wundt's laboratory psychology, Wertheimer and his colleagues Kurt Koffka (1886–1941), Wolfgang Kohler (1887–1967), and Kurt Lewin (1890–1947) believed that studying the whole of any experience was richer than studying individual aspects of that experience. The saying "the whole is greater than the sum of its parts" is a Gestalt perspective. Consider that a melody is an additional element beyond the collection of notes that comprise it. The Gestalt psychologists proposed that the mind often processes information simultaneously rather than sequentially. For instance, when you look at a photograph, you see a whole image, not just a collection of pixels of color. Using Gestalt principles, Wertheimer and his colleagues also explored the nature of learning and thinking. Most of the German Gestalt psychologists were Jewish and were forced to flee the Nazi regime due to the threats posed on both academic and personal freedoms. In America, they were able to introduce a new audience to the Gestalt perspective, demonstrating how it could be applied to perception and learning (Wertheimer, 1938). In many ways, the work of the Gestalt psychologists served as a precursor to the rise of cognitive psychology in America (Benjamin, 2007).

Behaviorism emerged early in the 20th century and

became a major force in American psychology. Championed by psychologists such as John B. Watson (1878–1958) and B. F. Skinner (1904–1990), behaviorism rejected any reference to mind and viewed overt and observable behavior as the proper subject matter of psychology. Through the scientific study of behavior, it was hoped that laws of learning could be derived that would promote the prediction and control of behavior. Russian physiologist Ivan Pavlov (1849–1936) influenced early behaviorism in America. His work on conditioned learning, popularly referred to as classical conditioning, provided support for the notion that learning and behavior were controlled by events in the environment and could be explained with no reference to mind or consciousness (Fancher, 1987).

For decades, behaviorism dominated American psychology. By the 1960s, psychologists began to recognize that behaviorism was unable to fully explain human behavior because it neglected mental processes. The turn toward a cognitive psychology was not new. In the 1930s, British psychologist Frederic C. Bartlett (1886–1969) explored the idea of the constructive mind, recognizing that people use their past experiences to construct frameworks in which to understand new experiences. Some of the major pioneers in American cognitive psychology include

Jerome Bruner (1915–), Roger Brown (1925–1997), and George Miller (1920–2012). In the 1950s, Bruner conducted pioneering studies on cognitive aspects of sensation and perception. Brown conducted original research on language and memory, coined the term "flashbulb memory," and figured out how to study the tip-of-the-tongue phenomenon (Benjamin, 2007). Miller's research on working memory is legendary. His 1956 paper "The Magic Number Seven, Plus or Minus Two: Some Limits on Our Capacity for Processing Information" is one of the most highly cited papers in psychology. A popular interpretation of Miller's research was that the number of bits of information an average human can hold in working memory is 7 ± 2. Around the same time, the study of computer science was growing and was used as an analogy to explore and understand how the mind works. The work of Miller and others in the 1950s and 1960s has inspired tremendous interest in cognition and neuroscience, both of which dominate much of contemporary American psychology.

Psychology And Society

Given that psychology deals with the human condition, it is not surprising that psychologists would involve themselves in social issues. For more than a century, psychology and psychologists have been agents of social action and change. Using the methods and tools of science, psychologists have challenged assumptions, stereotypes, and stigma. Founded in 1936, the Society for the Psychological Study of Social Issues (SPSSI) has supported research and action on a wide range of social issues. Individually, there have been many psychologists whose efforts have promoted social change. Helen Thompson Woolley (1874–1947) and Leta S. Hollingworth (1886–1939) were pioneers in research on the psychology of sex differences. Working in the early 20th century, when women's rights were marginalized, Thompson examined the assumption that women were overemotional compared to men and found that emotion did not influence women's decisions any more than it did men's. Hollingworth found that menstruation did not negatively impact women's cognitive or motor abilities. Such work combatted harmful stereotypes and showed that psychological research could contribute to social change (Scarborough & Furumoto, 1987).

Among the first generation of African American psychologists, Mamie Phipps Clark (1917–1983) and her husband Kenneth Clark (1914–2005) studied the psychology of race and demonstrated the ways in which school segregation negatively impacted the self-esteem of African American children. Their research was influential in the 1954 Supreme Court ruling in the case of Brown v. Board of Education, which ended school segregation (Guthrie, 2003). In psychology, greater advocacy for issues impacting the African American community were advanced by the creation of the Association of Black Psychologists (ABPsi) in 1968.

In 1957, psychologist Evelyn Hooker (1907–1996) published the paper "The Adjustment of the Male Overt Homosexual," reporting on her research that showed no significant differences in psychological adjustment between homosexual and heterosexual men. Her research helped to de-pathologize homosexuality and contributed to the decision by the American Psychiatric Association to remove homosexuality from the Diagnostic and Statistical Manual of Mental Disorders in 1973 (Garnets & Kimmel, 2003).

WHAT IS PHSYCOLOGY

Psychology has evolved from the Greek word "psyche," which means "soul" or "mind," and "logos," which means speech. It is an academic and applied field concerning the study of the mind, brain, and behavior, both human and nonhuman. Psychology also refers to the practical application of such knowledge to diverse spheres of human activity, including problems of people's daily lives and the treatment of psychological illness.

In simple words, psychology involves study of the human mind and how it functions in different situations. In other words, basically it involves a deep analysis of how people think, behave and interact with one another in different type of situations and environments. This subject traces its roots to ancient civilizations of India, Egypt, China and Greece. Wilhelm Wundt, a German Doctor is the person responsible for bringing psychology into lab settings and also introducing the structural school of psychology. After that many eminent researchers and analysts have contributed a lot in this field as it is never possible to read and predict the human mind in totality. Perhaps this is something that can change even before you may imagine. That's the main beauty of this field because it deals with the most complex thing on the earth i.e.

human mind.

Various approaches to psychology include forensic, abnormal, computational, developmental, cognitive and quantitative psychology. Psychologists make use of three types of inferences which are deduction, induction and abduction to provide explanations on the way the mind works. As part of their efforts to understand the way the mind works, they make use of survey results. Surveys are used to record data which are needed to measure mood change patterns, attitude and traits, and other aspects of the human mind.

Psychology has evolved from the Greek word "psyche," which means "soul" or "mind," and "logos," which means speech. It is an academic and applied field concerning the study of the mind, brain, and behavior, both human and nonhuman. Psychology also refers to the practical application of such knowledge to diverse spheres of human activity, including problems of people's daily lives and the treatment of psychological illness.

Psychology differs from anthropology, economics, political science, and sociology in seeking to capture illustrative generalizations about the mental function and explicit behavior of individuals. However, contrary to this, other disciplines depend more heavily on field studies and historical methods for extracting expressive generalizations. In reality, however, there is much "cross-fertilization" that takes place among different fields. Psychology differs from biology and neuroscience in that it is mainly concerned with the interface between mental processes and behavior of a person. It also refers to the common procedures of a system and not merely the biological or neural procedures themselves.

However, subfields of psychology, such as neuropsychology, combine the study of the actual neural processes with the study of the mental effects they have intuitively produced. Psychology in literal terms means the study of the human mind. It illustrates and attempts to explain awareness, behavior, and social interaction. This study can be structured purely in terms of phenomenological descriptions of internal experiences or as a result of behavior, which includes social conduct. Empirical psychology is mainly dedicated to describing human experience and behavior as it actually occurs.

The study of the correlation between consciousness and the brain or nervous system has been undertaken only recently. However, it is still not clear in what ways they interact.

Psychology is a particularly extensive field, which includes various approaches to the study of mental processes and behavior. An understanding of brain function is gradually being included in psychological theory and practice, particularly in areas such as artificial intelligence, neuropsychological, and cognitive neuroscience. Mechanical and electronic computing has played an important role in developing the information-processing hypothesis of the mind.

Importance Of Psychology

Psychology is very important especially because it deals with the study of the mental processes and behaviour at the same time. It is also applied in our daily lives and in many things

There are many misconceptions regarding the field of psychology, especially because of its diversity and the different careers associated with the study of psychology. Psychology is actually a science and a discipline in both academic and applied field which deals with the human mind and its relation to human behaviour. The aim of psychology is to understand, explain, and predict the thought, emotion, and the behaviour of man. Psychology is involved in various areas of study and application in different subjects.

Psychology is very important especially because it

deals with the study of the mental processes and behaviour at the same time. It is also applied in our daily lives and in many things. How we behave, how we react to situations, and how we perform are all associated with psychology. That is because psychology studies our nature, how we think and how it is related to what we do, and why we think and act the way we do. It is actually very complicated because unlike the study of disease processes and the physical body, studying the human mind is very complicated and it is hard to study in an unbiased way. Its importance in the society has grown significantly over the years. Psychology is used to study various kinds of mental and life threatening diseases such as in Alzheimer's, Parkinson's, and many other types of neurological disorders. Psychology is also used to better understand and help those with pervasive developmental disorders such as autism. The study of psychology in these disorders and diseases has helped the medical professionals in developing cure and treatment for certain diseases.

With psychology, we are able to learn about ourselves. To fully understand ourselves we have to know about the causes of our own behaviour and our perspectives in life. By knowing ourselves and learning our own personality, we can develop goals for ourselves. Also, by learning about ourselves, we are able to learn about other people and their differences. Gaining understanding of oneself and of others can help improve the way relationships and communications work. These are only some of the common uses and the importance of studying psychology.

Psychology allows people to understand more about how the body and mind work together. This knowledge can help with decision-making and avoiding stressful situations. It can help with time management, setting and achieving goals, and living effectively.

The science not only allows people to be more successful, but it can also impact their health. It helps many tackle their mental illnesses so that they can continue living their lives. Psychological studies have also aided in drug development and the ability to diagnose various diseases (such as Alzheimer's and Parkinson's).

I can personally testify to the importance of the subject. Psychology has helped me as a writer because I have become more determined to do the things I will enjoy and write on the topics that I like. I can understand who I am and look at events on a more positive aspect. Whenever I have a problem, I can handle it better. Down to the choices over the projects I will work on and the way I will handle my time, psychology helps me make better decisions within my life.

HOW PSYCHOLOGYCAN HELP YOU LIVE A BETTER LIFE

How can psychology apply to your everyday life? Do you think that psychology is just for students, academics, and therapists? Then think again. Because psychology is both an applied and a theoretical subject, it can be utilized in a number of ways.

While research studies aren't exactly light reading material for the average person, the results of these experiments and studies can have significant applications in daily life. The following are some of the top ten practical uses for psychology in everyday life.

Get Motivated

Whether your goal is to quit smoking, lose weight, or learn a new language, some lessons from psychology offer tips for getting motivated. To increase your motivational levels when approaching a task, utilize some of the following tips derived from research in cognitive and educational psychology:

- ✓ Introduce new or novel elements to keep your interest high

- ✓ Vary the sequence to help stave off boredom

✓ Learn new things that build on your existing knowledge

✓ Set clear goals that are directly related to the task

✓ Reward yourself for a job well done

Improve Your Leadership Skills

It doesn't matter if you're an office manager or a volunteer at a local youth group, having good leadership skills will probably be essential at some point in your life. Not everyone is a born leader, but a few simple tips gleaned from psychological research can help you improve your leadership skills.

One of the most famous studies on this topic looked at three distinct leadership styles. Based on the findings of this study and subsequent research, practice some of the following when you are in a leadership position:

✓ Offer clear guidance, but allow group members to voice opinions

✓ Talk about possible solutions to problems with members of the group

✓ Focus on stimulating ideas and be willing to reward creativity

Become A Better Communicator

Communication involves much more than how you speak or write. Research suggests that nonverbal signals make up a huge portion of our interpersonal communications. To communicate your message effectively, you need to learn how to express yourself nonverbally and to read the nonverbal cues of those around you.

- ✓ A few key strategies include the following:

- ✓ Use good eye contact

- ✓ Start noticing nonverbal signals in others

- ✓ Learn to use your tone of voice to reinforce your message

Learn To Better Understand Others

Much like nonverbal communication, your ability to understand your emotions and the emotions of those around you plays an important role in your relationships and professional life. The term emotional intelligence refers to your ability to understand both your own emotions as well as those of other people.

Your emotional intelligence quotient is a measure of this ability. According to psychologist Daniel Goleman, your EQ may actually be more important than your IQ.

What can you do to become more emotionally intelligent? Consider some of the following strategies:

- ✓ Carefully assess your own emotional reactions

- ✓ Record your experience and emotions in a journal

- ✓ Try to see situations from the perspective of another person

Make More Accurate Decisions

Research in cognitive psychology has provided a wealth of information about decision making. By applying these strategies to your life, you can learn to make wiser choices. The next time you need to make a big decision, try using some of the following techniques:

Try using the "six thinking hats" approach by looking at the situation from multiple points of view, including rational, emotional, intuitive, creative, positive, and negative perspectives

Consider the potential costs and benefits of a decision

Employ a grid analysis technique that gives a score for how a particular decision will satisfy specific requirements you may have

Improve Your Memory

Have you ever wondered why you can remember exact details of childhood events yet forget the name of the new client you met yesterday? Research on how we form new memories as well as how and why we forget has led to a number of findings that can be applied directly in your daily life.

What are some ways you can increase your memory power?

- ✓ Focus on the information.

- ✓ Rehearse what you have learned.

- ✓ Eliminate distractions.

Make Wiser Financial Decisions

Nobel Prize-winning psychologist Daniel Kahneman and his colleague Amos Tversky conducted a series of studies that looked at how people manage uncertainty and risk when making decisions. Subsequent research in this area known as behavior economics has yielded some key findings that you can use to make wiser money management choices.

One study found that workers could more than triple their savings by utilizing some of the following strategies:

- ✓ Don't procrastinate. Start investing in savings now

- ✓ Commit in advance to devote portions of your future earnings to your retirement savings

- ✓ Try to be aware of personal biases that may lead to poor money choices

Get Better Grades

The next time you're tempted to complain about pop quizzes, midterms, or final exams, consider this;research has demonstrated that taking tests actually helps you better remember what you've learned, even if it wasn't covered on the test.

Another study found that repeated test-taking may be a better memory aid than studying. Students who were tested repeatedly were able to recall 61 percent of the material while those in the study group recalled only 40 percent. How can you apply these findings to your own life? When trying to learn new information, self-test frequently in order to cement what you have learned into your memory.

Become More Productive

Sometimes it seems like there are thousands of books, blogs, and magazine articles telling us how to get more done in a day, but how much of this advice is founded on actual research? For example, think about the number of times have you heard that multitasking can help you become more productive. In reality, research has found that trying to perform more than one task at the same time seriously impairs speed, accuracy and productivity.

So what lessons from psychology can you use to increase your productivity? Consider some of the following:

- ✓ Avoid multitasking when working on complex or dangerous tasks

- ✓ Focus on the task at hand

- ✓ Eliminate distractions

Be Healthier

Psychology can also be a useful tool for improving your overall health. From ways to encourage exercise and better nutrition to new treatments for depression, the field of health psychology offers a wealth of beneficial strategies that can help you to be healthier and happier.

Some examples that you can apply directly to your own life:

- ✓ Studies have shown that both sunlight and artificial light can reduce the symptoms of seasonal affective disorder

- ✓ Research has demonstrated that exercise can contribute to greater psychological well-being.

- ✓ Studies have found that helping people understand the risks of unhealthy behaviors can lead to healthier choices

PHSYCOLOGY AND HUMAN BEHAVIOR

Human behaviour is a curious thing. A range of factors, including our upbringing, what we've been taught, our culture, and our religious beliefs, influence the way we behave. It's also influenced by what we see happening around us and how effectively people encourage us to change our preconceived ideas.

Behaviour change marketing helps people assess what they believe by offering new insights into issues. It's not about coercing people into believing something new, but looking into an issue that's current or relevant. It can encourage them to think about issues that they would not normally take notice of.

You cannot force someone to think in a certain way, but by explaining issues around a topic, you can get a community talking and encourage change. Behaviour change marketing focuses on this innate need for people to discuss matters that affect them. Even matters that are being discussed by others can become important to someone who would normally not even think about an issue.

Take climate change. Because the topic has become an issue that interests the general public, it is able to affect the way people act. People are now more likely to recycle, reduce and reuse, try to buy less or consume less, and to think about their habits. This topic has entered the public arena because people have been educated about what they can do to reduce climate change. Even people who do not change their behaviour have been encouraged to think about climate change as an issue.

Part of behaviour change marketing is to persuade or convince people of the need to change. This could be through promoting behaviour change as good or necessary. Sometimes the reasons people behave the way they do has less to do with their beliefs or any strongly held convictions and more to do with following trends. If people believe that others are conscientiously recycling, then they are more likely to do it themselves.

Other ways behaviour change marketing can work is to appeal to people's morality, to promote the costs or benefits of making a change, or to show that it is socially good to make a change. There are obvious moral and social issues with drink driving, for example, as you are potentially affecting others and not just yourself. Then there may be cost benefits to making a change: for example, buying ecologically friendly light bulbs may actually save you money.

As fantastically (and fanatically) self-aware organisms, we humans tend to ascribe great importance to our intellectual processes: We're rational and reasoning creatures, we assert, capable of stepping back and assessing our own behavior through an analytical lens.

Like any other biological entity, however, we're interacting with and responding to our environment in myriad ways well beyond the realm of our conscious perception. We usually take these subconscious, autonomic aspects of our being for granted, but naturally, they're fundamental to both our appreciation of the world around us and, critically, our day-to-day survival.

We don't need to compel ourselves to shiver when the mercury drops; our hand recoils at the lick of the flame or the bite of the dog. Thankfully, we don't have to think our way through the mechanics of walking in order to pull it off – start trying to, and you're liable to beeline for the pavement.

The conscious and the subconscious, the voluntary and the involuntary: When it comes to Homo sapiens, these processes aren't either-or propositions. They're thoroughly intertwined, influencing and echoing one another. In short, human beings (breaking news) are complicated systems, and the study of human behavior a complex task. Parsing out behavioral and emotional nuances requires zoomed-in looks at the tempos and intensities of all kinds of physical and psychological networks – and a holistic, big-picture perspective of how those networks interface with one another.

Understanding human behavior

The reason most people fail to understand human behaviour correctly is that they look at their behaviour without taking other variables into consideration.

If you had the goal of understanding a car's wheel, can you analyze the wheel alone without trying to understand its relationship with the other parts of the car?

If you did so then you might get the wheel incorrectly or fail to understand its function. For example you might never understand why the wheel has certain holes in the middle and even assume that its faulty but when you come to know that this wheel will fit into a rotating shaft then the holes in the center will make all the sense in the world.

The same goes for humans, You wont understand human behavior correctly before you take into consideration the person's beliefs, values, lifestyle, way of thinking and all other variables that affect him directly or indirectly.

A perfect real life example for understanding human behaviour

Brian,a self made millionaire, was a confident and charming person. Brian was so proud of himself and the main psychological identity he used to identify with was being a self made millionaire.

One day Brian discovered that he developed a weird obsessive compulsive disorder that forced him to check whether he left his car's door unlocked or not every few minutes!

For the first instance it might seem to a person who knows little about psychology that a problem happened with Brian's brain chemistry, which is a part of the truth, but he will never be able to guess what was going on unless he analyzes Brian's personality in more details.

In the past few weeks Brian has been seeing a recurring dream where his car gets stolen. Again to a person who knows little about the human nature it might seem that Brian is afraid to lose his car and that his fears were fed by this dream but that conclusion is wrong as well.

In the past couple of months Brian faced serious problems with his business that threatened its continuity and threatened his main and most important psychological identity. After all if he went out of business he wont be that self made millionaire anymore and he will lose his money.

Understanding Human nature by connecting the elements together

Because dreams always come in the form of symbols the loss of the car in Brian's dream was just a reflection of his fear of loss of his status. In other words the dream meant that Brian was concerned about losing his status or prestige! (see what does your dream mean)

Because the subconscious mind thinks using symbols and because logic is ignored to a certain extent during its operation Brian's mind forced him to develop that obsessive compulsive disorder because it was so concerned about the threat of the loss of his status.

In other words, Brian developed that disorder because he was too afraid to lose his status and checking whether the car was locked or not was a reflection of his fear of losing his car if he became poor.

This is how to understand human behaviour

When trying to understand human behaviour don't ever examine a single item without examining all the items in the system.

If a woman fears cats then instead of quickly assuming that a traumatic experience with cats happened to her when she was young you should try to look at other aspects of her life.

Could this fear of cats be a reflection of her fear of other women?

Could her low self esteem made her vulnerable to the presence of other women who were symbolized in the form of cats by her subconscious mind?

Of course i am not asking you to study the previous examples by hard then say that each man who develops such a disorder is afraid to lose his status or that each woman who fears cats has low self esteem but instead i am asking you to take a deeper look in order to understand the human behaviour perfectly.

Human behavior is very much inconsistent. In behavior, we aren't able to assume one pair blueprint of behavior. Levitt classified behavior as; (Id) triggered behavior, (ii) determined behavior, (iii) Goal-oriented behavior. From these observations, it may be known that behavior is a reliant element. By understanding behavior, an individual may predict, direct, transform and control behavior of group or individuals. There are generally four standard assumptions concerning character of folks: individual distinctions, a great person, caused behavior (motivation) and worthiness of the individual (human dignity).

11 Main Aspects of Human Behaviour

1.Psychology

Psychology is the science of human behaviour, Behaviour of an individual refers to anything an individual does.

An act of behaviour has three aspects:

Cognition-to become aware of or know something,

Affection-to have a certain feeling about it, and

Conation-to act in a particular way or direction after the feeling.

Human behaviour may be covert (expressed inside) or overt (expressed outside). While symbolic adoption is an example of covert behaviour, use adoption is an example of overt behaviour.

2. Personality

Personality is the unique, integrated and organized system of all behaviour of a person. Personality is the sum total of one's experience, thoughts and actions; it includes all behaviour patterns, traits and characteristics that make up a person. A person's physical traits, attitudes, habits and, emotional and psychological characteristics are all parts of one's personality.

Genetically influence on personality is seen clearly in the effect of physiology on physique and temperament, their interaction, and the role of nervous system in the acquisition of personality traits.

The cultural influence commences at birth with the infant's response to environment and continues throughout life as the influence of the home, community and society increases during growth and maturity of the individual. Parents, teachers and friends exercise great influence on the formation of attitudes and of the personality as a whole.

Sme commonly used personality types are introverts and extroverts. According to Guilford (1965), the introverts are people whose interests are turned inward upon themselves and their own thoughts, whereas the extroverts are those whose interests are turned outward upon the environment.

The introvert generally shuns social contacts and is inclined to be solitary, whereas the extrovert seeks social contacts and enjoys them. Lying in between are found people who are neither extrovert nor introvert, they are called ambiverts.

3. Interest

An interest is a preference for one activity over another. The selection and ranking of different activities along a like- dislike dimension is known as expressed interest. An interest is made manifest (visible), when a person voluntarily participates in an activity.

There is no necessary relationship between expressed interest and manifest interest, though in many situations they tend to coincide or overlap. Many individuals engage in some activities which they claim to dislike and just on the reverse, many people may refuse to engage in activities which they claim to enjoy.

4. Attitude

Allport (1935) defined attitude as a mental state of readiness, organized through experience, exerting a directive and dynamic influence upon the individual's response to all objects and situations with which it is related.

Attitudes have certain characteristics:

1. Attitudes are formed in relation to objects, persons and values. Attitudes are not innate, but are formed as a result of individual's contact with the environment.

2. Attitudes have direction; positive or favourable, negative or unfavourable. They also vary in degrees.

3. Attitudes are organized into a system and do not stand loosely or separately.

4. Attitudes are rooted in motivation and provide a meaningful background for individual's overt behaviour.

5. Attitudes develop through a consistency among responses. They are more stable and enduring than opinions.

6. Attitudes are prone to change. Changes in attitude may be brought about by training and, other instructional methods and aids.

5. Emotions

Emotions denote a state of being moved, stirred up or aroused and involve impulses, feelings and physical and psychological reactions. A negative emotional response may lead to non-cooperation and non-participation in programmes, stoppage of work or even destruction of the work done. In a programme of planned change, the extension agent should take care of the state of emotion of the client system.

Guilford (1965) suggested the following rules for emotional control:

(i) Avoid emotion provoking situations,

(ii) Change the emotion provoking situation,

(iii) Increase skills for coping with the situation,

(iv) Re-interpret the situation,

(v) Keep working towards the goal,

(vi) Find substitute outlets, and

(vii) Develop a sense of humour.

6. Wishes

According to Chitambar (1997), a wish is a pattern of behaviour which involves:

(a) Anticipated future satisfaction,

(b) Which the person believes is reasonably likely of attainment, and

(c) Towards which the individual usually relates some of his/her present behaviour.

While wish-goals are oriented toward achievement in the future, what is significant is its influence on behaviour in the present. Wishes are based on subjective judgement which may at times be irrational and otherwise faulty. At any one time, a person may have several wishes and it may become necessary to set priorities for their achievement.

7. Prejudice

PREJUDICE means pre-judgement. Judgement before due examination and consideration of facts, and based on certain assumptions generally lead to the formation of prejudice. Prejudice is normally negative and difficult to reverse. Prejudices may lead to hostile attitude towards persons or objects. Expressing ill feeling or hostility towards some minority or caste groups, or an innovation are examples of prejudice.

An effort in reducing prejudice must start with the understanding about its origin. Personal contact, use of mass media, suitable enactments having penal provision, economic changes resulting in greater security etc. may help in reducing prejudice.

8. Stereotype

Stereotypes are fixed images formed in one's mind about people, practices or various other social phenomena on the basis of experience, attitudes, values, impressions or without any direct experience, Stereotypes help in knowing how people perceive various groups of people or practice or various other social phenomena.

Stereotypes have certain characteristics:

Uniformity-members belonging to a particular group share the stereotype.

Direction-may be positive or negative.

Intensity-indicates strength of the stereotype.

Quality-refers to content, the kind of image provided by the stereotype.

9. Thinking and Reasoning

According to Garrett (1975), thinking is behaviour which is often implicit and hidden, and in which symbols (images, ideas, and concepts) are ordinarily employed. Group thinking, in which a number of persons participate in the solution of a problem, is usually more efficient than individual effort and is often more satisfactory.

In reasoning, the thinking process is applied to the solution of problems. There are, in general, two methods of solving problems-deductive and inductive. Deductive reasoning starts with a general fact or proposition, under which various specific items can be placed or classified.

Inductive reasoning, on the other hand, starts with observations and proceeds step by step to a general conclusion. Both methods are employed in most learning situations.

10. Frustration and Adjustment

A common pattern of human behaviour involves hopes for future achievement. Such ambitions and goals are generally termed as wish. Frustration is a condition in which an individual perceives the wish goal blocked or unattainable. This creates some tension in the individual. When faced with such a situation, the individual tries to make several kinds of adjustments in the behaviour pattern. This is achieved through defense mechanism.

A defense mechanism is a device, a way of behaving, that a person uses unconsciously to protect oneself from ego-involving frustrations. This helps the individual to reduce tension. Following Chitambar (1990) and Krech and Crutchfield (1984) some adjustment patterns i.e. defense mechanisms are presented in brief.

Rationalization occurs when a person unconsciously explains the situation to oneself by reasoning that, after all the individual never did really wish to achieve the goal. Example, 'grapes are sour'. Rationalization differs from alibis and excuses in that the first one is unconscious in nature, while the latter two are conscious.

Rationalization makes an individual feel comfortable by helping avoid unpalatable situations by justifying one's own behaviour in conformity with the existing social practices and values. Hence, rationalization functions as one of the major obstacles to change.

Aggression is caused by frustration of dominant motives. Aggression may be turned outwards i.e. directed towards other persons, or directed inwards i.e. makes oneself responsible for whatever has happened, or may be repressed without any overt expression.

Aggression may be expressed in the form of anger, actual physical violence against objects and people, verbal attacks and fantasies of violence.

Identification is a common form of adjustment in

which the individual lives through the achievement of others, participating vicariously (as a substitute) in their success. Parents could receive genuine satisfaction from their children's success, which they themselves could not achieve.

Projection means transferring one's emotion and ascribing the source of emotion to another object. Projection is a tendency to 'push out' upon another person, one's own unrealized frustrated ambitions, or to attribute to another one's own faults.

Projection may take two forms-(i) in order to escape from facing the reality that a person has failed, the individual may blame another or even a non-existent person or factor. In another type, (ii) the individual reasons that one's own faults are also found in others to an even greater degree.

Fantasy or Day dreaming is a common form of adjustment to frustration. The individual enters an imaginary world in which the person's all wish goals are realized. Compensation is a reaction to a feeling of inferiority. The inferiority feeling may be based on real or imaginary deficiency, which may be physical or otherwise, and compensation is an attempt to overcome or neutralize the deficiency.

Compensation may take two forms:

(i) Substitution-when a new goal is substituted for a goal which is blocked and

(ii) Sublimation-when the substitution involves moral consideration i.e. changing a particular emotion in a socially valued and socially acceptable way. An individual may work hard and try to shine out to compensate for one's own deficiencies.

Regression means going back to a less mature level of behaviour. In certain frustrating situation, the behaviour of the individual tends to become primitive. The actions become less mature, more childish; the sensitivity of discriminations and judgements diminishes; feelings and emotions become more poorly differentiated and controlled, like those of a child. Example, a farmer dissatisfied with an innovation, may discontinue it and revert to the previous practice which may be old and uneconomic.

Repression is the mechanism by which wishes are not allowed to come out of the unconscious or thrown down into the unconscious. For example, a sex relationship not sanctioned by the society is generally repressed and gradually forgotten.

11. Deviant Behaviour

Some individuals' personality traits and behaviour

differ considerably more than others' from the norms. Such behaviour is termed as deviant behaviour and the individuals are known as deviants.

Three essential aspects of deviant behaviour are presented, following Chitambar (1997):

1. Deviation is culturally defined. The same behaviour considered as deviant in one culture, may be regarded as normal or highly valued in another culture.

2. Deviation develops through the process of socialization, in the same way as normal behaviour does.

3. Deviation is a matter of degree. If the personality traits and behaviour of individuals in a society are placed on a continuum, the majority would be near the centre, which would represent the area of accepted social norms. Outside this, will lie those individuals referred to as social deviants.

On one side-the 'high side'-will be those social deviants whose deviancy not only is approved by society, but also secures for them status, high recognition and praise. These 'desirable' deviants can bring about rapid social change.

On the other side, lie those deviants who by virtue of

the extreme difference of their personality traits and behaviour are conspicuously set apart and disapproved by the society. They are considered as 'undesirable' deviants.

PSYCHOLOGY AND MINDSET

The media these days has sure created a whole lot of hype about "mindset?" So I'm officially giving my two cents of what mindset development is, and how you can actually change it. You can because there really is a psychology to mindset. Wouldn't you like to know what it is? Just do a search in your favorite Web browser for the word "Mindset." You'll get thousands of searches, but you'll also be hard-pressed to find one source online that understands how mindset works. Some might, sure. But with so many gurus and experts claiming to be able to help you evolve just by changing one (not so) teeny thing, wouldn't it be useful to know the truth? The truth about the psychology BEHIND the curtain of mindset? I think so too! So here it is. Mindset is really just about mind-shift. It's about the way you see the world. Think of mindset as the pair of lenses you choose to look through at the world.

You can wear rosy or gray. The truth is, your consistent thoughts only add to the positive, or negative, outlook of your life. This is what they mean by "self-fulfilling prophecy." Those media gurus and I agree that you must change your mindset to have the happiness you want. But it's simply NOT ENOUGH for me to tell you to simply "change your mindset" and wait for the magic happen. That's like me saying, "I'll drop a little fairy dust on your head, and your mind will instantly be cleared of all the goo." Sorry, mindset change doesn't work that way. No wonder so many frustrated humans are scurrying about in our society, looking for the NEXT guru that can answer, "How can you make me happy?" Wait no more. I can answer that question. The truth about mindset change is that it's so easy, you might wonder if fairy dust is involved. And you might wonder why you spent thousands of hours paying someone to help you be happy when I'm giving it to you for free. (You're welcome!) I'm going to describe something I call the "Mind Tree." Draw this out on a piece of paper as I explain it so it makes more sense. The trunk of your tree is a simple formula: thoughts create emotions; emotions create actions. Then two main branches spawn from thoughts: conscious and subconscious.

Those are the two types of thoughts--the first you can easily tap into and are aware of and the second you can't easily access. These subconscious thoughts lurk in the background of your mind. Your habitual thoughts are your mindset. These are the thoughts you have to change if you want to change your mindset. But here's the kicker: Your conscious thoughts make up only about 15% of your total thoughts, maybe less! Your subconscious thoughts make up the other 85%. Draw this on your mindset tree. Let it sink in. That means in order to change your mindset, you have to tap into those thoughts you don't even know you're thinking. Bad news, right? Well, not so fast. You can change your subconscious programming. There are so many ways, and that's where a GOOD guru comes in! From my pre-frontal cortex to yours (that's where your conscious thoughts are stored), here are just a few to get you started: First, identify what subconscious thoughts are ones that are no longer serving you well. They may sound something like this: "I am never good enough. Money doesn't grow on trees and doesn't come easy. Hard work is the only work that pays, etc." You can see how just one subconscious thought can create a whole heap of trouble, can't you? Second, choose to change.

Oh, yes, you know I had to say it. CHOOSE to change! The reality is, most people figure out what subconscious thoughts are actually holding them back but then won't do anything about it. Making the decision to take action is a very big step. And it's vital. (The reasons for not taking action are a whole therapy session in itself, so we'll save that for another time!) Three, implement tools. Create new habitual thoughts, affirm what is truth, post sticky notes all over your house and in your car, use EFT, journal ad nauseum, use a "change buddy" for motivation, have lucid dreams, talk about your change efforts until you are sick, and keep moving in THAT direction, not the OTHER direction. You have so many ways to change your negative subconscious programming. One popular phrase is "Just Do It!" But what happens when "Just Do It" doesn't work? No, it's not a matter of willpower or strength. And it's not an issue of character. It's about sticktoitiveness, practice, and consistent follow-through. Yes, there is a psychology to mindset. Can you call it a day just by knowing that? No, but once you face those negative subconscious thoughts, you can shout from the rooftop "JOB DONE!"

A mindset is a belief that orients the way we handle situations — the way we sort out what is going on and what we should do. Our mindsets help us spot opportunities but they can trap us in self-defeating cycles.

This essay isn't about all the beliefs we might hold. It is about the beliefs that make a difference in our lives — the beliefs that distinguish people who are successful at what they do versus those who continually struggle.

THE STANFORD UNIVERSITY PSYCHOLOGIST CAROL DWECK (2006) POPULARIZED THE IDEA OF MINDSETS BY CONTRASTING DIFFERENT BELIEFS ABOUT WHERE

OUR ABILITIES COME FROM.

If we have a fixed mindset that our ability is innate then a failure can be unsettling because it makes us doubt how good we are. In contrast, if we have a growth mindset then we expect that we can improve our ability — and a failure shows us what we need to work on. People with a fixed mindset are out to prove themselves, and get very defensive when someone suggests they made a mistake — they measure themselves by their failures. People with a growth mindset often show perseverance and resilience when they've committed errors — they become more motivated to work harder. You can imagine how much this fixed vs growth mindset can affect our lives.

My investigation of the nature of insight turned up a major difference between people (and organizations) who concentrate on ways to reduce errors versus others who, in addition to worrying about errors, are also excited about chances to make discoveries. The preoccupation with errors — the belief that the only way to improve performance is by reducing errors — seems to fit the fixed mindset, and the interest in discoveries — the belief that performance improvements depend both on cutting errors and on making insights — maps onto the growth mindset.

Other types of mindset can also make a big difference.

A few years ago my wife Helen and I studied police officers, soldiers and marines who had shown outstanding skills in dealing with civilians. We wanted to see what set them apart from colleagues who typically intimidated civilians in order to get them to comply. We discovered that these "Good Strangers" (as they were called) shared one trait — they all had a mindset that their colleagues didn't. Sure, they worried about their own safety, and that of their buddies. Sure, they wanted to achieve the mission, and to follow the rules. But in addition, the Good Strangers sought to gain the trust of civilians. One police officer explained to us that in every encounter with civilians, even when he was arresting a lawbreaker, he tried to conduct himself so that the civilian trusted him more at the end of the encounter than the beginning. He believed that being a professional meant doing his job in a way that fostered trust. Think back to your encounters with police — I suspect some of these encounters did not increase your trust in the officer.

We found a fourth important mindset in our work with police and military. Many of them believed that the way to get someone to do what you want is to command obedience, through intimidation or in other ways. But the Good Strangers believed that they often could get cooperation voluntarily. It took skill and took more time but it had a long-term payoff. And it built trust.

Mindsets aren't just any beliefs. They are beliefs that orient our reactions and tendencies. They serve a number of cognitive functions. They let us frame situations: they direct our attention to the most important cues, so that we're not overwhelmed with information. They suggest sensible goals so that we know what we should be trying to achieve. They prime us with reasonable courses of action so that we don't have to puzzle out what to do. When our mindsets become habitual, they define who we are, and who we can become.

We've looked at four mindsets that distinguish people who are doomed to struggle versus those who can be successful: a) fixed/growth, b) preoccupation with failure versus eagerness for discoveries, c) wanting to build trust, and d) seeking voluntary cooperation. Here is a fifth mindset that emerged from a project my research team did with Child Protective Services caseworkers. The mediocre caseworkers believed that their job was to follow procedures, but the best caseworkers saw the job as continually solving problems.

We found this same following procedures/solving problems contrast in other groups such as nurses and petrochemical plant operators. We also found it in another study of police officers. Recent academy graduates tried to add to their playbook, believing that if they learned enough procedures they could do the job. In contrast, the seasoned police officers appreciated that there were never enough procedures, and they had to be ready to solve unique problems. In fact, some of the seasoned police officers got a little bored when everything went too smoothly. They appreciated a good challenge — obviously they had a growth mindset.

The wrong mindsets can get in our way. A fixed mindset about our ability will inhibit our progress. So will a procedural mindset, governed by the belief that adding more plays in our playbook will turn us into experts. A mindset to eliminate mistakes will stifle our curiosity. A mindset about dominating civilians will damage a police officer's interactions with civilians and will result in more physical fights and reduced safety.

One of the most powerful aspects of mindsets is how quickly they can be shifted, and how powerful the consequences can be. Unlike skills that have to be practiced again and again, mindsets sometimes show dramatic shifts. Reading Dweck's book Mindset for an hour or two is enough to alter our beliefs about our abilities and motivate us to change to the growth mindset. In my work with police officers I heard many stories of officers who expected to demand obedience until they saw a supervisor speaking quietly and getting compliance.

One police officer remembered an event, decades earlier, at the beginning of his career. It was a dark night in a dangerous neighborhood. He and his supervisor, Raymond, had spotted a suspect and were closing in to make the arrest. On the way, they passed a mildly inebriated homeless man, sitting on a stoop, and the man whispered, "He's got a gun, Raymond." Sure enough, the suspect was armed and they were able to make the arrest safely. Afterwards, he asked his supervisor why the vagrant had warned them. Raymond explained that the man was harmless and he had tried to look out for him and get him to shelters when necessary. And in that instant, the rookie officer decided he wanted to have that kind of Good Stranger relationship with the people in the community. He wanted them to trust him and look out for him, rather than fear him.

Of course, it doesn't always go this easily — some of the police and military I encountered were just too determined to take no unnecessary risks. And I suspect some of the people Dweck has encountered couldn't let go of their fear of failures. But others are able to shift their beliefs and mindsets. Dweck tells the story of Jimmy, a junior high school student who had shown little interest in his classes. Then he sat through a session describing the growth mindset and tearfully asked, "You mean I don't have to be dumb?" From that point, Jimmy became a hard-working student. Mindsets are powerful, and shifting them can be sudden and transformative.

UNDERSTANDING HOW YOUR MIND WORKS

Our brains perform so many functions that living with one can sometimes become a confusing mess. How many times have you had mixed thoughts, feelings, ideas, solutions, and memories clammoring for some mental real estate, all while trying to stay focused on something else?

Cognitive psychologists have tried to make sense out of this for many years, but most of their output has been impractical. However, over the past 20 years a major theme emerged that was a breakthrough, which isn't something new to regular Psychology Today readers. The key finding was that our brains have two major types of processes: those that operate automatically (usually called System 1) and those that are more effortful (System 2). The research that demonstrated this won Daniel Kahneman the Nobel Prize.

I found this rough distinction to be somewhat helpful for my counseling clients, but it has been difficult to translate it into useful tools. So I have been working to find a better application for therapy, and recently arrived at what I call the Three Frames of Mind. All three have a purpose, none of them are superior to any other, and there are variations on each. Readers familiar with Kahneman's research will notice that the first two Frames, (Engaged & Automatic) are both forms of System 1 and the other (Analytic) is a practical way of looking at System 2.

Frames of Mind

For the descriptions below to make sense, I invite you to think of a great example for each one from your own life. You may have even used all 3 in the past couple of minutes reading this book. Once you get a good sense of them, they should become more obvious and easy to work with. I will also provide an example of each that happened to me recently hanging out with a friend.

1. Engaged Mind: this is the state of being totally immersed in, or connected to, what we are doing in the present moment. When we are fully present in a conversation, skiing down a mountain, crying after hearing about a friend having cancer, or taking the first bite of the best slice of pizza in the world; basically when our thoughts and attention are fully connected to what is happening here-and-now, that is Engaged Mind. People that are able to Engage in their daily activities (rather than zoning out or being distracted by other thoughts), are generally happier and more

satisfied with their lives and relationships. Recent research even shows that being in Engaged mind reduces base levels of the stress hormone cortisol.

Being Engaged doesn't mean an absence of pain, since what might be happening at any given moment could be physically or emotionally painful. It just means being connected to whatever is going on. Current counseling approaches based on mindfulness are designed to help people improve their experience of Engagement, and this is often one of the goals my clients have in therapy. You can read my post on Mindfulness here: An Introduction to Mindfulness.

Example: When I am hanging out with my friend I am totally caught up in listening to a story and then telling one of my own. I feel connected and the interactions are spontaneous and free of impression management. I am fully present in each moment, unconcerned with anything else that is happening outside of that conversation. Time flies by.

2. Automatic Mind: our brain is constantly conducting an enormous range tasks. For example, we become aware of any changes in the environment (new sounds, changes in light or temperature, quick movements, etc) and any pains or bodily sensations that deserve to be noticed (and some that don't). We effortlessly

make evaluations and judgments about things being positive or negative (including ourselves), categorize our experiences, and make decisions about things we need to do and have to remember. We have scenes from our past triggered and have feelings and sensations about things that might occur in the future. We form habits to Automate major parts of our lives, and are pulled out of moments with memories or questions. This non-stop flow of information is part of being human, and we spend a large percentage of our lives swimming in this stream. This is Automatic Mind.

The content of Automatic Mind is determined by current internal and environmental conditions, instincts, perceptions, and prior learning. The flow is essential for our survival and helps us adapt among countless other things, but it is also full of misinformation, distortions, and biases. Although they can be beneficial, the immediate judgments and impulses, engrained habits, and intense moods that Automatically grip us are usually the source of our greatest problems and pain, especially when it becomes routine. If Automatic thoughts and feelings are pleasant, then spending a lot of time in this frame is great! But when those things are more negative or troubling, or are so strong that we can't stay Engaged, then Automatic Mind can become an unbearable place that we try to escape from. Most people come to counseling for things related to Automatic Mind.

Example: During a slow moment of the conversation with my friend, my mind wanders to what I am doing after we part. I mentally run through a list of things to get at the grocery store, and also replay an argument I got into with someone else a few hours earlier that makes me get a bit anxious. I am not completely present in what is happening here-and-now, but am off and running with this Automatic flow, losing track of the details of the conversation in the process, and feeling anxious.

3. Analytic Mind: since we are self-aware creatures, we have the ability to intentionally step back from our current thoughts, feelings, and experiences to observe them, manipulate information in our minds, and solve problems. All of the complex reasoning we can do is what I call Analytic Mind.

Since there are so many different ways Analytic Mind can work, I offer 6 broad categories below. Also, many of these thought processes also take place in Automatic Mind. The difference here is that Analytic Mind is when we intentionally choose to use these abilities.

-Observe: we can observe other people, as well as the workings or our own minds.

-Reflect: we can replay events in our memories, and arrive at new perspectives.

-Solve: we can take immediate issues and problems and find solutions or understanding.

-Plan: we can plan deep into the future and create backup options.

-Focus: we can sustain attention on something important

-Imagine: we can use our imaginations to run through how something may play out.

Most of our complex reasoning skills come online at the beginning of adolescence and develop into adulthood. When we make decisions after Analyzing a situation, we are less likely to make mistakes or have biased perspectives. Other problems can arise here when we stay in this frame too much by "over-Analyzing" things, develop a rigidity of thinking, or don't use it enough! Our Analytic Minds also come into conflict with Automatically generated emotions and intuition, which can leave us in a states of confusion, indecision, or "cognitive dissonance." You can read more about that here: Resolving Cognitive Dissonance.

Example: After noticing my anxiety, I decided to try and

re-Engage in the conversation. However, I stayed anxious and kept having difficulty being involved. I decided to take a couple minutes to take a closer look at my anxiety to understand why it was so strong, and to reason through it. I reflected on the earlier argument, and realized that I made a critical mistake, and I then focused on developing a plan of how to apologize and make things right again. After doing this, I was able to Engage again with my friend.

Mastering Your Mind

You may think your success is determined by your intelligence, experience, environment, or even your personality. But research suggests that it's your point of view – your mindset – that may be the key.

The mindset you adopt for yourself profoundly affects the way you lead your life, says Carol Dweck, PhD, author of Mindset: The New Psychology of Success.

Your mindset -- the difference in how you react to feedback or accomplishment -- can affect your performance in school, relationships, business and even parenting.

Dweck's research suggests there are just two different mindsets: fixed and growth. Those with a fixed mindset need to keep proving themselves over and over, while those with a growth mindset believe their basic qualities can be cultivated through their own efforts.

What type of mindset do you have?

Here's one quick way to find out: Think back to your school days. If you got a bad grade in school, would you often give up, saying the class was just a waste of time, or would you tend to tell yourself you just needed to study harder?

If you were likely to give up, you are likely to have a fixed mindset; if you decided to work harder, you probably have a growth mindset.

Someone with a fixed mindset is typically quick to interpret disappointments as utter failure. "Nothing ventured, nothing lost," becomes their philosophy, as they get increasingly reluctant to attempt new things and believe in themselves. They're also likely to under- or over-estimate their abilities, setting themselves up for frustration and failure.

On the other hand, those with a growth mindset tend to be quick to create a simple strategy to deal with problems as they occur. And they're better able to accurately identify their own strengths and weaknesses.

Interestingly, Dweck says that research done in the brain-wave lab at Columbia University, in New York, shows a link between actual brain activity and one's perspective.

In the study, participants with both types of mindsets were asked hard questions. When they got feedback, those with a fixed mindset were only interested in how well they scored, and didn't want to learn the right answer. Those with a growth mindset listened to information that would enhance their knowledge, and seemed less focused on how they did on the questions themselves.

The good news is that you can actually change your mindset. But there are some things Dweck says you should know:

Your mindset is part of your make-up. Understanding your mindset can help you think and react in a different way.

If you have a fixed mindset, everything is about outcome: getting the grade, or rising to the top of the organization, for example. If you have a growth mindset, it's about valuing what you do regardless of the outcomes.

Generally, those with a fixed mindset prefer effortless

success. It helps them prove their talent.

You're not always in your dominant mindset. Many people have elements of both mindsets, and you can have different mindsets in different areas of your life. For example, you might think your artistic ability is fixed ("I just can't draw") but you hope to develop athletic ability by taking golf lessons. Whatever mindset people have in a particular area will guide them in that realm.

If you have a growth mindset, you most likely believe that abilities can be cultivated. But you should know some things probably can't be cultivated, such as preferences or values.

People with fixed mindsets have just as much confidence as those with growth mindsets. But someone with a fixed mindset tends to be more fragile and susceptible to setbacks.

Those with growth mindsets don't always feel confident. In fact, they sometimes plunge into something just because they're not good at it. They just want to try.

If you want to re-adjust your mindset, how do you do it? Start by catching yourself giving up when something starts to get difficult -- say when you're doing a crossword puzzle, or playing video game or a sport. "Put yourself in a growth mindset. Picture your brain forming new connections as you meet the challenge and learn. Keep on going," Dweck suggests.

She also encourages people to leave their comfort zones and seek constructive criticism. "We can choose partners, make friends, hire people who make us feel faultless. But think about it – do you want to never grow?"

Why You Need To Develop A Growth Mindset

"If you imagine less, less will be what you undoubtedly deserve." ~ Debbie Millman

It is said that you have a growth mindset if you are one of those people who believe that—by investing enough time, effort and study—you will be able to acquire any ability. If you believe abilities are innate and that, simply, there is no way of doing that for what you were not born, then you have a fixed mindset.

Those with a fixed mindset are very afraid of failure because they see it as a sign of weakness or lack of ability in a given field. People with a growth mindset don't care much about failure because they know that they can learn from it and therefore improve their performance.

Carol Dweck, Ph.D. in Psychology and professor at Standford University, has studied how these types of mindsets influence peoples' lives. She has concluded that people with growth mentality are more successful in every aspect of their lives and live with lower stress levels (you can read the outcome of her research in her book of 2006, Mindset: The New Psychology of Success).

Someone with a fixed mindset sees effort as something unnecessary. They will tend to avoid challenges, surrender when obstacles appear, ignore criticisms and feel threaten with someone else's success. As a consequence, they will become stagnant and will never reach their potential.

Someone with a growth mindset perceives effort as the necessary path to mastery. They will accept challenges despite the risk, fight against adversities, learn from criticisms and find inspiration in someone else's success.

Good news is that it's possible to work on a fixed mindset and transform it into a growth one. The best way to achieve this is through deliberate practice. You have to take active part, and take some steps which are against your beliefs. It's your daily actions the ones that change the perception of yourself.

For example, if you have given up doing sports because you think it's not your thing, try to run only one kilometer at a pace you feel comfortable with. Do it again another day, and another... and another. In a few days you will be easily running two kilometers and in some weeks, five. As months go by you will see that you can even increase your speed little by little and achieve decent times. Contrary to what you believe, your identity could end up including the word "athlete".

If you think that "being organized" is not for you and that you are a natural procrastinator, then you are limiting very much your personal development and you'll waste a good part of your life just by not trying to improve. Start by practicing the steps that will make you more productive. Concentrate on the process, not on the final outcome (it will come later), and the transformation will happen.

HOW TO USE PSYCHOLOGY TO BATTLE PROCRASTINATION

I have read a lot about procrastination (mainly because I've done it all my life), and found many different reported causes. But it all boils down to the age-old battle of pleasure versus pain. It is said that all human behavior falls into two categories: acquiring pleasure or avoiding pain. Our decisions and actions are really efforts to either gain pleasurable feelings or avoid some sort of pain or uncomfortable feeling.

So how does this relate to procrastination? Procrastinators are focused on doing activities that are pleasurable while avoiding activities that have perceived pain.

Watching TV, playing video games, reading, and napping are all activities that can be more pleasurable than working. These may be obvious but work-related tasks can also reinforce delay. Tasks such as checking email, looking at website stats, doing research, and training are all ways that we can feel busy without really getting anything accomplished. Sometimes it's more fun to learn about how to do things than actually doing them.

For some, the pain is the discomfort of the work

needed to complete their task. These people look at what the job requires and want to avoid the process. It can also be that many procrastinators tie their self-worth with their performance and the fear of being criticized for their work overcomes the need to complete it.

Many strive for perfectionism, but their fear of failure motivates them to avoid the task altogether. The perceived pain of making a mistake, being criticized, or letting someone else down can be too much to bear. There is more to procrastination than just being lazy.

Procrastination is one of the biggest obstacles to productivity and a guilty refuge of creatives everywhere. It's something we're all guilty of, and something we all have our own tactics (with varying degrees of success) to combat. What makes us procrastinate? Why is the temptation so great, even when we know we need to complete the task at hand? First, let's look at the psychology of procrastination.

While everyone procrastinates to some extent, not everyone is a chronic procrastinator. There are relatively harmless instances of procrastination—not starting a project until you've gone to the washroom, checked Facebook, refilled your coffee and organized everything in your top desk drawer, or leaving your least favourite task for Friday afternoon. But there are also the unhealthy procrastination habits that find you staring at a blank computer screen for an hour, or that leave you awake in the middle of the night in a cold sweat, agonizing over the work you didn't complete, wondering how you'll ever get it done the next day.

Understand Procrastination

There are a lot of misconceptions about what causes procrastination. For many years, I felt that procrastination meant that I was lazy and unfocused. Whether it was a university paper due or a client presentation I had to have ready at 9 am, I'd find myself awake in the middle of the night skimming articles on the Battle of the Bulge or the care and feeding of chinchillas (I've never had a chinchilla) while sweating about all the work I hadn't done. Conventional wisdom denotes the source of procrastination to be a lack of willpower or poor time management, and so that was what I believed my problem to be.

However, in more recent studies psychologists have understood procrastination to be closely related to our emotional brain—a coping mechanism driven by our own fear of failure. By avoiding tasks that are intimidating and overwhelming, and focusing on something less stressful, we give our brain temporary relief. Unfortunately, as all procrastinators know, the end result is usually the last-minute rush to complete projects, coupled with intensified anxiety, a lack of sleep, and reduced quality of work.

Once we understand that procrastination is mostly fear and anxiety based, we can learn more meaningful methods to overcome it. The age-old "just get started!" advice doesn't fit as neatly into the narrative of procrastination when we are aware that most people are avoiding things they are anxious about.

"It really has nothing to do with time-management," says Association for Psychological Science Fellow Joseph Ferrari, a professor of psychology at DePaul University. "To tell the chronic procrastinator to just do it would be like saying to a clinically depressed person, cheer up."

Why Do We Procrastinate and Wait Until the Last Minute?

We all procrastinate at some time or another, and researchers suggest that the problem can be particularly pronounced among students. An estimated 25 to 75 percent of college students procrastinate on academic work.

One 2007 study found that a whopping 80 to 95 percent of college students procrastinated on a regular basis, particularly when it came to completing assignments and coursework. A 1997 survey found that procrastination was one of the top reasons why Ph.D. candidates failed to complete their dissertations.

According to Ferrari, Johnson, and McCown, there are some major cognitive distortions that lead to academic procrastination.

Students tend to:

Overestimate how much time they have left to perform tasks

Overestimate how motivated they will be in the future

Underestimate how long certain activities will take to complete

Mistakenly assume that they need to be in the right frame of mind to work on a project

As you read through that list, you can probably recall a few times in the past that the same sort of logic has led you to put things off until later. Remember that time that you thought you had a week left to finish a project that was really due the next day? How about the time you decided not to clean up your apartment because you "didn't feel like doing it right now."

We often assume that projects won't take as long to finish as they really will, which can lead to a false sense of security when we believe that we still have plenty of time to complete these tasks. One of the biggest factors contributing to procrastination is the notion that we have to feel inspired or motivated to work on a task at a particular moment.

The reality is that if you wait until you're in the right frame of mind to do certain tasks (especially undesirable ones), you will probably find that the right time simply never comes along and the task never gets completed.

Self-doubt can also play a major role. When you are unsure of how to tackle a project or insecure in your abilities, you might find yourself putting it off in favor of working on other tasks.

The Negative Impact Of Procrastination

It's not just students who fall into the "I'll do it later" trap. According to Joseph Ferrari, a professor of psychology at DePaul University in Chicago and author of Still Procrastinating: The No Regret Guide to Getting It Done, around 20 percent of U.S. adults are chronic procrastinators.

These people don't just procrastinate occasionally; it's a major part of their lifestyle. They pay their bills late, don't start work on big projects until the night before the deadline, delay holiday shopping until Christmas Eve, and even file their income tax returns late.

Unfortunately, this procrastination can have a serious impact on a number of life areas, including a person's mental health. In a 2007 study, researchers found that at the beginning of the semester, students who were procrastinators reported less illness and lower stress levels than non-procrastinators. This changed dramatically by the end of the term when procrastinators reported higher levels of stress and illness.

Not only can procrastination have a negative impact on your health; it can also harm your social relationships. By putting things off, you are placing a burden on the people around you. If you habitually turn in projects late or dawdle until the last minute, the people who depend on you such as your friends, family, co-workers, and fellow students can become resentful.

The Reasons Why We Procrastinate

In addition to the reasons why we procrastinate, we often come up with a number of excuses or rationalizations to justify our behavior.

According to Tuckman, Abry, and Smith, there are 15 key reasons why people procrastinate:

- ✓ Not knowing what needs to be done

- ✓ Not knowing how to do something

- ✓ Not wanting to do something

- ✓ Not caring if it gets done or not

- ✓ Not caring when something gets done

- ✓ Not feeling in the mood to do it

- ✓ Being in the habit of waiting until the last minute

- ✓ Believing that you work better under pressure

- ✓ Thinking that you can finish it at the last minute

- ✓ Lacking the initiative to get started

- ✓ Forgetting

✓ Blaming sickness or poor health

✓ Waiting for the right moment

✓ Needing time to think about the task

✓ Delaying one task in favor of working on another

How Do Procrastinators Differ From Non-Procrastinators?

In most cases, procrastination is not a sign of a serious problem. It's a common tendency that we all give in to at some point or another. It is only in cases where procrastination becomes so chronic that it begins to have a serious impact on a person's daily life that it becomes a more serious issue. In such instances, it's not just a matter of having poor time management skills; it's an indication of what Ferrari refers to as a maladaptive lifestyle.

"Non-procrastinators focus on the task that needs to be done. They have a stronger personal identity and are less concerned about what psychologists call 'social esteem'—how others like us—as opposed to self-esteem which is how we feel about ourselves," explained Dr. Ferrari in an interview with the American Psychological Association.

According to psychologist Piers Steel, people who don't procrastinate tend to be high in the personality trait known as conscientiousness, one of the broad dispositions identified by the big 5 theory of personality. People who are high in conscientiousness also tend to be high in other areas including self-discipline, persistence, and personal responsibility.

Falling prey to these cognitive distortions is easy, but fortunately, there are a number of different things you can do to fight procrastination and start getting things done on time.

HOW TO USE PSYCHOLOGY TO BOOST YOUR CONFIDENCE

Society offers us plenty of advice on how to be confident. "Just be yourself." "Fake it til you make it." "Dress for success." Tips fly at us from every direction, from mothers to magazine covers. Some of this advice can be useful, but it can ultimately feel ineffective or empty when we don't really believe in ourselves. We all battle core feelings about ourselves that can be negative and demoralizing. In response, we may find ourselves either sinking into self-shame or trying to build up our ego just to get through the day.

To truly construct a solid foundation of self-confidence, we have to dig a little deeper. There are many positive, psychological steps we can take to feel good about ourselves. Most importantly, we have to do two things: 1. Challenge the inner critic we all possess and 2. Practice self-compassion. With these goals in mind, we can start to take practical actions to feel more comfortable in our skin. Here are some powerful tools that can help us all feel more self-possessed.

How To Be Confident: Practice Self-Compassion

It's valuable to move through life with what mindfulness expert and interpersonal neurobiologist Dr. Daniel Siegel calls a COAL attitude, in which we are Curious, Open, Accepting, and Loving toward ourselves no matter what we're going through. That way, even if we feel humiliated and defeated, or our self-confidence has taken a hit, we won't waste time beating ourselves up. Instead, we learn from our experiences. Enhancing our self-compassion is an adaptive process that allows us to feel more self-acceptance, while simultaneously making real efforts to develop, both which help to establish our confidence.

Groundbreaking research by Dr. Kristin Neff has shown that self-compassion can actually be more valuable and adaptive than self-esteem. For instance, compared to self-esteem, self-compassion was associated with "greater emotional resilience, more accurate self-concepts, more caring relationship behavior, [and] less narcissism." When wondering how to be confident, practicing self-compassion is a great place to start. To fully understand why self-compassion is so crucial to our confidence, it's helpful to break down the three elements of self-compassion as defined by Neff.

Self-kindness vs Self-judgment – When we get carried

away with judging and evaluating ourselves, our confidence tends to plummet. Imagine berating yourself before a date or a job interview. "You're not dressed right." "You're gonna be so awkward." These thoughts will likely increase our anxiety and even impair our ability to act natural and be ourselves. Now, imagine being kind to yourself instead, as if a friend is sitting beside you, offering encouragement and warmth. This "friend" doesn't have to build us up or offer false praise. It can simply say, "It's okay that you're nervous, but there's absolutely nothing wrong with you. I'm proud that you showed up and are trying this." While self-esteem is still often based on evaluation, self-compassion comes from having a kind attitude toward ourselves no matter what we're going through or taking on.

Mindfulness vs Over-identification with thoughts – Because our thoughts can go so negative at times, it's helpful to practice mindfulness as a way to avoid being consumed by this negativity. Mindfulness is a way of focusing our attention and accepting our thoughts and feelings without judgment, while also letting them go. Think about how athletes or performers have to actively focus on clearing their minds before they march onto the field or step out on the stage. It's hard to feel self-possessed and capable when our hearts are racing and heads are spinning with doubt and self-criticism. Whether through meditation or breathing exercises, mindfulness allows us to stay in our bodies in the moment and allow our thoughts to pass like cars on a train. We can notice and acknowledge them, but we don't board the train and get swept away. By not over-identifying with our negative or self-critical thoughts, we learn to live more in the moment and feel more self-possessed, both which can be key to feeling confident.

Common humanity vs Isolation – In her examination, Neff found that it's much easier to have self-compassion when we accept that we are all part of a shared human experience. In other words, we all make mistakes, and we all suffer. It's easy to attack ourselves when we view ourselves as different or alone in our struggle. Our confidence can be shattered by both seeing ourselves as outsiders in some negative sense and failing to embrace that we are unique in a very positive sense. When we see ourselves as human, we are less likely to feel like we need to be the best or like we're already the worst. We are less likely to feel victimized and more likely to look directly at our shortcomings and make real efforts to grow and change.

How To Be Confident: Get To Know Your Inner Critic

Dr. Robert Firestone, author of Overcoming the Destructive Inner Voice has written extensively about the role of the "critical inner voice" in injuring people's confidence and limiting their ability to fully be themselves. This "voice" is like a sadistic coach that attacks us from every angle and undermines our goals. It affects us in all areas of our lives. Sometimes, this destructive thought process can seem subtle, even soothing, like a parent whispering in our ear: "No need to try anything new," it says. "That will only make you anxious. Why not just stay in your comfort zone and feel safe?" Other times, that voice is outright vicious and punishing. "You literally can't do anything right. Why try? You will fail!" Whether whispering or shouting, the critical inner voice has one goal, which is to reinforce old, critical ways we have of seeing ourselves that hurt us but feel familiar, as if they're part of our identity. As Dr. Firestone put it in his blog "How to Befriend Yourself:"

The enemy within can be thought of as a negative identity. This negative identity is a byproduct of negative ways you were labeled as a child, the negative attitudes toward yourself that you incorporated from any mistreatment you were exposed to and the defensive strategies that you formed to cope with psychological pain that further bent you out of shape. You mistake the identity that you formed under these circumstances as being the truth and act as though it were. Catching on to this misconception of yourself allows you to challenge and alter this mistaken identity and can help you to become your authentic self.

Firestone has developed a series of steps people can take to help them identify and overcome their critical inner voice as well as a therapy methodology called Voice Therapy. Practicing these steps whenever our critical inner voice starts to crush our confidence is a process that can be incredibly empowering and can help bring us back to ourselves and our real, more compassionate point of view. Initially, when we challenge this inner critic (and the more we accomplish and ignore it), we may notice this voice grow even louder. However, if we're persistent and continue to cast these thoughts aside or "starve the monster," eventually, the voice will shrink down and lose power over us.

This effort to conquer our inner critic and adopt a more self-compassionate attitude is part of a lifelong process. Over and over again, we have to become aware of when that critical inner voice is creeping in and attempting to take the wheel. As we do, we can keep returning to a compassionate attitude that will help us through the hard times. In addition to this ongoing goal, there are also some actions we can take each day to boost our confidence. Here are some science-backed tips for doing just that:

* Reflect on a moments when you felt accomplished – One study recently showed that recalling an event in which we felt proud or recognized can help strengthen our confidence. These types of thoughts can also act as natural counters to our critical inner voice. These don't need to be major events – maybe just a time we were acknowledged for being generous or overcame a fear. We shouldn't get carried away, feeling like we need to pull up old victories just to believe that we're okay. Instead, we should just allow the memory itself to make us feel good and serve as a small reminder of who we really are.

 * Exercise – There's no debate that being active makes us feel good. Studies have shown that even light exercise can boost our confidence. This doesn't mean we have to do an extreme body makeover or obsess over any physical result. It just means getting moving to release some mood-boosting endorphins and enjoying the perk of feeling more confident throughout the day.

 * Stand tall – Yup, that annoying reminder from

teachers and parents turns out to have some merit; standing up straight can make us more confident. It may sound silly, but according to one study from Harvard and Columbia University researchers, better posture actually makes people feel more confident and powerful.

* Dress in ways that make you feel your best – No matter how minuscule our interest in fashion may be, our personal style is part of who we are. Studies have shown that how we dress can affect our performance, mood, and self-esteem, which has led some researchers to suggest that "we should put on clothes that we associate with happiness, even when feeling low."

 * Practice generosity – Being generous is a natural way to reduce stress, boost one's immune system and feel a sense of purpose. Anything from volunteering to performing a favor for a friend can enhance our sense of self. "Generosity is a natural confidence builder and a natural repellent of self-hatred. Not only does it make us feel better about ourselves, but it actively combats feelings of isolation and depression," said Dr. Lisa Firestone, who co-authored Conquer Your Critical Inner Voice.

* Find tools to help reduce your anxiety – When we

feel anxious, it can be very difficult to connect with feelings of confidence. There are many exercises anyone can learn to help them deal with anxiety and return a sense of inner calm and presence. We can find many techniques for alleviating anxiety here. Practicing these methods can help us feel more calm and comfortable in our skin.

Confidence is simply the degree to which you believe that your actions will result in a positive outcome.

This is not the same as self-esteem.

Self-esteem is a more general feeling you have about yourself, where as confidence is the belief you have in your skills in a given situation. When most people say they want to be more confident, what they mean is that they want more self-esteem.

Unsurprisingly however, the more areas you become confident in, the more you are likely to naturally develop self-esteem.

Why Do We Want Confidence?

Confidence is an evolutionary advantage that can help you approach whatever task is in front of you without hesitation or anxiety. It can allow us to do what we really want to do with our lives.

The problem is that most of the time the advice we get about how to be more confident can be a little generic.

"Fake it till you make it," "Talk louder" or "Dress the part."

To be fair, this isn't terrible advice, it can actually have a positive impact on how you feel, but it doesn't really instill you with the kind of deep confidence that results in real change.

Here Are 5 Hidden qualities Of Confident People.

They manage their outcome dependence

Confident people don't worry about the outcome of a situation. Their attention is focused on the action or activity as opposed to the external result.

In the event that they fail, they see it as a learning experience as opposed to a reflection of who they are as a person or even how much they're worth.

They assess themselves accurately

This might seem counter-intuitive, but to develop true confidence you need to have a little bit of brutal self-honesty.

If you have unrealistic expectations about your

capabilities, you're likely to get shocked and disheartened when things don't go as you expected. On the other hand if you have an objective assessment of your skills, this is less likely to be the case.

Another important thing to consider here is that they are able to accept constructive criticism from others without getting defensive. The attention of confident people isn't focused on whether others perceive them as competent but on how they can improve for the future.

They practice Positive Visualization

Ours brains have a difficult time distinguishing real memories and constructed ones. Self-assured people use this to their advantage by visualizing their competence in a certain area until their neural networks have been rewired for success.

One study revealed that weightlifters that practiced positive visualization found the practice almost as effective as the physical practice itself for performance enhancement.

They choose their activities carefully

You can't be the best at everything and self-assured people know this. Instead they stick to what they known is going to make them confident.

For example, if they want to be a confident swimmer they might spend a lot of time running, because some of the skills are complimentary. But they're not going to spend hours writing creative stories, because the overlap between the two activities is less significant

Sometimes it's simple enough to realize that if you want to feel confident, you should spend time just doing things your confident in.

This might not be what you want to hear, but it's the truth. If you want to develop self-esteem, you need to need to push your comfort zone in a number of areas, but it is slow growth over time that will lead to deeper, long lasting confidence.

They develop their skills

To feel more confident you need to better yourself in the area you want to feel confident in, and the only way to do so is practice.

Again, this is pretty obvious, but it means being able to focus on one area for a sustained period of time until you're competent, instead of letting your attention drift all over the place and getting what is known as 'shiny objective syndrome.'

They take action!

As Dale Carnegie said:

"Inaction breeds doubt and fear. Action breeds confidence and courage. If you want to conquer fear, do not sit home and think about it. Go out and get busy."

HOW TO USE PSYCHOLOGY
TO MOTIVATE YOURSELF

Understanding the psychology of motivation can help you when you know you need a push to get you going. When motivation is desired, there are really only two factors that will get a human being moving. The first is an anticipation of pleasure and the second is fear of pain. You can paint all kinds of pretty words around these two things like expectation of rewards or fear of reprisal, but the psychology of motivation always boils down to these same two things.

You know that when your morale is down, your productivity goes down the tubes, right. So then the best thing for you to do would be to figure out what your greatest motivators are. It is usually much healthier and less stressful to be motivated by the positive emotion of anticipation. But there are certainly those times - especially when you are under the gun - when only fear will do the trick. The key is to not let it get to that point, at least not all the time anyway.

The Psychology of Motivation Can Work For You Or Against You

Knowing that the psychology of motivation can work for you or against you, you can get yourself prepared. If you know ahead of time what it is that most motivates you, you can infuse your thinking with these ideas beforehand and keep yourself from the triple threats of procrastination, discouragement and guilt - and all the evil things that come out of them.

One of the easiest things you can do ahead of time is to take 15 or 20 minutes and write down all of the long-term goals you have. Make them juicy. Don't just write down "I want to make more money." A dollar more is still more and you know you don't just want that. If your goal is to make more money - decide what that money will get you like a cruise or an all inclusive vacation to Antigua (my personal favorite) or a fancy new car. Put a few pictures where you can easily see them and when you find yourself down think about these things and how happy they make you.

Can You "Trick" Yourself Into Feeling Motivated?

You can also use the psychology of motivation to "trick" you into feeling better and getting more done. Have you ever noticed the difference in how you feel when you are moping around compared to when you are jumping up and down excited? Big difference, right? If you want to trick yourself into feeling more motivated, just start jumping up and down and laughing. You'll get an instant boost of endorphins and it will be almost impossible to crawl back into that mopey state and you'll be more inclined to get going.

I used to believe that I simply needed to power through—use whatever energy I had left to keep working and hope for better results. But, finally, exhausted and unsatisfied with the results that I was achieving, I turned to behavioral psychology to learn how to get "unstuck" and perform at my best.

I'm going to cover the psychology behind how rewards influence our behavior and offer some techniques that you can practice to get and stay motivated.

Why We Crave Rewards

Alexander Rothman's theory of behavior maintenance suggests that your ability to maintain a positive behavior or habit is dependent on your perception of the benefits:

Decisions regarding behavioral initiation are predicted to depend on favorable expectations regarding future outcomes, whereas decisions regarding behavioral maintenance are predicted to depend on perceived satisfaction with received outcomes.

However, challenging and ambitious projects don't always provide immediate rewards. Sometimes you even get negative feedback for prolonged periods.

When we receive positive feedback, we become more motivated. And when our motivation increases, we perform better. It's a cycle that feeds on itself.

If we perceive the rewards resulting from a given behavior as insufficient, or if we receive negative feedback, we lose motivation. This lack of motivation might manifest itself as procrastination or a lack of energy. We experience this because our brains are telling us to stop investing energy in something that is not helping us.

Douglas Lisle, a psychologist who specializes in motivation, describes moods and emotions as "feedback systems" that can indicate the effectiveness of our actions. He says that anxiety is actually an important and valuable emotion:

Anxiety is generally a useful guide—signaling us that our proposed endeavor may require our very best effort to succeed and, in fact, may require talent beyond our current abilities... The survival value of anxiety is obvious—if you are contemplating a trek across dangerous terrain, you had better be anxious. You had better consider carefully whether this is an intelligent undertaking. And, if it is, your anxiety will help to facilitate careful planning, checking and rechecking of supplies, the rehearsing of potentially needed skills, worrying about things that could go wrong, and so forth.

Anxiety is a signal that we may need to rethink our strategy. When you are overly anxious, you won't feel motivated or energized. The lack of motivation hinders your ability to perform, which hinders your ability to achieve goals.

When you're in this negative feedback loop, it's difficult to get up off the couch and get to work. You just want to sit around and do nothing. You can't seem to cross items off your to-do list, even though they've been there for weeks. But as you begin to take action and pick up small wins, you start feeling less stuck.

After making more progress, you're still not quite at your peak level of performance because there's still some uncertainty about your ability to succeed and achieve results. You still have some degree of stress, but it's healthy stress that's enough to motivate you to keep taking action. As you continue to gain momentum, you reach a state of optimal motivation and performance, before reaching a new plateau.

How We Measure Success

Behind most of the decisions we make is a cost-benefit analysis. This analysis may be done consciously or unconsciously. We compare the benefits that we expect to receive to the costs that we expect will be required.

While money is one of the most obvious forms of benefit, rewards can come in many forms. Humans also seek social status and positive feedback from peers. Rewards validate your cost-benefit analysis. It's evidence that gives you more confidence that you're moving in the right direction.

For example, say that you decide to start freelancing on the side because you're confident that you can make some extra money and build your portfolio. When you get positive feedback, in the form of a new client, your cost-benefit analysis gains validation. Your initial hypothesis, that you can start a freelancing business, is more likely to be correct.

As a result of the monetary reward from closing the new client, your cost-benefit balance further tips toward motivation (the left side of the graphic above). The benefits outweigh the costs, motivating you to continue freelancing.

Conversely, if you were to spend months trying to find a freelancing client but never manage to land one, your brain may interpret freelancing as a poor return on investment. This would limit your energy for seeking clients.

If your brain doesn't understand both the costs of inaction and the benefits of action, you won't feel very motivated.

Some people are more motivated by fear. Rather than moving toward something—such as a freelancing business—they are motivated to move away from something else. They may be motivated to get out of student debt or quit their day job. It's important to think in terms of the desired action (freelancing in this case) as well as the undesired action or the status quo. If your brain doesn't understand both the costs of inaction and the benefits of action, you won't feel very motivated.

This may seem straightforward, but it gets more interesting when you consider that we don't always do a good job of interpreting feedback. Many people don't internalize the rewards they receive. Some may even be succeeding but actually believe they're failing.

Failures can generally be grouped into two categories: real and imagined. If you have ambitious goals, you will inevitably experience a real failure. You might shut down your business, take a loss on an investment, or get dumped by a partner. However, it's far more often that your perceived failures are actually just small missteps moving you in the right direction. You simply need to reinterpret the feedback you receive.

Techniques For Boosting Motivation

Regardless of whether the negative feedback you're getting is real or imagined, there are techniques you can use to regain or sustain motivation during challenging times. Imagined failure—in the form of overreacting to negative feedback or lacking appreciation for positive feedback—can be solved through changing the way you think about your work and results. You can overcome real failure by changing your strategy.

The techniques below can help break a cycle of negative feedback and get you back into a positive feedback loop.

Change Your Thinking

Oftentimes, feelings of failure are merely figments of imagination. In these cases, you don't actually need more money or more pats on the back from your peers. Rather, you simply need to change the way you interpret your situation and internalize the rewards you're already receiving.

Set achievable goals. Studies have found that when people make progress toward goals, they are more motivated to continue. Progress reduces the perceived costs and increases confidence in future benefits. Achieving a goal also gives you data that indicates your cost-benefit analysis was correct and you are moving in the right direction. One strategy is to break big goals into smaller goals that you can achieve on a consistent basis. Your long-term goal may be to sell your company for $1 billion, but that will take years. Without some smaller wins along the way, you may lose motivation. Consider setting a weekly goal, such as shipping a new feature, or publishing a piece of content. Accomplishing shorter-term goals will keep you motivated to achieve your longer-term goals.

Acknowledge intangible rewards. According to a study by researchers at Princeton, money can make you happier, but you reach diminishing returns once you make $75,000 per year. Your biology is more concerned with simply surviving than climbing up Maslow's hierarchy of needs and realizing your full potential. Rewards such as supporting your community or increasing your financial safety net are still important. But you won't necessarily gain a dopamine hit of motivation from these things like you will from landing a new job that pays $75,000 a year. You'll need to remind yourself of the less tangible rewards you are receiving.

Change your interpretation of failure. When you fail at something, you lose motivation. Your brain tells you to stop investing time and money in an opportunity that might not lead to success. However, failure is also a learning opportunity. Now that you've failed, you know what doesn't work. You can try something new that's more likely to work. When you fail, don't identify it as a failure. Instead of telling yourself, "I'm a loser," tell yourself, "I lost this time, but I'll win in the long run." Also remember that there's an element of chance in most pursuits. The loss may not have even been a result of your performance.

Upgrade your definition of success. When you decide to start a business, your goal is probably to achieve profitability, or perhaps to sell it. However, there is a high degree of chance in starting a company. Sometimes even the most talented and hardworking entrepreneurs fail. You don't know how the economy will change, what new regulations will affect your market, how consumer preferences will shift, or what new competitors may appear. Instead of letting your motivation depend on factors outside your control, define success in terms of making good decisions and executing them to the best of your abilities.

Increase the cost of inaction. When you win at a video game, your brain thinks you've just done something beneficial, but you really haven't. Remind yourself that climbing to the top of the World of Warcraft leaderboard is not as rewarding as getting healthier, closing your next deal, or starting that nonprofit. In fact, spending too much time playing video games will only make it less likely that you will achieve your most important goals. Remind yourself that inaction has a cost and try to deprive yourself of the rewards you receive from inaction.

Change Your Behavior

Many personal development articles encourage suppressing negative emotions and forcing yourself through whatever comes your way. And, from a psychological perspective, it's easier to push through hardship than it is to accept that you are falling short. Suppressing negative feedback, though, allows you to avoid reconsidering your strategies and priorities. You may actually need less hustle and more strategic thinking.

Take on a new challenge. If the rewards you're

receiving are not meeting your expectations given your perceived abilities, they may not be motivating. Lisle writes that "people sometimes become depressed because their lives no longer require their very best efforts. Consistently operating at significantly less than your full capacity may save energy, but it often doesn't feel good." Find an opportunity to take on a new project at work or start a side project that challenges you.

Change your strategy. If you're unsatisfied with the results of your efforts, consider why you are not achieving sufficient rewards and what you can do to improve. It may turn out that you are working on the right project or pursuing a great opportunity but simply need to change the way you are doing it. For example, if your blog hasn't grown the way you'd hoped, you may need to shift from writing short articles frequently to more in-depth articles less frequently. Or you may need to learn or improve a skill that can help you succeed, such as SEO or Facebook ads.

Choose the right opportunity. The cost-benefit analysis that you ran to determine what you should be working on didn't pan out as expected. This is common because it's difficult to predict the future. If you determine that you are accurately measuring your results and changing your strategy is insufficient, it may be best to shift your focus to something new. While this realization may bruise your ego, it would be foolish to deny the reality that you are not achieving the results you are capable of. Consider your strengths, weakness, and values—and find your next big opportunity.

PSYCHOLOGY AND POSITIVE THINKING

Take for example, the cell phone that has become an indispensable gadget for every one all over the world today. It too once used to be an impossible dream, however, it was the positive attitude and will of one single individual that made it possible and accessible to billions of people today. If the inventor was pessimistic and had gotten depressed with the numerous failures he might have encountered on his way, we would not be talking to our dear ones on a handy and mobile phone today. It clearly manifests the applicability of the principle that what the mind can visualize, the human body is capable of achieving it.

Ones Psychology and Positive Thinking play a crucial role in countering negative tendencies

The feeling of joy born out of a positive and healthy existence is unbeatable. Ones life condition becomes such that one feels lively, happy and capable of taking on anything in this world. The future looks all bright and brimming with hope and fulfillment. One feels the thankfulness of being alive from ones core. Life just looks perfect - flawless!

In reality, however, it all sounds to good to be true. The people nowadays are surrounded by so many worries and fears stemming from various issues related to relationships, finance, career, family life, office etc. that taking out time to think positively becomes a rare activity. Positive thinking by its very meaning is all about the state of one?s mind rather than one?s actions. Of course the state of mind eventually gets manifested in the form of actions, but it all starts from ones brain. You must firmly believe and be confident about the fact that you are endowed with all sorts of capabilities, health and attitude to taste success. This is also known as positive affirmation.

A synonym often used for positive affirmation is self-suggestion. However, self-suggestion refers to the method by which one can rid oneself of all the negative thoughts that stop him/her from thinking positive. Subjecting oneself to repeated self-suggestions can work wonders on the individual by leading him/her to a life state full of positive thoughts.

You can even opt for the strategy of recording all your self-suggestions and positive affirmations on a CD with a background music score and playing it regularly while driving to work or when relaxing. This method helps immensely in driving certain thoughts home and ensuring their absorption and manifestation in a very successful manner.

Positive Thinking - A Self-Learning Process

It is often commented in the psychology parlance that what the mind visualizes, body is capable to achieve. It is the mind that is the center of ones existence and determines all the actions of a person. Thus, if you are able to visualize success in you mind, your body and your surroundings start working towards the accomplishment of that goal in a very spontaneous manner. The more positive thoughts you feed your mind with, the more positive results you will see in your environment.

It is very important that you do not confuse positive thinking with daydreaming. Positive thinking is much more rooted in the reality of our day-to-day existence as compared to dreaming. It instills in us the ability to respond to the situations in a positive manner, thus helping us change the circumstances for better.

Another great benefit that you stand to gain from the habit of positive thinking is that it will help you through the difficult times of your life. So even when the tides are not in your favor, you will be able to derive the strength to keep pushing on and emerge victorious over yourself.

Understanding the Psychology of Positive Thinking

You may have heard about positive thinking, but don't really know enough about to know exactly how it works. Positive thinking can provide many benefits in your life such as improving your health, opportunities in life, the way you relate to others and the way you see yourself.

The psychology behind the power of positive thinking is that you're more apt to take on life with a positive outlook and have more positive results than if you face the world negatively. That doesn't mean that you should gloss over the obvious, but it does mean that a bad circumstance can be made much brighter than viewing them in a negative way.

Some psychologists view positive thinking as how you explain what happens in your life. If you have an optimistic attitude, you're more likely to explain away bad things that happen by blaming something else for the circumstance. You're also more apt to view a negative happening as outside the norm or a temporary circumstance.

Abraham Lincoln once commented, "Most folks are about as happy as they make up their minds to be."

Abraham Lincoln once commented, "Most folks are about as happy as they make up their minds to be."

When you make up your mind to approach life's challenges with a positive attitude, you're not ignoring the bad stuff in the world, but it does mean that you're attempting to see the best both in people and in situations.

Positive thinking and positive psychology are often thought to be the same, but they're really not. With positive psychology, the focus is definitely on positive thinking, but most psychologists tend to think it's more beneficial to think realistically.

For example, positive thinking might lead a person to take risks that he or she shouldn't, such as investing money in a business that's extremely risky or thinking positively that you can swim across the lake without taking into consideration the distance.

However, it is clear that thinking more positively will ensure more positive outcomes in your life. The best thing you can do is to pay attention to your self-talk and realistically assess whether it's better to think that way – or not.

Health Benefits

In recent years, the so-called "power of positive thinking" has gained a great deal of attention thanks to self-help books such as The Secret. While these pop-psychology books often tout positive thinking as a sort of psychological panacea, empirical research has found that there are many very real health benefits linked to positive thinking and optimistic attitudes.

According to the Mayo Clinic, positive thinking is linked to a wide range of health benefits including:

✓ Longer life span

✓ Less stress

✓ Lower rates of depression

✓ Increased resistance to the common cold

✓ Better stress management and coping skills

✓ Lower risk of cardiovascular disease-related death

✓ Increased physical well-being

✓ Better psychological health

One study of 1,558 older adults found that positive

thinking could also reduce frailty during old age.

Clearly, there are many benefits of positive thinking, but why exactly does positive thinking have such a strong impact on physical and mental health.

One theory is that people who think positively tend to be less affected by stress. Another possibility is that people who think positively tend to live healthier lives in general; they may exercise more, follow a more nutritious diet and avoid unhealthy behaviors.

As you practice positive thinking, you'll become more adept at culling out the positive thoughts that aren't realistic as opposed to the thoughts that can have a positive impact on your life.

POSITVE THIKING VS POSITIVE PSYCHOLOGY

Affirmations in the New Age movement refer to the belief that the practice of positive thinking and holding a positive attitude are strong enough to allow anyone to achieve success in anything they do. The Secret has been the moving force in this believe system, as it has been advocated and supported by millions.

Everyone from Oprah, to Big Sean, to Montel has claimed The Secret works and has encouraged everyone to do the same. Positive Psychology is not the same as positive thinking and or affirmations and it is one of the largest misconceptions of this field, especially with the rise of the New Age movement.

In fact, some positive psychology researchers, such as Barbara Fredrickson, argue that it is detrimental to have insincere positive emotions and thoughts, as it will eventually backfire.

In the last decade, we have also seen the growth of positive psychology, a new branch of mental science which looks at the sunnier side of life (the study of human flourishing.) Positive psychology focuses on positive aspects of wellbeing including (but not limited to) positive emotions, happiness, hope, optimism and other constructs that relate to the idea of positive thinking.

To the uninformed, it would be easy to assume that positive psychology and positive thinking are strongly related. Some might even say, "Finally, science is proving what we have always thought to be true about positive thinking." But this is not exactly the case. While positive thinking and positive psychology may be related, they are more like third cousins than twin brothers. And anyone who uses one or the other would be benefited by understanding the differences:

Philosophical orientation: Positive thinking begins with the assumption that positive thinking is good for you. This is often based on personal or anecdotal experience and then extrapolated to other aspects of life as a general prescription for a better life. Positive psychology begins with scientific inquiry. Positive psychology takes some of those assumptions about positive thinking and says, "let's test them" to see where they hold true or don't.Ich liebe dich...

Positive thinking proponents, for example, argue that positivity is a powerful factor in our health and recovery from illness. Positive psychology has also found a strong link between happiness and health but seeks to understand the limitations of this relationship. Positive emotions seem to help more with prevention than with cure, and more with lifestyle illnesses than with genetic or environmental ones.

Positive emotions help build our social support network, encourage more positive lifestyle choices and buffer us from the negative health impacts of stress. But there are many serious health issues that positive emotions have little impact on. In fact, too much optimism could discourage people from seeking the treatment they need. Positive psychology is about using the scientific method to understand these nuances.

Positivity ratios: Positive thinking generally promotes the "more is better" approach to positivity. Some proponents of positive thinking would argue that if you don't have the wealth, health or happiness you want out of life, it's because you allowed some negativity to creep in. Only by shutting these thoughts out and focusing on the positive can you be successful.

Positive psychology on the other hand, is about understanding the purpose of positive emotions and understanding the different contexts when they may prove valuable. Positive psychology is also interested in negative emotions when they help us to flourish in our lives.   Barbara Fredrickson, for example, a researcher who specializes in positive emotions, has found an ideal ratio of 3 positive emotions to every 1 negative emotion for human flourishing. 3:1, not 3:0.

Many researchers in positive psychology are studying the benefits of mindfulness, which means accepting both positive and negative emotions (in whatever ratio they happen to exist) and then acting consciously, while staying true to personal values and goals. These researchers argue for the importance of a meaningful life over a happy one.

Optimism

positive thinking eschews an optimistic outlook even when one isn't warranted by the situation. Proponents will suggest "affirmations" for example, where people are told to say out loud things they wish to be true, even if they aren't (e.g. "I make a million dollars a year!") Positive psychology studies why optimism is sometimes beneficial (and sometimes not.) Psychology researchers don't generally promote uninhibited optimism in all situations.

As Martin Seligman, the author of Learned Optimism, says, "you don't want the pilot who is de-icing the wings of your plane to be an optimist." Another psychologist, Sandra Schneider, promotes "realistic optimism," which is a matter of trying to realistically get to the truth of a matter, but where ambiguity lies in the meaning of a situation, favor the more positive assumption that will bring you greater mental wellbeing.

Another researcher Acacia Parks, says that the positive psychology brand of optimism is not about being positive all the time but about "entertaining the possibility that things could work out." The benefit of optimism comes from being open to it, not from blindly following it even when it makes no sense to do so.

The reality is, much of what the positive thinking movement has proposed has shown some validity, and this is why people do get benefit out of reading The Secret or attending Tony Robbins' seminars. Barbara Fredrickson has identified "upward spirals" to show how our positive emotions tend to reverberate off of those around us, sustaining and amplifying their benefits. And Martin Seligman has studied the benefits of favoring more optimistic thinking styles. But positive thinking is a one-note song that falls flat in certain situations, while positive psychology is about understanding the rich complexity of the positive side of life.

THE POWER OF POSITIVE THINKING

Many times today people undermine the power of positive thinking. Most people never truly understand the power that positive thoughts have over our every day lives. It's these same people who believe that success comes from something outside of themselves and most seem to have a hard time creating success in their lives. I have created this article to talk you about the concept and power of positive thinking and how I have implemented certain basic pre-school techniques that have truly enhanced my life in every way, shape, and form.

I started my journey on to positive thinking and personal development through reading everyday. Reading is a powerful medium all in it's own. I read biographies and auto-biographies of some of the most successful people in the world. I started reading these types of books because I wanted to see how these people created success in their lives. As I began reading these books I noticed something amazing. Each successful person, no matter their field of study, utilized a certain step by step process that empowered them to first think positively then bring those positive thoughts into reality.

It may not be a new piece of advice to have someone

telling you that you will succeed in life as long as you think positive. However, is the power of positive thinking so strong that you will be guaranteed of success if you do not harbour negative thoughts in your mind? You may be surprise but the answer is a resounding 'Yes!' and today you will learn how having a positive mindset can bring you greater success in life.

As Buddha once said, "What You Have Become Is What You Have Thought", so you need to be positive in your thinking in order to attract the positive energies from the universe. Having a positive mindset means that you will not give up easily and that is especially important if you run a business. It will also affect your relationship with the people around you. It might not be an easy task to change your thoughts to being positive if you are someone who is not optimistic. However, if you want to achieve your dreams, you have to work on it because your mindset will directly affect your life.

The power of positive thinking has been around for many decades and there have been numerous studies done to prove that there is a direct relationship between what you think and the results you get at the end. I am sure you have heard of terminally ill cancer patients who recover miraculously because of their positive mindset and strong belief that they will survive.

Positive thinking has a new advocate these days. Dr. David R. Hawkins is a leading psychiatrist who has published numerous books about the power of positive thinking as well as the power of many forms of thought and spiritual teachings. Using the findings of kinesiology, Dr. Hawkins has made it easier to determine the power of positive thinking versus negative thinking and has shown how many people can alter their lives for the better. By using certain muscle testing techniques, Dr. Hawkins kinesiological research has helped to determine that certain systems of thought are actually more powerful than others in promoting the health and well being of all people.

According to the studies done with kinesiology, various statements, teachings, teachers and subjects of interest all carry a certain energy field along with their subject matter. When these different topics are held in mind by individuals, the reactions of their muscles are then monitored and can determine various strengths and levels of power in the fields present. Through the observation of the muscles reactions, scientists can determine if the individual statements evoke a positive reaction in the muscles or not. This has been shown to be useful in determining the actual power of some statements as opposed to others and of various persons, places or things as they affect the energy meridians in the body. The research is extremely beneficial to those who have examined the findings and has even spurned more studies which are all continuing today.

Dr. Hawkins has gone even further with his research than the simple testing of statements and their relative power. He has devised a scale of consciousness which can actually be used to determine the level of power for anything anywhere and he has used the reaction of the muscles to determine those levels of power according to the science of kinesiology. First, a scale of power was set up from 0 to 1000 and tested subjects were told that zero represented the absolutely lowest level or "no power" range. The highest level at 1000 represented the most power possible level for a human being to be capable of acquiring and the scale was set up as logarithmic so that it was representative of an increase in terms of exponential increments. Many statements, patterns of thought and even teachings were all proven again and again to have a certain level of power according to their kinesiological response in the body.

In terms of the power of positive thinking, there have been many teachers and teachings which have been reported to score very high on the consciousness scale.

Among some of the higher numbers were teachers such as the Buddha, Jesus and Krishna who all scored very high with all test subjects. Similarly, many Eastern teachers such as Ramana Maharshi, Nisargadatta Maharaj and Muktananda all scored in the 600 is and 700 is in terms of the way peoples bodies reacted to the teachings. The word "Love" has consistently scored extremely high at 500 and the word "peace" was also scored at 600. These findings were astounding and have become part of a widespread study and a series of publications which are now very popular in many countries. It is clear from these findings that there is an inherent power to positive thinking which can actually have a physical affect on your body if it is repeated and made to become part of your lifestyle. The findings of Dr. Hawkins suggest a number of things, one of which is that nothing is thought to have come about as a result of an accident or a "random" occurrence. Each thing carries with it a field of energy which largely affects the outcome of its existence. With the discovery that everything carries with it a certain level of power, it is also the case that nothing can be said to be part of an accident unless we were to ignore the recently discovered designations that have been made upon these various objects or thought patterns. Individual people themselves can be tested to be holding a certain amount of energy or "power" such that the reactions of the muscles can also show this level of power in many circumstances. With this discovery, brings the obvious conclusion that, not only are certain thoughts more or less powerful but everything which is capable of being held in mind is subject to a certain test of power.

We all must be aware of the law of attraction, which can show us how to feel positively about a certain topic or subject and it is these thoughts within us that influence how we feels, which is what makes us get attracted to something that we desire. For most people, being able to say that the product that they are selling is great is very easy, but when the same people are alone, it is not that easy to feel and think positively because they may be more preoccupied with worrying about paying their bills or having to play a role in which they will need to decide how to react under negative circumstances.

So, to harness the power of positive thinking and be full of optimism and have a bright outlook requires paying close attention to your innermost thoughts and being able to focus on being aware of these thoughts and learning to direct them in a direction where they are most needed, which is really a manifestation of feeling positive rather than negative. Having a positive attitude and being attentive to positive thoughts isn't something that is taught to us as children and it is not a natural expression of our inner self. In fact, it is common to be careful about what we are saying and not pay enough attention to what are our thoughts.

The Law of Attraction works with the power of thoughts and feelings. What you think of most is what happens most. Now just imagine if you could create pathways of only positive thoughts in your brain. That will attract only more positive things in your life. Start focusing on positive thoughts to experience the power of positive thinking.

'Nothing is good or bad but thinking makes it so'. Our ancestors had discovered this secret. Now you have the chance to use it to its fullest potential. Stay in the moment. Stop accepting everything you hear around you.

The Healing Power Of Positive Thinking With Mind Power

Do you remember when you were sick last? I'm sure it felt horrible. And, what's worse, as you develop illness, big or small, you eventually succumb to negative thoughts as you unconsciously stare the sickness down into the illnesses beady little eyes. You focus on the illness. It usually happens as you permit our thoughts to focus on what's wrong, the negative. Now, try to remember when a loved one looks after you and continues to assure you that you will get better soon. You shift your focus on the healthy, more positive future and you lose site of the negative aspect, you only have positive thoughts.

Positive thinking is no medical miracle, no quick fix pill that eliminates all illnesses instantly. But, in a short time, comparatively, you're better. The same concept is used in placebo medicine, it's as if it causes your mind to have a strong belief that everything is going to be alright and you are going to get better soon. This is the power of Positive thoughts, the belief that you will get better, and along with the real results or the implied results from the medicine, this work hand in hand for a positive result.

There's been test after tests, researches after researches about the power of positive thinking on healing. Most studies have proven that positive thoughts can indeed speed up a persons healing.

There was a scientific research done to see how a persons thoughts can impact their health. It was proven that when people are stressed, our ability to fight off illnesses or diseases, the immune system of the body, gets weaker. Now, when that same person transforms their thoughts to a positively nature, hence minimizing their stress, the immune system strengthens.

Here are few tips to attain positive thinking:

1) Feel Positive - let positive feelings flow through you. Use mental images (go to your happy place). Find the feeling of happiness, success and strength.

2) Be Near Positive - surround yourself with people who positive and just in their thoughts but in their actions also. It can be contagious, either Positive or negative feelings. Being around those whose moods are negative, the glass is half empty people can also make your spirits negative. But bring those positive folks around whose outlook on life is positive then so will yours. Remember, you are the sum total of the people you surround yourself with!

3) Say Positive, Think Positive - Hear Positive, Think Positive. Always use positive words and listen to positive music, not only when speaking but also when you are thinking. Words like "I am capable" and "I can" are powerful mood changers.

Growing a positive thought process is the key to inner self-healing. It's not that easy to do, especially when we are always around negative people but it is do-able. A positive outlook in life will empower you, motivate you, even if your situation or circumstances is far from where or what you want it to be, just be positive and you can expect positive results, even if it is only in your spirit. Guaranteed, with a positive adjustment to your life, your life will change.

In self-healing by thinking positive, I should also say that you should still need to seek out the help of a doctor for that professional opinion and advice, when you are not feeling well. I'm also not advising to not take medicines anymore and that all you need is to think positive about your condition and you'll get better. I'm trying to tell you to use positive thinking side by side with your current treatment.

If you are being treated and you are also in a negative thought process about your life and condition, you will definitely get worse. On the other hand, if you are in an unfortunate state of affair and you focus on positive thinking side by side with your treatment, then it will seriously strengthen your odds dramatically. Your thoughts and your mind and have enormous power on your body and life!

7 Ways To Increase Positive Thinking

A positive thinking pattern is a thought process that helps you approach everything in life in a more productive, positive way, thinking only the best will happen to you. Here are 7 ways to increase your sense of optimism and boost your positive outlook on life:

1. Positive Self talk:

One of the best positive thinking tips, positive self talk can help you change the way you think and talk to your mind.

Filling your mind with positive thoughts and conveying positive messages to your brain can help you gradually kick negativity out of your life. Immediately say "Stop" when you notice yourself thinking of negativity and pessimism.

Saying this aloud will be even more helpful, which will make you aware as to how many times you are shunning negative thoughts that may run through your head innumerable times every day.

2. Change limiting beliefs:

When you say you can't or won't do something, you are only building up resistance against doing that thing.

Remember, self-limiting beliefs cannot do you any good. Challenge yourself every time you entertain such a belittling thought or belief, changing "I can't" to "why can't I." Start saying I can and you will notice a huge difference in your thought processes, clearing the way for positive thoughts to set in!

3. Replace negative influences:

One of the simplest ways to change positive thinking is to replace negative influences with positive ones.

If you are constantly surrounded by people who are always negative, you tend to adopt their thoughts gradually and become a victim of negativity without conscious choice on your part.

Limit your exposure to such people, who do not speak encouraging words and are always unsupportive of your goals and dreams. Surround yourself with positive and successful minds, who always inspire and motivate you to face and deal with challenges and obstacles in life.

Such people vibrate positive energy that will inspire you to entertain positive thoughts and think positive for yourself too.

4. Focus on the present:

Ask yourself, "Can I change my past"?

The answer will be No, because you cannot control or change what has already happened.

However, you can always control your future. You can learn from your past and tell yourself that you can influence your future and won't repeat your mistakes again. Thus such positive thinking will certainly help you build a better tomorrow.

Be grateful for everything you have at present. A state of contentment and gratitude can sometimes do wonders to your psyche, and can change how to tackle the issues in your life with better clarity.

5. Focus on happy moments:

When you remember happy moments, it eases stress. Remember, there are happy and sad moments in everybody's life.

Tell yourself that everybody must face ups and downs in life. Make it a conscious habit to remember good events, rather than difficult times.

6. Read books or watch movies:

When you think negative thoughts, you tend to believe that the worst happens with you alone.

But if you read inspiring books and quotes or watch inspirational movies, you realize that the greatest men on earth even had to overcome troubles and hardships before they have attained great success and wealth.

Reading motivational books or biographies of successful people will help flood your mind with good thoughts and encourage you to develop positive thinking skills as well.

7. Learn to Meditate:

Meditation is one of the best ways to increase positive thinking and clarity. It allows you to connect with your inner self and change your thought pattern, clearing your soul of negativity.

A great quote by Buddha said, "The mind is everything. What you think you become." If you can transform your thought process, you can control everything that transpires in your life.

PSYCHOLOGY AND MINDFULNESS

There is growing interest in the applications of mindfulness in applied psychological settings. However, the speed at which it is being assimilated by Western psychological and public healthcare disciplines has led to concerns about whether the evidence for mindfulness-based interventions justifies this growing popularity. Concerns have also been raised over the 'authenticity' of contemporary Western approaches and whether they bear any resemblance to the traditional Buddhist model. This article examines these issues and discusses whether the current popularity of mindfulness is likely to be just a passing trend, or 'a breath of fresh air' in terms of alleviating suffering and advancing understanding of the human mind.

Research into the attributes, correlates, and applications of mindfulness has increased greatly during recent decades. In fact, mindfulness is arguably one of the fastest-growing areas of psychological research. During 2013 almost 600 scientific papers concerning mindfulness were published, representing a tenfold increase compared to the number of mindfulness papers published during 2003 (Shonin et al., 2013a).

However, due to the speed at which mindfulness has been taken out of its traditional Buddhist setting and assimilated by Western psychological and medical disciplines, concerns and integration issues have inevitably arisen. One such concern is whether the quality of empirical evidence tallies with the numerous claims concerning the efficacy and utility of mindfulness-based interventions (MBIs).

This article briefly discusses current empirical research directions and provides what we believe is timely critical opinion on key issues in mindfulness research, including whether the current popularity of mindfulness in psychology is likely to be just a passing trend, or 'a breath of fresh air' in terms of advancing understanding of the human mind.

Our life can quickly pass us by when we're not focused on what matters. We have a bad habit of emphasizing the negative and overlooking the positive. Being mindful can help. Mindfulness is a state of active, open attention on the present. When we are mindful, we carefully observe our thoughts and feelings without judging them as good or bad. Mindfulness can also be a healthy way to identify and manage hidden emotions that may be causing problems in our personal and professional relationships. It means living in the moment and awakening to our current experience, rather than dwelling on the past or anticipating the future. Mindfulness is frequently used in meditation and certain kinds of therapy. It has many positive benefits, including lowering stress levels, reducing harmful ruminating, improving our overall health, and protecting against depression and anxiety. There is even research suggesting that mindfulness can help people cope better with rejection and social isolation.

A person's experience of time tends to be subjective and is heavily influenced by their emotional state. Fears and insecurities about the past and the future can make it difficult to fully enjoy the present. The key is learning how to pay attention and focus on the here and now. Mindfulness is a tool that allows people to be more aware of their physical and emotional conditions without getting bogged down in self-criticism and judgment. Mindfulness done well allows one to regain control over destructive feelings and even to capture positive memories that can be savored at a later date.

What Is Mindfulness and How Does It Work?

You may have heard the term "Mindfulness" and have a rough idea of what it's about but in this article, you'll get a very clear understanding of what it is and why it's important to you.

With the growth of mindfulness meditation as an

intervention for stress, tension, anxiety, depression, pain, rumination, sleeplessness, and many other common ailments, this is quickly becoming a big question arising all over North America and world wide.

Mindfulness is that gap where you, the awareness, are aware of what's happening within your mind. You become clear and alert to what you think, say and do. Often people meditate as a way of being clearer without all the distractions the flood through the senses. However, becoming aware of your breath and focusing on the air flowing in and out of the lungs can also do it.

This may not sound like any big deal, but it's a monumental leap of what any other creature can do. Humans are the only species on this planet that can do this. This is because every other species doesn't identify with the mind to create an ego, they simply accept things as they are and are one with it.

For example, a cat doesn't sit there and think, what does that human think of me, should I make my coat shinier so that he'll pat me and give me food? No, they simply accept this moment and do what they do through instinct and being in alignment with the present moment.

In this way animals have an advantage over humans, but what we have is the next phase of evolution, where we have an amazing capacity to not only survive but also thrive like no other species.

The issue is though, our quest to survive and thrive has become out of balance with our essential nature of oneness with all. This imbalance causes us to experience pain, which ultimately leads us to not only search for but also to find what the Truth is for us. It's life's way of restoring balance and when you consider that we are not separate to life, it's our way of restoring balance within ourselves.

So can you see why this is important now?

In a nutshell, the illusion of living day to day through entirely mind based activity (usually in hope or in fear that tomorrow will be different than today) causes pain, NOW. The way to begin to find your way through the pain is to bring awareness to your breath and from there, seeing what you think, say and do. The awareness creates a gap between you and what is perceived and through that a choice can be made for what is real, you the awareness or what your mind is telling you through a perception!

When you go on a binge, just before you start you always have these overwhelming feelings of cravings for food. Before starving yourself you have feelings of aversion or disgust with yourself and your body - so you stop eating.

With mindfulness you will be able to see your eating disorder as a foreign voice (or a person) who is sitting inside you, telling you what to do. When you practice mindfulness you will be able to separate yourself from this foreign voice and be free.

Mindfulness is a subset of meditation practices. To be mindful first of all you must learn to meditate. Mindfulness and meditation are similar but not exactly the same. Like we have already explained that mindfulness is the awareness of the present moment. But Meditation is the intentional self regulation of attention. During meditation you regulate and control your attention. And this is a development of mindfulness.

In mindfulness you learn not to judge and not to react. Observing what passes by nonjudgmentally, from moment to moment, with no reactivity whatsoever towards any part of the experience, whether the thought or the sensation. By decreasing our overactivity in the judgmental part of the mind and the reactive part of the mind, our nervous system learns to change its pattern. It becomes less judgmental, less reactive, more objective, providing us with more opportunities to manage life whatever the problem is.

This method is not limited to eating disorders, anxieties, fears or depression. People of different faiths practice this method in different ways for thousands of years. This is certainly not limited to psychological or emotional problems.

Everyone will benefit from decreasing reactivity, decreasing biased judgments, giving new parameters to the nervous system, and more insight and focused attention. In a nutshell, the purpose of practicing mindfulness training is to develop a degree of acceptance towards one's experience, and of course an equal degree of awareness. When things become acceptable on the inside, it seems that people find things more acceptable on the outside as well. The world becomes a better place.

How Mingling Mindfulness With Positive Psychology Makes You Great

According to a recent study, the key to our survival as a species is the survival of the kindest, not merely the fittest. Thus, having kindness as the dominant trait in a person would be key to both evolution and personal successes. Another recent study reveals that mixing both mindfulness and positive psychology would result in optimized well-being and elevate one's compassionate trait and resistance to stress and negativity.

With resistance to stress and negativity, we can be our best selves, hence being a "super human," who can achieve many things and be useful to society. With minimal stress and negativity in aggregate, assuming billions of individuals are also in this state of mind, civilization can progress positively.

Now, let's discuss the theory of "survival of the kindest," what mindfulness and positive psychology are, their benefits, how they're linked with each other, and how to integrate them in life to eliminate stress and negativity.

Survival of the Kindest

According to Dacher Keltner, the director of the Berkeley Social Interaction Laboratory, in his book, Born to Be Good: The Science of a Meaningful Life, the evolution has crafted the human species that comes with remarkable tendencies toward generosity, kindness, reverence, self-sacrifice, and play. They play important roles in survival, gene replication, and smooth functioning.

Despite the misconception that violence,

competitiveness, and self-interest were the natural state of human beings, which were responsible for our evolution, Charles Darwin, on the contrary, had a different understanding. Darwin argued that human beings' tendencies toward compassionate social instincts were stronger than the instinct of self-preservation. Otherwise, our species would have been extinct already, which says a lot about the survival of the kindest.

The Link between Mindfulness and Positive Psychology

According to Vago and Silbersweig in Frontiers in Human Neuroscience:

mindfulness is a trait or mental state involving intentional focusing of the attention on an object, like breathing, while observing thoughts, emotions, and sensations as they emerge in the present moment.

Mindfulness itself is beneficial to health in five ways: attention regulation, increased body awareness, emotional regulation, emotional-exposure regulation, and changes in the perspective of the self.

Positive Psychology is the scientific study of the positive traits that enable individuals and communities to thrive. It was pioneered by Martin Seligman in 1998 and was also co-initiated by Mihaly Czikszentmihalyi and Christopher Peterson. This new field of psychology isn't based on pathology model. Instead, it's based on the belief that people want to lead meaningful and fulfilling lives by cultivating their best selves.

The practice of mindfulness is used as one of the tools of positive psychology, as it has been linked to increased positive feelings, a greater sense of coherence, improved quality of life, greater empathy, greater satisfaction in relationships, and more hope (Vago and Silbersweig, 2012). Other tools include gratitude journaling, reframing from negativity to positivity, self-compassion, and listing personal strengths.

Another link between mindfulness and positive psychology is that mindfulness increases well-being and positive mental qualities, including compassion. Mindfulness-based meditation has been used in compassion training, which would result in increased sensitivity to one's self and others' needs. By being empathetic, we would be more motivated to help others. In return, this facilitates greater compassion and gives us feelings of joy and satisfaction. In other words, they create a circle of joy (Cebolla, 2017).

Integrating Mindfulness and Positive Psychology in Life

Once we've been able to create and close the positive

circle and repeated the process in loops, negativity and stress would diminish over time. It's probably something like the antithesis of depression. Thus, it allows for optimized activities, both in quality and quantity.

It might sound like a utopia that combining mindfulness and positive psychology would make us "super humans." However, many educators are already teaching mindfulness in elementary classrooms worldwide.

Studies have shown that mindfulness taught since childhood would do more than increased positivity, greater compassion, and diminishing stress and negativity. It would also help with focus, emotion regulation, engagement, and future career satisfaction, which would solve many problems.

You can begin with integrating mindfulness meditation, walking meditation, gratitude journaling, reminding ourselves of our strengths and positive traits, self-compassion, and reframing negativity with positivity. It doesn't require any money to begin, just a motivation to start and turn the activities into a lifelong habit.

As Einstein once said:

We cannot solve our problems with the same thinking we used when we created them.

We've found the answer. With greater positivity and compassion, the world's problems can be solved. And it starts with one person: You.

7 Great Benefits of Mindfulness in Positive Psychology

In the most basic sense, mindfulness is being consciously aware of your thoughts and emotions. For one to practice good mindfulness it involves the 'self-regulation' of attention so that it is focused on adopting a neutral attitude toward one's experiences in the present moment.

There are many beneficial effects on developing and practicing mindfulness. Below are 7 great benefits of mindfulness.

1. Being mindful of your thoughts and emotions promotes well-being

The concept of self-regulation is somewhat paradoxical in that regulation in the strictest sense of the word such as self-control is not 'mindful'. Rather, mindfulness is a state that is characterized by introspection, openness, reflection and acceptance of oneself.

Recently in the field of psychology, there has been strong evidence demonstrating that mindfulness is significantly correlated with positive affect, life satisfaction, and overall well-being.

Mindfulness itself, however, is not a new concept; it has existed in Buddhism for over two thousand of years. Modern day research has made several interesting findings suggesting this 'enhanced self-awareness' diminishes stress and anxiety and, in turn, reduces the risk of developing cancer, disease, and psychopathology. It is useful to practice mindfulness in positive psychology as a tool for general physical and mental health.

2. Being mindful can improve your working memory

Working memory is the memory system that temporarily stores information in our minds for further recall and future processing. Many studies have been undertaken that suggest a strong interrelationship between attention and working memory.

van Vugt & Jha (2011) undertook research that involved taking a group of participants to an intensive month-long mindfulness retreat. These participants were compared with a control group who received no mindfulness training (MT). All participants from both groups first undertook a memory recognition task before any MT had been providing. The second round of a memory recognition task was then undertaken by all participants after the month's training.

Results were positive – while accuracy levels were comparable across both groups, reaction times were much faster for the group that had received mindfulness training. These results suggested that MT leads to attentional improvements, particularly in relation to quality of information and decisional processes, which are directly linked to working memory.

mindfulness vs depressive symptoms3. Mindfulness acts as a buffer against the depressive symptoms associated with discrimination

A self-report study conducted at the University of North Carolina measured the level of discrimination experienced by participants and also the presence and/or severity of their depressive symptoms. Participants also completed a questionnaire that measured their level of mindfulness as a trait, which is characterized by a conscious awareness of the present.

The results showed that the more discrimination participants experienced the more depressive symptoms they had. It was also found that the more mindful people were, the less depressed they were.

Finally, and most importantly, the findings suggested that mindfulness might be a protective factor that mitigates the effects of discrimination on the development of depressive symptoms. That is, although discrimination was associated with depressive symptoms, the association became much weaker as mindfulness increased. So, it appears that practicing mindfulness may be one way of preventing the onset of depression!

4. Mindfulness can help you make better use of your strengths

"Mindfulness can help an individual express their character strengths in a balanced way that is sensitive to the context and circumstance they are in."(Niemiec, 2012)

A lot of research has shown that mindfulness influences mental health and personality (Baer, Smith & Allen, 2004). Not surprisingly, mindfulness is related to character strengths as well.

Mindfulness and Strengths

Mindfulness and strengths joined forces a long time ago. In Buddhism, mindfulness meditation not only relieves suffering but also cultivates positive characteristics and strengths such as compassion, wisdom, and well-being. Even the meaning of mindfulness, defined by Thich Nhat Hanh (Niemiec, 2014), includes some dimensions of strengths. He saw mindfulness as a means "to keep one's attention alive in the present reality. And this 'aliveness' captures both the self-regulation of attention and the approach of curiosity."

Relationship of Mindfulness and Strengths

According to research by Bishop and colleagues (2004), experiencing mindfulness begins with making a commitment to maintain curiosity about the mind wandering and looking at differences in other objects.

Other research (Ivtzan, Gardner & Smailova, 2011) found that curiosity is one of the strengths that is correlated to living a satisfied, meaningful, and engaging life.

According to a study by Niemiec, Rashid & Spinella (2012), transcendence strengths can become more meaningful in mindfulness practice as they connect mindfulness with spiritual meaning.

In addition, during the practice of mindfulness, people may face both internal and external obstacles including boredom, wandering mind, physical discomfort, and difficulty in commitment, and this requires the strength of courage and perseverance to overcome and keep going.

Mindfulness, strengths, and acknowledgment

"Mindfulness opens a door of awareness to who we are and character strengths are what is behind the door since character strengths are who we are at core" (Niemiec, 2014)

Mindfulness can help you make better use of your strengths. One needs attention to their inner states and behavior to pursue a goal (Brown, Ryan & Creswell, 2007). Therefore, to be able to see your strength, you need to access your inner state of mind. To access your strengths or your true self, mindfulness is the path.

Research by Carlson (20013) showed that we have many blind spots, such as information barrier and motivation barrier, which is modest and meager in self-evaluation. It also decreases the bias we have in ourselves since practicing mindfulness reduces the defensiveness of your ego as you start to have more reality-based thoughts.

Mindfulness and Neuroplasticity

The term neuroplasticity refers to structural and

functional changes in the brain related to experience. It has been known that musical training and language learning promote structural changes in our brain and cognitive abilities.

Mindful awareness is a form of experience that changes not only structure, but also the function of our brain throughout our lives.

You can think of mindfulness as a mental muscle. Every time we lift weight, we strengthen the muscle we are working on. In the same way, every time we pay attention to the present moment without judgment, connectivity of the attention, self-regulation and compassion circuitry grows in our brain.

5. Mindfulness practice raises your happiness set-point

Our brain is divided into left and right hemispheres. It has been shown that our brain has high activity in the right prefrontal cortex (front part of the brain) when we are in a depressed, anxious mood.

Our brain has high activity in left prefrontal cortex when we are happy and energetic. This ratio of left-to-right activity shows our happiness set-point throughout daily activities. So, what happens to this ratio when we practice mindfulness meditation?

The research of Richard Davidson and Jon Kabat-Zinn shows that only 8-week of 1-hour daily mindfulness practice leads to significant increase in left-sided activation in the brain and this increase is maintained even after 4 months of the training program (Davidson, Kabat-zinn et al., 2003). In brief, this finding demonstrates that short-term mindfulness practice increases our happiness level significantly, even at a physical level.

"Short-term mindfulness practice increases our happiness level significantly"

6. It makes you more resilient

Resilience, in most basic terms, is individual's ability to recover from setbacks and adapt well to change. Similarly, in our brain, we have a region called anterior cingulate cortex (ACC), located deep inside our forehead. ACC plays important role in self-regulation and learning from the past experience to promote optimal decision making.

The research findings of Tang and his colleagues show that mindfulness training groups that went through only 3-hour practice have higher activity in ACC and also show higher performance on the tests of self-regulation and resisting distractors, compared to the control group (Tang et al., 2007, 2009). This means that with the help of mindfulness practice, we can change our brain in the way we react to setbacks and make decisions in our life.

7. It shrinks the stress region in your brain

Remember that time you rush through life with sweat palms and trouble sleeping at night? Every time we get stressed, the 'amygdala' takes over control.

Amygdala is a key stress-responding region in our brain and plays important role in anxious situations. It's known that high amygdala activity is associated with depression and anxiety disorders (Siegle et al., 2002).

The good news is that mindfulness practice can actually shrink the size of amygdala and increase our stress reactivity threshold.

Recent research performed by Taren and colleagues shows a connection between long-term mindfulness practice and a decreased size of amygdala (Taren et al., 2013). By practicing mindfulness, we can change how we react to stressful situations and improve our mental and physical well-being.

"There's a connection between long-term mindfulness practice and a decreased size of the amygdala"

How long should you practice mindfulness?

According to Richie Davidson, one of the world's most renowned contemplative neuroscientists, even 1.5 hours of mindfulness practice leads to structural changes in the brain.

CONCLUSION

When you ask most people what it takes to become successful, they'll tell you that success comes from hard work. The psychology of success is often overlooked entirely. While yes, hard work is part of the equation, they are missing a large part. You can never become successful if you don't have the right mindset.

The right mindset cures everything. Your mindset will determine if you're successful or if you're unsuccessful. Your mindset will tell you that you're a failure and you should just give up or that you're on the right track to success. Which voice are you listening too?

Becoming an entrepreneur will be the hardest challenge of your life because you're becoming a different person than everyone else. When that happens, you will question yourself. Are you on the right path? Why don't you just work for someone else? If you continue to ask yourself these questions, you will lose. When you have the right mindset, no matter what you face, you will come out the other side.

The key to developing a growth mindset is to understand why "fake it until you make it" is actually quite effective — it results in small wins, which then lead to genuine confidence.

That is exactly what you should do: focus on creating small wins through changing your habits. Make daily "micro quotas" (10 minutes of working out a day) that are so easy you can't say no.

In short, nail it then scale it. Over time, this creates a key trait in the growth mindset: a passion for learning rather than the need for approval.

Initial progress creates the desire to move forward. The innate mindset is what stops most people from starting ("I'm not a fit person…"), but the growth mindset will blossom after just a few small wins prove, "Hey, I can definitely do this."

It is a useful reminder that the things we want need to be claimed. They aren't a given for anyone. You don't receive an education, you claim it. You don't receive athletic success, you claim it. You don't receive mastery in your work, you claim it.

Do not go yet; One last thing to do

If you enjoyed this book or found it useful I'd be very grateful if you'd post a short review on Amazon. Your support really does make a difference and I read all the reviews personally so I can get your feedback and make this book even better.

Thanks again for your support!

Introducing

COGNITIVE BEHAVIORAL THERAPY

By

Daniel Anderson

Table of Contents

CHAPTER ONE

TAKING COGNIZANCE OF THE COMMON MENTAL HEALTH ISSUES

Anxiety

Feeling worried or nervous is a normal part of everyday life. Everyone frets or feels anxious from time to time. Mild to moderate anxiety can help you focus your attention, energy, and motivation. If anxiety is severe, you may have feelings of helplessness, confusion, and extreme worry that are out of proportion with the actual seriousness or likelihood of the feared event. Overwhelming anxiety that interferes with daily life is not normal. This type of anxiety may be a symptom of generalized anxiety disorder, or it may be a symptom of another problem, such as depression.

Jane's story

"Jane has always been a worrier, but it never interfered with her life before. Lately, however, she's been feeling keyed up all the time. She's paralyzed by an omnipresent sense of dread, and worries constantly about the future. Her worries make it difficult to concentrate at work, and when she gets home she can't relax. Jane is also having sleep difficulties, tossing and turning for hours before she falls asleep. She also gets frequent stomach cramps and diarrhea, and has a chronic stiff neck from muscle tension. Jane feels like she's on the verge of a nervous breakdown."

What is GAD?

Everyone gets worried sometimes, but if you have generalized anxiety disorder (GAD),it is overwhelming and can dominate one's day with inappropriate and exaggerated worries and tension, even when there is nothing present to worry about. GAD is often accompanied by physical symptoms or sensations like a racing heart, breathlessness, nausea, can't sleep,chest pains and sweating for example.

Generalized anxiety disorder (GAD) involves anxiety and worry that is excessive and unrelenting. This high-level anxiety makes normal life difficult and relaxation impossible. If you have generalized anxiety disorder (GAD) you may worry about the same things that other people do: health issues, money, family problems, or difficulties at work. But you take these worries to a new level.

Normal worry vs. Generalized Anxiety Disorder (GAD)

"Normal" Worry:

- Your worrying doesn't get in the way of your daily activities and responsibilities.

- You're able to control your worrying.

- Your worries, while unpleasant, don't cause significant distress.

- Your worries are limited to a specific, small number of realistic concerns.

- Your bouts of worrying last for only a short time period.

Generalized Anxiety Disorder:

- Your worrying significantly disrupts your job, activities, or social life.

- Your worrying is uncontrollable.

- Your worries are extremely upsetting and stressful.

- You worry about all sorts of things, and tend to expect the worst.

- You've been worrying almost every day for at least six months.

GAD sufferers seem unable to eliminate or ignore their concerns, even though they usually realize that their anxiety is more intense than the situation warrants.

GAD sufferers may often feel light-headed or out of breath. They may also feel nauseated or have to go to the bathroom frequently. Generalized anxiety is constant and can cause anxiety/panic attacks during the day and night. Night time anxiety and panic attacks are especially disturbing and can often wake the sufferer from deep sleep feeling particularly frightened. Night time anxiety can be minimized with some practical steps which minimize the impact of such things as blood sugar level fluctuations during sleep.

Individuals with GAD seem unable to relax, and they may startle more easily than other people. They tend to have difficulty concentrating and often, they have trouble falling or staying asleep.

The sort of symptoms you can experience in generalized anxiety are generally milder than those experienced during an anxiety / panic attack. Although distressing, they are usually much less extreme but may include some of the symptoms outlined on our anxiety symptoms list.

Your stomach may churn, your heart races or beats slower or you may get palpitations you may also feel sweaty or clammy, dizzy or shaky and general unrest.

You may just feel as if you have the Flu with shaky or weak legs and clamminess. You might get disturbing thoughts or feel depressed, this is perfectly normal and will pass, it is purely a response to anxiety and must not be mistaken for depression. Remember, these thoughts and feelings are harmless but unpleasant none the less.

So let us look some levels of anxiety, such as: "Mum there's a great big spider in my bedroom" cries a child and the child gets anxious about the spider, a specific creature she imagines can hurt her. Anxiety always relates to hurt. This is a controllable anxiety, get rid of the spider equals getting rid of the anxiety, (carefully looking to see there are no other spiders lurking there). I would call this third-line-anxiety. A learned anxiety, overcome with reason and action. This anxiety is a learned one, where the growing person has learned that certain things can harm us and being little (in psyche if not body) there is a need for immediate help from others perceived as being stronger than the self. This is usually enough and can be used in a creative and useful manner. An example would be learning self-defence to ward off bullies at school. There is also the chronic worrier who perceives their worry as an anxiety state, and rightly so, we may say anxiety at a lesser level. I would call this second-line anxiety. Overcome with specific understanding of the self. This is also reasonably easy to overcome by getting to know who you really are. This is not as hard as you may think.

However there is also another anxiety, of varying degrees, one where it 'takes over' the emotions and won't go away. A terrifying emptiness of blackness filled with 'spiders' of our deep inner psyche's creation, not simply one in the bedroom that can be overcome by a bit of reason, muscle and mum's trusty broom. I would call this first-line anxiety. This is often very difficult to clear, not because it can't be cleared, but by the very nature of distrust on which all anxiety is founded. Anxiety is a very real but unconscious form of expression of the hurting child

Let's understand where anxiety comes from. This may be a bit heavy, but stay in there and you'll be supplied with information you need to give you a foundation of knowledge to underpin your new, productive actions. You see, all life must express itself in its own way. You are special part of that life and you have been since you were first united as one by the penetration of daddy's sperm into mummy's egg. The life then created was a NEW and powerful life. Very different to the first two living creatures (egg and sperm) and already eager to get stuck into life into mummy's womb where it forms into another new life (life meeting life again). Then you grow into a baby, and all the experiences of mother as she carries you are recorded in your little psyche. Then you are born. What an experience! Life (baby) meeting life (the world baby will live in).

Here is how it ideally works:

Essentially the growing baby wants mother's attentions at all times. Baby has already gone through the amazing life series of development of all the organs of the body and has broken from being dependent on the mother, has travelled the sometimes very scary birth canal and is eager to go on to new things. All this at an emotional level. Then baby goes through a series of transitional developments... firstly the need for acceptance. This is the prime essential and we all carry that through life to the grave. From acceptance baby moves to Being. A genuine, real little bundle of life that has father as a guarantee of strength and mother as an assurance of sustenance, both vital to the growing child. Then with mother and father there to sustain life as a right, baby moves to what can be called Wellbeing. From there on to Identification where baby identifies with mother to gain his personal identity and from father for his social identity. Further development for the well-parented child leads to Status as a person and then on to Production.

But what if there is a blockage somewhere along that ideal chain? What if mother does NOT come when called upon by baby's very real needs? What would happen if the normal cycle was BLOCKED, for whatever reason, at the first stage when mother was NOT there to supply her loving acceptance/ sustenance? The inner pain can be endured for a time, but then baby may feel that mother will never come and a panic starts to become a pathway within the developing psyche. This pathway has no name as it's an indefinable feeling,but it's REAL to baby and it starts to develop its own pathways within the psyche. There starts a despair, a hopelessness and the ability to wait for the second stage of BEING by mother's coming is weakened. Infantile death! Baby doesn't know this of course, and it's all pushed into the feeling unconscious to be drawn on at any time later in life when similar experiences are presented.

Here is the foundation of hopelessness, the substance for anxiety.

Let me give you an illustration:

A lady came to me with a terrible anxiety about money. She was single, attractive, intelligent. Money was a terrifying agent for her anxiety on a large scale, permeating all she did. However her older brother was a millionaire by age 21! Same parents, same parental love shared by both. Both accepted. What was the difference? It appeared that her father was a very successful businessman in a middle eastern country. His livelihood was taken away from him by an antagonistic government action. The very lives of the father, mother and son were seriously at risk so they fled to United States as immigrants with absolutely no money at all. The mother was devastated at all this and my client was conceived during this calamitous period. She wore her mother's grief (loss of livelihood) mother's desperation (lack of money) mother's shame (social scorn) and now mother's contribution to poverty (becoming pregnant) In US, the father resumed his business talents and again became wealthy, the son following dad's social example, but the girl only knew, among all the love shared in the family, the distress that associated with money. The son felt prosperity. That was HIS inner picture. The girll felt poverty-anxiety. THAT was her inner picture. She was able to step out of that state with the adult mind of CHOICE leaving behind the anxiety-feeling mind of the inner CHILD.

I will show you how you can do that also a little later.

At each stage of acceptance, being, wellbeing, identification, status, productivity, varying degrees of blocking can take place, leaving behind it's legacy of anxiety. Here is first line trauma. Bearing in mind that we are a complex of genetics, ego strength, ancestral and cellular memories, and family dynamics so it would be difficult indeed for a therapist to get to the bottom of it all.

So let's look at the basics of anxiety and as we go, if you feel (note the word feel) something stirring within you, take note of it, maybe write it down for your attention later on.

WE are a complex of many ingredients and all of these ingredients and circumstances join together to make the strength of our ego (who we believe ourselves to be). If a person has a strong ego they will act accordingly and if a weak ego (or none at all) they will act accordingly.

Makes sense. But for the growing child the sense of power lies in the parenting, especially mother. So the little ego will react to the bad as well as the good in it's own strength. This is why you are unique. No one is the same as you and YOU have the inner answer to your inner anxiety.

Let's look at how it can operate:

Baby can, and does, suffer from mental anguish at the loss of BEING through the loss of mother's attentions, for whatever reason, (don't go blaming mum as it quite often, indeed almost always, someone else messing up her routine with baby) and this results in dread sometimes with rage attached and sometimes beyond rage with depressions as a result. Different babies, different ego-responses. What happens in this case is baby develops a feeling, nay, a TERROR of the death of the spirit. Baby (you and me) has been through.

The joys and energetic drives of LIFE! LIVING! Taking LIFE as LIFE itself with all of the energetic joys of getting 'stuck into life' in mother's endometrium. BLISS! And now being denied this feeling of LIFE! and an emerging sense of DEATH! This once LIFE! Being somehow blocked and this blocking taking away that BEING so essential to baby's growth - a growth that cannot be stopped except by death. So: delusional fears of death (self or close persons). Being preoccupied with impending death. Doom. Disaster.

Hell. So with this mind-set there is an entry into a panic state, intense apprehension, ANXIETY as a first-line anxiety.

A sense of despair 'takes over'. Various phobias are revealed that are peculiar to the experiences of the little baby/child. The ability to wait for 'the good' to come in the form of some accepting person is almost nil. The BEING is challenged by a feeling of separation that will never be satisfied. Therefore no sustenance. A hopelessness called anxiety. This feeling was once REAL and the feeling is still REAL to the inflicted person. However note that it is a FEELING and as such cannot harm you in any way. A harmless but intense feeling that simply 'takes over' as it did when baby was experiencing the FACT of non-BEING.

Anxiety at this level can lead to endless talking about their terrible plight. Feeling 'locked in' to endless bad relationships. Difficult to maintain true friendships, which fuels the anxiety. Shutting one's self off from help. Isolated by others. More anxiety.

Indeed there are so many paths that can be developed by the human psyche regarding anxiety we could wonder if there is ANY real, basic relief from it's malevolent attacks. Let's look at some of the expressions of this malady, remembering that if baby was caught in this terrifying experience the deepest REPRESSION covers this desperate infantile deprivation and can lead to the death of the spirit in dread. It is a basic TERROR.

Caught in a RAGE Catch 22: Not to rage as a baby/child is to die by isolation. To rage is to both destroy and be destroyed. Have you had that feeling? If so, this is your story. Anxiety releases infantile RAGE and dreams (nightmares?) of how to destroy the whole rotten anxiety mess. The mother delay becomes an intolerable bondage, forced into the unconscious, but wanting to DO something (fright, flight, fight) which translates into the physical counterparts of: tense head feelings, buzzing in the ears, head throbbing, nose often congested, vision blurred, tight chest, breathing irregular, heart beating fast, blood pressure up, loss of appetite, nervous dyspepsia, tight stomach, constipated, loss of weight, muscles tight and aching, pains in the neck and limbs, tremors, fidgeting, sweating, blotchy skin, menstruation preceded by tension, irritable, angry scenes, sexual libido often lost, and there are others. Survival is therefore by fight as mounting rage is an attempt to force a response. This is all an active aggressive response to this separation-anxiety.

Or we may go into the phobic areas of expression of our anxiety. there is only one anxiety, but many expressions of it: Agoraphobia, Claustrophobia, Fears of loss of consciousness, Hospitals, Separation, Being sick. etc.

Attention seeking can become a fixation with infantile dependent behaviour attached.

Any usual output is thereby lost, the energies being put to the inner world of the child within, unconsciously fighting from a platform of dire distress. Weakness or tiredness takes over. Not wanting to either start or finish a task.

Fatigue can become persistent and quite strong.

Loss of concentration. Can't read and remember what has been read. Little if any concern for others. Small problems become major events. Easily distracted. Antisocial. Not a party-goer. Only partial attempts to become party to activities.

Moods are gloomy with heavy, stony grief. Irritable, whining, always lamenting. All the good times are in the past. Memory selects past grievances. All is experienced as painful, even any happy times, and can't feel love for family or show or feel real grief.

Depersonalised and incapable of emotion. Unreality feelings include being 'outside myself' or 'not there'. Time drags. Colours look drab, or all is seen as grey.

The spirits are low, especially in the morning o after sleep. Negative people, Denies inner hostility. God is seen as distant, angry and rejecting.

As personalities before the trigger of anxiety in this level is activated, they could well have been well adjusted and outgoing. Others cold have been dependent and anxious with a record of hard work, anxiously, meticulously and over-conscientiously performed.

In this case they would have been denied mother, as a baby, but also had attentions not of their satisfaction, as a surrogate mother, or nurse. So you can see that there could be many variants and only YOU would have that, unconsciously, in your psyche.

Anxiety can cause physical and emotional symptoms. A specific situation or fear can cause some or all of these symptoms for a short time. When the situation passes, the symptoms usually go away.

Physical symptoms of anxiety include:

• Trembling, twitching, or shaking.

• Feeling of fullness in the throat or chest.

• Breathlessness or rapid heartbeat.

• Light-headedness or dizziness.

• Sweating or cold, clammy hands.

• Feeling jumpy.

• Muscle tension, aches, or soreness (myalgias).

• Extreme tiredness.

Sleep problems, such as the inability to fall asleep or stay asleep, early waking, or restlessness (not feeling rested when you wake up).

Anxiety affects the part of the brain that helps control how you communicate. This makes it harder to express yourself creatively or function effectively in relationships. Emotional symptoms of anxiety include:

• Restlessness, irritability, or feeling on edge or keyed up.

• Worrying too much.

• Fearing that something bad is going to happen; feeling doomed.

• Inability to concentrate; feeling like your mind goes blank.

Anxiety disorders

Anxiety disorders occur when people have both physical and emotional symptoms. Anxiety disorders interfere with how a person gets along with others and affect daily activities. Women are twice as likely as men to have problems with anxiety disorders. Examples of anxiety disorders include panic attacks, phobias, and generalized anxiety disorder.

Often the cause of anxiety disorders is not known. Many people with an anxiety disorder say they have felt nervous and anxious all their lives. This problem can occur at any age. Children who have at least one parent with the diagnosis of depression are more likely to have an anxiety disorder than other children.

Anxiety disorders often occur with other problems, such as:

Mental health problems, such as depression.

Substance use problems.

A physical problem, such as heart or lung disease. A complete medical examination may be needed before an anxiety disorder can be diagnosed.

Panic attacks

A panic attack is a sudden feeling of extreme anxiety or intense fear without a clear cause or when there is no danger. Panic attacks are common. They sometimes occur in otherwise healthy people. An attack starts suddenly and usually lasts from 5 to 20 minutes but may last even longer. You have the most anxiety about 10 minutes after the attack starts.

Symptoms include feelings of dying or losing control of yourself, rapid breathing (hyperventilation), numbness or tingling of the hands or lips, and a racing heart. You may feel dizzy, sweaty, or shaky. Other symptoms include trouble breathing, chest pain or tightness, and an irregular heartbeat. These symptoms come on suddenly and without warning.

Sometimes symptoms of a panic attack are so intense that the person fears he or she is having a heart attack. Many of the symptoms of a panic attack can occur with other illnesses, such as hyperthyroidism, coronary artery disease, or chronic obstructive pulmonary disease (COPD). A complete medical examination may be needed before an anxiety disorder can be diagnosed.

People who have repeated unexpected panic attacks and worry about the attacks are said to have a panic disorder.

Depression

While everyone feels sad from time to time, major depression is very different. Major depressive disorder or clinical depression causes you to experience feelings of sadness, loneliness, or a loss of interest in things you once enjoyed. When these feelings occur for more than two weeks, doctors may diagnose this as major depressive disorder. These symptoms are a sign that you need to seek professional help. Talk to your doctor if you have symptoms that may indicate depression.

Common symptoms of depression

Symptoms of depression can vary. They may manifest themselves differently from person to person. However, for most people, depression symptoms affect their ability to perform daily activities, interact with others, or go to work or go to school. If you suffer from depression you may often experience several of the following:

Sadness

The most common symptom of depression is a feeling of sadness or emptiness that lasts for more than two weeks. A person may describe this symptom as a feeling of "hopelessness." They may feel as if life will not get better and that this intense level of sadness will last forever. If this feeling lasts longer than two years it's known as dysthymia. This is a type of chronic depression in which a person's moods are consistently low.

Worthlessness

Continual feelings of worthlessness, guilt, or helplessness often accompany the condition. People tend to focus on personal shortcomings or past failures. They often blame themselves when their life isn't going the way they would like. Teenagers who experience depression commonly report feelings of worthlessness. They may report feeling misunderstood and start to avoid interactions with others.

Irritability

Depression may cause people to get easily frustrated or angered, even over small or insignificant matters. This often relates back to a person experiencing levels of tension and fatigue that makes it difficult to get through the day. Men and women may display irritability symptoms differently from each other. Women often report feeling angry at one moment, and then tearful at the next. Men may appear volatile or aggressive due to their depression. Traditional male roles in society may also mean that a man displays irritability for not being able to "get it together" and overcome depressive symptoms.

Fatigue

People with depression often experience lack of energy or feel tired all the time. Small tasks, like showering or getting out of bed, may seem to require more effort than one can muster. Fatigue can play a role in other symptoms associated with depression, such as withdrawal and apathy. You may feel overwhelmed at the mere thought of exertion or going outdoors.

Guilt

Depression is often the result of imbalanced chemicals in the brain. However, people experiencing depression may blame themselves for their symptoms instead. Statements such as "I can't do anything right" or "everything is my fault," become the norm for you.

Crying spells

People who have depression may find themselves crying frequently for no apparent reason. Crying spells can be a symptom of post-partum depression, which can occur in a woman after she's given birth.

Apathy

People with depression commonly lose interest or stop finding pleasure in activities that they once enjoyed, including sex.

Anxiety

Anxiety is a feeling of impending doom or danger, even when there isn't a justifiable reason. Depression can cause a person to feel anxious all the time. A person may say they are constantly tense, but there's no direct threat or identifiable source for this tension.

Restlessness

Agitation and restlessness, including pacing, an inability to sit still, or hand wringing, may occur with depression.

Lack of concentration

People with depression may have a difficult time remembering, maintaining focus, or making decisions. Fatigue, feelings of worthlessness, or feeling "numb" can turn decision-making into a talk that is difficult to accomplish. Friends or family members may discuss specific dates or events, but you may not remember just moments later due to concentrating lack of concentration. This inability to concentrate can lead to withdrawal in a depressed person.

Withdrawal

Many people with depression shut themselves off from the world. They may isolate themselves, not answer the phone, or refuse to go out with friends. You feel as if you're "numb," and that nothing will bring you joy.

Sleep problems

People's sleep habits are likely to change as a result of depression. They may not be able to fall asleep or stay asleep. They may wake up in the middle of the night and not go back to sleep at all. You may sleep for long periods and find that you don't want to get out of bed. These symptoms lead to fatigue that can exacerbate additional symptoms of depression, such as a lack of concentration.

Overeating or loss of appetite

Depression can often cause a lack of interest in food and weight loss. In other people, depression leads to overeating and weight gain. This is because a person may feel so frustrated or miserable that they turn to food as a means to escape their problems. However, overeating can lead to weight gain and cause you to exhibit low levels of energy. Not enough food can also cause you to also have low energy levels and feel weak.

Thoughts of suicide

Thinking or fantasizing about death is a serious sign that needs to be addressed right away. According to the Mayo Clinic, thoughts of suicide are symptoms common in older men. Loved ones may not initially notice this thinking and pass a person's depression symptoms off as age-related mental health changes. However, depression and especially suicidal thoughts are never normal emotions.

If you or a loved one is thinking of hurting themselves, seek immediate medical attention. At the emergency room, a doctor can help you get mental health care until these feelings subside.

Physical pain

Physical symptoms, such as body pain, headaches, cramps, and digestive problems also can occur. Younger children with depression commonly report physical pain symptoms. They may refuse to go to school or behave particularly clingy due to the worry about their aches and pains.

Phobias

Fear is a powerful and primitive human emotion. It alerts us to the presence of danger and it was critical in keeping our ancestors alive. Fear can be divided into two responses, biochemical and emotional. The biochemical response is universal, while the emotional response is highly individual.

Biochemical Reaction

Fear is a natural emotion and a survival mechanism. When we confront a perceived threat, our bodies respond in specific ways. Physical reactions to fear include sweating, increased heart rate, and high adrenaline levels that make us extremely alert. This physical response is also known as the "fight or flight" response, in which your body prepares itself to either enter combat or run away. This biochemical reaction is likely an evolutionary development. It's an automatic response that is crucial to our survival.

Emotional Response

The emotional response to fear is highly personalized. Because fear involves some of the same chemical responses in our brains that positive emotions like happiness and excitement do, feeling fear under certain circumstances can be seen as fun, like when you watch scary movies. Some people are adrenaline junkies, thriving on extreme sports and other fear-inducing thrill situations. Others have a negative reaction to the feeling of fear, avoiding fear-inducing situations at all costs. Although the physical reaction is the same, fear may be perceived as either positive or negative, depending on the person.

Causes of Fear

Fear is incredibly complex. Some fears may be a result of experiences or trauma, while others may actually represent a fear of something else entirely, such as a loss of control. Still other fears may occur because they cause physical symptoms, such as being afraid of heights because they make you feel dizzy and sick to your stomach, even if you're simply watching a video or looking at a picture and in no actual danger.

Scientists are trying to understand exactly what fear is and what causes it, but this is a supremely difficult undertaking in light of the differences between individuals in terms of what they fear and why. Not to mention that there is no agreement between scientists who study fear as to whether it's a sort of behavior that's only observable or something our brains are physically wired to do.

Fear is the basis of anxiety but it is not the only anxiety attack symptom. Treatment for your anxiety needs to address this fear first, however, because it is the trigger for anxiety.

You'll likely want to look at natural anxiety relief, rather than drug-induced treatments because at some point, you will want to be drug and anxiety free.

So let's talk about fear itself and how you can start treating yourself now.

Where does this fear come from? Why does it cause such distress and feed anxiety as well as it does? What can you do to stop it?

There have been many theories around fear and its role as an anxiety attack symptom. Treatment options are equally diverse. Some are scams while others have proven to be highly effective, regardless of how long you've suffered anxiety attack symptoms.

Having suffered years of anxiety, I underwent the related medical treatments. The medications merely kept me calm while I went through 3 years of therapy, but when it was over, the fear had eased but it hadn't gone away.

Then one day, I discovered the secret behind that fear. Today, I immediately recognize when the fear is stirring and can halt it immediately.

If you can identify your fear, you will be able to do the same.

First let me say that I disagree with the approach that you don't have to know what causes the fear, and that it's only important to know that the fear is simply an anxiety attack symptom. For me, it was imperative I figure out the fear so I could deal with it. And when I did, my anxiety attacks subsided.

I hope this secret I'm about to reveal helps you too.

The first thing to realize is that fear comes from your subconscious. Your body senses a danger or perceived danger and responds with fear. Fear causes your body to increase its adrenalin so it can fight to preserve itself. Today, however, much of the fear is internalized rather than from an outside source, like a threat from a wild animal.

It's true that over time our experiences have taught us to respond automatically with this fear instinct. When it gets out of control, as when it becomes an anxiety attack symptom, treatment must be sought.

Let's start with your thoughts, because that's where the fear hides.

If you listen closely when you feel an anxiety attack coming on, you'll get a sense that something just happened to scare you. You know that feeling you get when you go into a room and forget why you went there? Fear as an anxiety attack symptom feels much the same. Inside, you feel uncomfortable. It's a feeling that's difficult to pinpoint or explain. You just sense something isn't right.

I firmly believe that the fear builds because now you are afraid of the fear itself, just as popular programs say. You don't understand where it's coming from and this makes you believe something terrible is going to happen.

This 'something' that caused your unease might be a memory your subconscious has suppressed. For instance, let's say you had a bad experience years ago when you had to go to a meeting. Perhaps you were asked to make a brief presentation, but you hadn't been notified in advance and weren't prepared. You immediately felt fear. This is a natural response to such an unexpected event.

One day, you're going about your business and something reminds you of that nerve-wracking event and the fear you felt resurfaces, but you try to suppress it. This time, you can't pinpoint what's causing it. You have now set up an automatic fear response that will continue until you find a way to deal with it.

When you sense your fear, stop and think about what just happened. What were you thinking about? Are you anxious about something in your life? Often, we have day-to-day 'fears' about things. We worry over finances, health, career, family, retirement, an expected move.

Perhaps you're having trouble meeting your bill payments. Maybe you have to do something you don't particularly feel comfortable doing. Maybe you are going somewhere and you're nervous about the trip for some reason.

Take time to sit down and write out the things that make you nervous, fearful, stressed. Cover your personal traits - for example, if you're a homebody and would rather keep to yourself than attend a meeting or go to a social gathering. Include any traumatic events in your life, going right back to the beginning.

Have you lost loved ones recently? Are you concerned about your life without them? This is particularly tough and might require help from bereavement support groups. Be sure to take advantage of them, because they can provide tremendous help in moving on.

How's your self esteem? Do you feel good about yourself? You might have to really think critically to discover just who you are and why you are the way you are. Write it all down and see if you can identify the things that trigger your fear.

See, my occasional lack of confidence will make me uncertain when I have to take on certain tasks. I'm not sure I can handle them, or that I'll do a good job. Now I know this is a threat to my self-esteem. If I fail, it shows I'm not as good as I'd like to believe.

Failing only reveals my weaknesses and limitations. Because self-esteem is necessary to live comfortably, fear results from this 'threat'. And yes, that fear can soon turn into an anxiety attack if I don't take those few minutes to catch those fleeting thoughts that caused it.

First you need to work on fear - your anxiety attack symptom. Treatment begins at home, as they say.

I've discovered that just the act of halting my fear to stop and think about what just went through my mind was enough to bring the anxiety attack to an end in a matter of seconds. As soon as that happened, I was able to think about the fear and focus on solutions, rather than on the fear itself.

Have you ever wakened from a dream and immediately forgotten what it was, but it felt important to remember? You struggled to recall it so you could find out what happened or resolve the problem. Think of your fear as a dream - something in your subconscious that you can resolve.

Remember too, that most fear is fear of the unknown. Identify your fear and it no longer has control over you. You have control over it, and your anxiety.

I wish I could better explain this process, but the best I can advise is to watch your thinking. Listen to yourself, to your thoughts. Understand who you are. Take the time to sit down and truly evaluate what makes you tick.

Be honest in your personal evaluation. It can be difficult, but it's absolutely necessary for this to work. Often we don't recognize how we think, especially when we're talking about the subconscious. For instance, you might believe you have good self esteem and that you're upbeat and forward-thinking. You can be almost certain this is not entirely true in all situations. Ask your partner or family member for feedback if necessary. Sometimes an outside source can pick up things you'll miss.

Acclimation

Repeated exposure to similar situations leads to familiarity. This greatly reduces both the fear response and the resulting elation, leading adrenaline junkies to seek out ever new and bigger thrills. It also forms the basis of some phobia treatments, which depend on slowly minimizing the fear response by making it feel familiar.

Psychology of Phobias

One aspect of anxiety disorders can be a tendency to develop a fear of fear. Where most people tend to experience fear only during a situation that is perceived as scary or threatening, those who suffer from anxiety disorders may become afraid that they will experience a fear response. They perceive their fear responses as negative and go out of their way to avoid those responses.

A phobia is a twisting of the normal fear response. The fear is directed toward an object or situation that does not present a real danger. Though you recognize that the fear is unreasonable, you can't help the reaction. Over time, the fear tends to worsen as the fear of fear response takes hold.

CHAPTER TWO

BECOME FAMILIAR WITH THE BASIC PRINCIPLES OF CBT AND UNDERSTAND HOW IT WORKS

The History Of Cognitive Behavioral Therapy

Cognitive behavioral therapy is an approach used by psychotherapists to influence a patient's behaviors and emotions. The key to the approach is in its procedure which must be systematic. It has been used successfully to treat a variety of disorders including eating disorders, substance abuse, anxiety and personality disorders. It can be used in individual or group therapy sessions and the approach can also be geared towards self help therapy.

Cognitive behavioral therapy is a combination of traditional behavioral therapy and cognitive therapy. They are combined into a treatment that is focused on symptom removal. The effectiveness of the treatment can clearly be judged based on its results. The more it is used, the more it has become recommended. It is now used as the number one treatment technique for post traumatic stress disorder, obsessive compulsive disorder, depression and bulimia.

Cognitive behavioral therapy first began to be used between 1960 and 1970. It was a gradual process of merging behavioral therapy techniques and cognitive therapy techniques. Behavioral therapy had been around since the 1920's, but cognitive therapy was not introduced until the 1960's. Almost immediately the benefits of combining it with behavioral therapy techniques were realized. Ivan Pavlov, with his dogs who salivated at the ringing of the dinner bell, was among the most famous of the behavioral research pioneers. Other leaders in the field included John Watson and Clark Hull.

Instead of focusing on analyzing the problem like Freud and the psychoanalysts, cognitive behavioral therapy focused on eliminating the symptoms. The idea being that if you eliminate the symptoms, you have eliminated the problem. This more direct approach was seen as more effective at getting to the problem at hand and helping patients to make progress more quickly.

As a more radical aggressive treatment, behavioral techniques dealt better with more radical problems. The more obvious and clear cut the symptoms were, the easier it was to target them and devise treatments to eliminate them. Behavioral therapy was not as successful initially with more ambiguous problems such as depression. This realm was better served with cognitive therapy techniques.

In many academic settings, the two therapy techniques were used side by side to compare and contrast the results. It was not long before the advantages of combining the two techniques became clear as a way of taking advantage of the strengths of each. David Barlow's work on panic disorder treatments provided the first concrete example of the success of the combined strategies.

Cognitive behavioral therapy is difficult to define in a succinct definition because it covers such a broad range of topics and techniques. It is really an umbrella definition for individual treatments that are specifically tailored to the problems of a specific patient. So the problem dictates the specifics of the treatment, but there are some common themes and techniques. These include having the patient keep a diary of important events and record the feelings and behaviors they had in association with each event. This tool is then used as a basis to analyze and test the patient's ability to evaluate the situation and develop an appropriate emotional response. Negative emotions and behaviors are identified as well as the evaluations and beliefs that lead to them. An effort is then made to counter these beliefs and evaluations to show that the resulting behaviors are wrong. Negative behaviors are eliminated and the patient is taught a better way to view and react to the situation.

Part of the therapy also includes teaching the patient ways to distract themselves or change their focus from something that is upsetting or a situation that is generating negative behavior. They learn to focus on something else instead of the negative stimulus, thus eliminating the negative behavior that it would lead to. The problem is essentially nipped in the bud. For serious psychological disorders like bipolar disorder or schizophrenia, mood stabilizing medications are often prescribed to use in conjunction with these techniques. The medications give the patient enough of a calming effect to give them the opportunity to examine the situation and make the healthy choice whereas before they could not even pause for rational thought.

Cognitive behavioral therapy has been proven effective for a variety of problems, but it is still a process, not a miracle cure. It takes time to teach patients to understand situations and identify the triggers of their negative behaviors. Once this step is mastered, it still takes a lot of effort to overcome their first instincts and instead stop and make the right choices. First they learn what they should do, and then they must practice until they can do it.

The Basics of Cognitive Behavioral Therapy

The underlying concept behind CBT is that our thoughts and feelings play a fundamental role in our behavior. For example, a person who spends a lot of time thinking about plane crashes, runway accidents and other air disasters may find themselves avoiding air travel.

The goal of cognitive behavior therapy is to teach patients that while they cannot control every aspect of the world around them, they can take control of how they interpret and deal with things in their environment.

Cognitive behavior therapy has become increasingly popular in recent years with both mental health consumers and treatment professionals. Because CBT is usually a short-term treatment option, it is often more affordable than some other types of therapy. CBT is also empirically supported and has been shown to effectively help patients overcome a wide variety of maladaptive behaviors.

Cognitive behavioral therapy is a psychotherapeutic approach that aims to teach a person new skills on how to solve problems concerning dysfunctional emotions, behaviors, and cognitions through a goal-oriented, systematic approach. This title is used in many ways to differentiate behavioral therapy, cognitive therapy, and therapy that is based on both behavioral and cognitive therapies. There is empirical evidence that shows that cognitive behavioral therapy is quite effective in treating several conditions, including personality, anxiety, mood, eating, substance abuse, and psychotic disorders. Treatment is often manualized, as specific psychological orders are treated with specific technique-driven brief, direct, and time-limited treatments.

Cognitive behavioral therapy can be used both with individuals and in groups. The techniques are often adapted for self-help sessions as well. It is up to the individual clinician or researcher on whether he/she is more cognitive oriented, more behavioral oriented, or a combination of both, as all three methods are used today. Cognitive behavioral therapy was born out of a combination of behavioral therapy and cognitive therapy. These two therapies have many differences, but found common ground on focusing on the "here and now" and on alleviating symptoms.

Evaluating cognitive behavioral therapy has led to many believing that it is more effective over psychodynamic treatments and other methods. The United Kingdom advocates the use of cognitive behavioral therapy over other methods for many mental health difficulties, including post-traumatic stress disorder, obsessive-compulsive disorder, bulimia nervosa, clinical depression, and the neurological condition chronic fatigue syndrome/myalgic encephalomyelitis. The precursors of cognitive behavioral therapy base their roots in various ancient philosophical traditions, especially Stoicism. The modern roots of CBT can be traced to the development of behavioral therapy in the 1920s, the development of cognitive therapy in the 1960s, and the subsequent merging of the two therapies. The first behavioral therapeutic approaches were published in 1924 by Mary Cover Jones, whose work dealt with the unlearning of fears in children.

The early behavioral approaches worked well with many of the neurotic disorders, but not so much with depression. Behavioral therapy was also losing in popularity due to the "cognitive revolution." This eventually led to cognitive therapy being founded by Aaron T. Beck in the 1960s. The first form of cognitive behavioral therapy was developed by Arnold A. Lazarus during the time period of the late 1950s through the 1970s. During the 1980s and 1990s, cognitive and behavioral therapies were combined by work done by David M. Clark in the United Kingdom and David H. Barlow in the United States. Cognitive behavioral therapy includes the following systems: cognitive therapy, rational emotive behavior therapy, and multimodal therapy. One of the greatest challenges is defining exactly what a cognitive-behavioral therapy is. The particular therapeutic techniques vary within the different approaches of CBT depending upon what kind of problem issues are being dealt with, but the techniques usually center around the following:

• Keeping a diary of significant events and associated feelings, thoughts, and behaviors.

• Questioning and testing cognitions, evaluations, assumptions, and beliefs that might be unrealistic and unhelpful.

• Gradually facing activities that may have been avoided.

• Trying out new ways of behaving and reacting.

In addition, distraction techniques, mindfulness, and relaxation are also commonly used in cognitive behavioral therapy. Mood-stabilizing medications are also often combined with therapies to treat conditions like bipolar disorder. The NICE guidelines within the British NHS recognize cognitive behavioral therapy's application in treating schizophrenia in combination with medication and therapy. Cognitive behavioral therapy usually takes time for patients to effectively implement it into their lives. It usually takes concentrated effort for them to replace a dysfunctional cognitive-affective-behavioral process or habit with a more reasonable and adaptive one, even when they recognize when and where their mental processes go awry. Cognitive behavioral therapy is applied to many different situations, including the following conditions:

Anxiety disorders (obsessive-compulsive disorder, social phobia or social anxiety, generalized anxiety disorder)

Mood disorders (clinical depression, major depressive disorder, psychiatric symptoms)

Insomnia (including being more effective than the drug Zopiclone)

Severe mental disorders (schizophrenia, bipolar disorder, severe depression)

Children and adolescents (major depressive disorder, anxiety disorders, trauma and posttraumatic stress disorder symptoms)

Stuttering (to help them overcome anxiety, avoidance behaviors, and negative thoughts about themselves)

Cognitive behavioral therapy involves teaching a person new skills to overcome dysfunctional emotions, behaviors, and cognitions through a goal-oriented, systematic approach. There is empirical evidence showing that cognitive behavioral therapy is effective in treating many conditions, including obsessive-compulsive disorder, generalized anxiety disorder, major depressive disorder, schizophrenia, anxiety, and negative thoughts about oneself). With the vast amount of success shown by the use of this therapy, it is one of the most important tools that researchers and therapists have to treat mental disorders today.

Automatic Negative Thoughts

One of the main focuses of cognitive-behavioral therapy is on changing the automatic negative thoughts that can contribute to and exacerbate emotional difficulties, depression, and anxiety. These negative thoughts spring forward spontaneously, are accepted as true, and tend to negatively influence the individual's mood.

Through the CBT process, patients examine these thoughts and are encouraged to look at evidence from reality that either supports or refutes these thoughts. By doing this, people are able to take a more objective and realistic look at the thoughts that contribute to their feelings of anxiety and depression. By becoming aware of the negative and often unrealistic thoughts that dampen their feelings and moods, people are able to start engaging in healthier thinking patterns.

Types of Cognitive Behavior Therapy

According to the British Association of Behavioural and Cognitive Psychotherapies, "Cognitive and behavioral psychotherapies are a range of therapies based on concepts and principles derived from psychological models of human emotion and behavior. They include a wide range of treatment approaches for emotional disorders, along a continuum from structured individual psychotherapy to self-help material."

There are a number of specific types of therapeutic approaches that involve CBT that are regularly used by mental health professionals. Examples of these include:

Rational Emotive Behavior Therapy (REBT): This type of CBT is centered on identifying and altering irrational beliefs. The process of REBT involves identifying the underlying irrational beliefs, actively challenging these beliefs, and finally learning to recognize and change these thought patterns.

Cognitive Therapy: This form of therapy is centered on identifying and changing inaccurate or distorted thinking patterns, emotional responses, and behaviors.

Multimodal Therapy: This form of CBT suggests that psychological issues must be treated by addressing seven different but interconnected modalities, which are behavior, affect, sensation, imagery, cognition, interpersonal factors and drug/biological considerations.

Dialectical Behavior Therapy: This type of cognitive-behavioral therapy addresses thinking patterns and behaviors and incorporates strategies such as emotional regulation and mindfulness.

While each type of cognitive-behavioral therapy offers its own unique approach, each centers on addressing the underlying thought patterns that contribute to psychological distress.

The Components of Cognitive Behavior Therapy

People often experience thoughts or feelings that reinforce or compound faulty beliefs. Such beliefs can result in problematic behaviors that can affect numerous life areas, including family, romantic relationships, work, and academics.

For example, a person suffering from low self-esteem might experience negative thoughts about his or her own abilities or appearance. As a result of these negative thinking patterns, the individual might start avoiding social situations or pass up opportunities for advancement at work or at school.

In order to combat these destructive thoughts and behaviors, a cognitive-behavioral therapist begins by helping the client to identify the problematic beliefs. This stage, known as functional analysis, is important for learning how thoughts, feelings, and situations can contribute to maladaptive behaviors. The process can be difficult, especially for patients who struggle with introspection, but it can ultimately lead to self-discovery and insights that are an essential part of the treatment process.

The second part of cognitive behavior therapy focuses on the actual behaviors that are contributing to the problem. The client begins to learn and practice new skills that can then be put in to use in real-world situations. For example, a person suffering from drug addiction might start practicing new coping skills and rehearsing ways to avoid or deal with social situations that could potentially trigger a relapse.

In most cases, CBT is a gradual process that helps a person take incremental steps towards a behavior change. Someone suffering from social anxiety might start by simply imagining himself in an anxiety-provoking social situation.

Next, the client might start practicing conversations with friends, family, and acquaintances. By progressively working toward a larger goal, the process seems less daunting and the goals easier to achieve.

The Process of Cognitive Behavior Therapy

During the process of CBT, the therapist tends to take a very active role.

CBT is highly goal-oriented and focused, and the client and therapist work together as collaborators toward the mutually established goals.

The therapist will typically explain the process in detail and the client will often be given homework to complete between sessions.

Cognitive-behavior therapy can be effectively used as a short-term treatment centered on helping the client deal with a very specific problem.

Uses of Cognitive Behavior Therapy

Cognitive behavior therapy has been used to treat people suffering from a wide range of disorders, including:

1. Anxiety

2. Phobias

3. Depression

4. Addictions

5. Eating disorders

6. Panic attacks

7. Anger

CBT is one of the most researched types of therapy, in part because treatment is focused on highly specific goals and results can be measured relatively easily.

Compared to psychoanalytic types of psychotherapy which encourage a more open-ended self-exploration, cognitive behavior therapy is often best-suited for clients who are more comfortable with a structured and focused approach in which the therapist often takes an instructional role. However, for CBT to be effective, the individual must be ready and willing to spend time and effort analyzing his or her thoughts and feelings. Such self-analysis and homework can be difficult, but it is a great way to learn more about how internal states impact outward behavior.

Cognitive behavior therapy is also well-suited for people looking for a short-term treatment option for certain types of emotional distress that does not necessarily involve psychotropic medication. One of the greatest benefits of cognitive-behavior therapy is that it helps clients develop coping skills that can be useful both now and in the future.

Although therapy must be tailored to the individual, there are, nevertheless, certain principles that underlie cognitive behavior therapy for all patients. I will use a depressed patient, "Amy," to illustrate these central tenets and to demonstrate how to use cognitive theory to understand patients' difficulties and how to use this understanding to plan treatment and conduct therapy sessions.

Amy was an 18-year-old single female when she sought treatment with me during her second semester of college. She had been feeling quite depressed and anxious for the previous 4 months and was having difficulty with her daily activities. She met criteria for a major depressive episode of moderate severity according to DSM-IV-TR (the Diagnostic and Statistical Manual of Mental Disorders, Fourth Edition, Text Revision; American Psychiatric Association, 2000). The basic principles of cognitive behavior therapy are as follows:

Principle No. 1: Cognitive behavior therapy is based on an ever-evolving formulation of patients' problems and an individual conceptualization of each patient in cognitive terms. I consider Amy's difficulties in three time frames. From the beginning, I identify her current thinking that contributes to her feelings of sadness ("I'm a failure, I can't do anything right, I'll never be happy"), and her problematic behaviors (isolating herself, spending a great deal of unproductive time in her room, avoiding asking for help). These problematic behaviors both flow from and in turn reinforce Amy's dysfunctional thinking.

Second, I identify precipitating factors that influenced Amy's perceptions at the onset of her depression(e.g., being away from home for the first time and struggling in her studies contributed to her belief that she was incompetent).

Third, I hypothesize about key developmental events and her enduring patterns of interpreting these events that may have predisposed her to depression (e.g., Amy has had a lifelong tendency to attribute personal strengths and achievement to luck, but views her weaknesses as a reflection of her "true" self).

I base my conceptualization of Amy on the cognitive formulation of depression and on the data Amy provides at the evaluation session. I continue to refine this conceptualization at each session as I obtain more data. At strategic points, I share the conceptualization with Amy to ensure that it "rings true" to her. Moreover, throughout therapy I help Amy view her experience through the cognitive model. She learns, for example, to identify the thoughts associated with her distressing affect and to evaluate and formulate more adaptive responses to her thinking. Doing so improves how she feels and often leads to her behaving in a more functional way.

Principle No. 2: Cognitive behavior therapy requires a sound therapeutic alliance. Amy, like many patients with uncomplicated depression and anxiety disorders, has little difficulty trusting and working with me. I strive to demonstrate all the basic ingredients necessary in a counseling situation: warmth, empathy, caring, genuine regard, and competence. I show my regard for Amy by making empathic statements, listening closely and carefully, and accurately summarizing her thoughts and feelings. I point out her small and larger successes and maintain a realistically optimistic and upbeat outlook. I also ask Amy for feedback at the end of each session to ensure that she feels understood and positive about the session.

Principle No. 3: Cognitive behavior therapy emphasizes collaboration and active participation. I encourage Amy to view therapy as teamwork; together we decide what to work on each session, how often we should meet, and what Amy can do between sessions for therapy homework. At first, I am more active in suggesting a direction for therapy sessions and in summarizing what we've discussed during a session. As Amy becomes less depressed and more socialized into treatment, I encourage her to become increasingly active in the therapy session: deciding which problems to talk about, identifying the distortions in her thinking, summarizing important points, and devising homework assignments.

Principle No. 4: Cognitive behavior therapy is goal oriented and problem focused. I ask Amy in our first session to enumerate her problems and set specific goals so both she and I have a shared understanding of what she is working toward. For example, Amy mentions in the evaluation session that she feels isolated. With my guidance, Amy states a goal in behavioral terms: to initiate new friendships and spend more time with current friends. Later, when discussing how to improve her day-to-day routine, I help her evaluate and respond to thoughts that interfere with her goal, such as: My friends won't want to hang out with me. I'm too tired to go out with them. First, I help Amy evaluate the validity of her thoughtsthrough an examination of the evidence. Then Amy is willing to test the thoughts more directly through behavioral experiments in which she initiates plans with friends. Once she recognizes and corrects the distortion in her thinking, Amy is able to benefit from straightforward problem solving to decrease her isolation.

Principle No. 5: Cognitive behavior therapy initially emphasizes the present. The treatment of most patients involves a strong focus on current problems and on specific situations that are distressing to them. Amy begins to feel better once she is able to respond to her negative thinking and take steps to improve her life. Therapy starts with an examination of here-and-now problems, regardless of diagnosis. Attention shifts to the past in two circumstances: One, when patients express a strong preference to do so, and a failure to do so could endanger the therapeutic alliance. Two, when patients get "stuck" in their dysfunctional thinking, and an understanding of the childhood roots of their beliefs can potentially help them modify their rigid ideas.

("Well, no wonder you still believe you're incompetent. Can you see how almost any child—who had the same experiences as you—would grow up believing she was incompetent, and yet it might not be true, or certainly not completely true?")

For example, I briefly turn to the past midway through treatment to help Amy identify a set of beliefs she learned as a child: "If I achieve highly, it means I'm worthwhile," and "If I don't achieve highly, it means I'm a failure." I help her evaluate the validity of these beliefs both in the past and present. Doing so leads Amy, in part, to develop more functional and more reasonable beliefs. If Amy had had a personality disorder, I would have spent proportionally more time discussing her developmental history and childhood origin of beliefs and coping behaviors.

Principle No. 6: Cognitive behavior therapy is educative, aims to teach the patient to be her own therapist, and emphasizes relapse prevention. In our first session I educate Amy about the nature and course of her disorder, about the process of cognitive behavior therapy, and about the cognitive model (i.e., how her thoughts influence her emotions and behavior). I not only help Amy set goals, identify and evaluate thoughts and beliefs, and plan behavioral change, but I also teach her how to do so. At each session I ensure that Amy takes home therapy notes—important ideas she has learned—so she can benefit from her new understanding in the ensuing weeks and after treatment ends.

Principle No. 7: Cognitive behavior therapy aims to be time limited. Many straightforward patients with depression and anxiety disorders are treated for six to 14 sessions. Therapists' goals are to provide symptom relief, facilitate a remission of the disorder, help patients resolve their most pressing problems, and teach them skills to avoid relapse. Amy initially has weekly therapy sessions. (Had her depression been more severe or had she been suicidal, I may have arranged more frequent sessions.) After 2 months, we collaboratively decide to experiment with biweekly sessions, then with monthly sessions. Even after termination, we plan periodic "booster" sessions every 3 months for a year. Not all patients make enough progress in just a few months, however. Some patients require 1 or 2 years of therapy (or possibly longer) to modify very rigid dysfunctional beliefs and patterns of behavior that contribute to their chronic distress. Other patients with severe mental illness may need periodic treatment for a very long time to maintain stabilization.

Principle No. 8: Cognitive behavior therapy sessions are structured. No matter what the diagnosis or stage of treatment, following a certain structure in each session maximizes efficiency and effectiveness. This structure includes an introductory part (doing a mood check, briefly reviewing the week, collaboratively setting an agenda for the session), a middle part (reviewing homework, discussing problems on the agenda, setting new homework, summarizing), and a final part (eliciting feedback). Following this format makes the process of therapy more understandable to patients and increases the likelihood that they will be able to do self-therapy after termination.

Principle No. 9: Cognitive behavior therapy teaches patients to identify, evaluate, and respond to their dysfunctional thoughts and beliefs. Patients can have many dozens or even hundreds of automatic thoughts a day that affect their mood, behavior, or physiology (the last is especially pertinent to anxiety). Therapists help patients identify key cognitions and adopt more realistic, adaptive perspectives, which leads patients to feel better emotionally, behave more functionally, or decrease their physiological arousal. They do so through the process of guided discovery, using questioning (often labeled or mislabeled as "Socratic questioning") to evaluate their thinking (rather than persuasion, debate, or lecturing). Therapists also create experiences, called behavioral experiments, for patients to directly test their thinking (e.g., "If I even look at a picture of a spider, I'll get so anxious I won't be able to think"). In these ways, therapists engage in collaborative empiricism. Therapists do not generally know in advance to what degree a patient's automatic thought is valid or invalid, but together they test the patient's thinking to develop more helpful and accurate responses.

When Amy was quite depressed, she had many automatic thoughts throughout the day, some of which she spontaneously reported and others that I elicited (by asking her what was going through her mind when she felt upset or acted in a dysfunctional manner). We often uncovered important automatic thoughts as we were discussing one of Amy's specific problems, and together we investigated their validity and utility. I asked her to summarize her new viewpoints, and we recorded them in writing so that she could read these adaptive responses throughout the week to prepare her for these or similar automatic thoughts. I did not encourage her to uncritically adopt a more positive viewpoint, challenge the validity of her automatic thoughts, or try to convince her that her thinking was unrealistically pessimistic. Instead we engaged in a collaborative exploration of the evidence.

Principle No. 10: Cognitive behavior therapy uses a variety of techniques to change thinking, mood, and behavior. Although cognitive strategies such as Socratic questioning and guided discovery are central to cognitive behavior therapy, behavioral and problem-solving techniques are essential, as are techniques from other orientations that are implemented within a cognitive framework. For example, I used Gestalt-inspired techniques to help Amy understand how experiences with her family contributed to the development of her belief that she was incompetent. I use psychodynamically inspired techniques with some Axis II patients who apply their distorted ideas about people to the therapeutic relationship. The types of techniques you select will be influenced by your conceptualization of the patient, the problem you are discussing, and your objectives for the session.

These basic principles apply to all patients. Therapy does, however, vary considerably according to individual patients, the nature of their difficulties, and their stage of life, as well as their developmental and intellectual level, gender, and cultural background. Treatment also varies depending on patients' goals, their ability to form a strong therapeutic bond, their motivation to change, their previous experience with therapy, and their preferences for treatment, among other factors. The emphasis in treatment also depends on the patient's particular disorder(s). Cognitive behavior therapy for panic disorder involves testing the patient's catastrophic misinterpretations (usually life- or sanity-threatening erroneous predictions) of bodily or mental sensations. Anorexia requires a modification of beliefs about personal worth and control. Substance abuse treatment focuses on negative beliefs about the self and facilitating or permission-granting beliefs about substance use.

How does it work?

Cognitive behavioural therapy (CBT) can help you make sense of overwhelming problems by breaking them down into smaller parts.

Some forms of psychotherapy focus on looking into the past to gain an understanding of current feelings. In contrast, CBT focuses on present thoughts and beliefs.

CBT can help people with many problems where thoughts and beliefs are critical. It emphasizes the need to identify, challenge, and change how a person views a situation.

According to CBT, people's pattern of thinking is like wearing a pair of glasses that makes us see the world in a specific way. CBT makes us more aware of how these thought patterns create our reality and determine how we behave.

In CBT, problems are broken down into five main areas:

• situations

• thoughts

• emotions

• physical feelings

• actions

CBT is based on the concept of these five areas being interconnected and affecting each other. For example, your thoughts about a certain situation can often affect how you feel both physically and emotionally, as well as how you act in response.

How CBT is different

CBT differs from many other psychotherapies because it's:

Pragmatic – it helps identify specific problems and tries to solve them

Highly structured – rather than talking freely about your life, you and your therapist discuss specific problems and set goals for you to achieve

Focused on current problems – it's mainly concerned with how you think and act now rather than attempting to resolve past issues

Collaborative – your therapist won't tell you what to do; they'll work with you to find solutions to your current difficulties

Stopping negative thought cycles

There are helpful and unhelpful ways of reacting to a situation, often determined by how you think about them.

For example, if your marriage has ended in divorce, you might think you've failed and that you're not capable of having another meaningful relationship.

This could lead to you feeling hopeless, lonely, depressed and tired, so you stop going out and meeting new people. You become trapped in a negative cycle, sitting at home alone and feeling bad about yourself.

But rather than accepting this way of thinking you could accept that many marriages end, learn from your mistakes and move on, and feel optimistic about the future.

This optimism could result in you becoming more socially active and you may start evening classes and develop a new circle of friends.

This is a simplified example, but it illustrates how certain thoughts, feelings, physical sensations and actions can trap you in a negative cycle and even create new situations that make you feel worse about yourself.

CBT aims to stop negative cycles such as these by breaking down things that make you feel bad, anxious or scared. By making your problems more manageable, CBT can help you change your negative thought patterns and improve the way you feel.

CBT can help you get to a point where you can achieve this on your own and tackle problems without the help of a therapist.

Exposure therapy

Exposure therapy is a form of CBT particularly useful for people with phobias or obsessive compulsive disorder (OCD).

In such cases, talking about the situation isn't as helpful and you may need to learn to face your fears in a methodical and structured way through exposure therapy.

Exposure therapy involves starting with items and situations that cause anxiety, but anxiety that you feel able to tolerate. You need to stay in this situation for one to two hours or until the anxiety reduces for a prolonged period by a half.

Your therapist will ask you to repeat this exposure exercise three times a day. After the first few times, you'll find your anxiety doesn't climb as high and doesn't last as long.

You'll then be ready to move to a more difficult situation. This process should be continued until you have tackled all the items and situations you want to conquer.

Exposure therapy may involve spending six to 15 hours with the therapist, or can be carried out using self-help books or computer programs. You'll need to regularly practice the exercises as prescribed to overcome your problems.

CBT sessions

CBT can be carried out with a therapist in one-to-one sessions or in groups with other people in a similar situation to you.

If you have CBT on an individual basis, you'll usually meet with a CBT therapist for between five and 20 weekly or fortnightly sessions, with each session lasting 30-60 minutes.

Exposure therapy sessions usually last longer to ensure your anxiety reduces during the session. The therapy may take place:

In a clinic

Outside – if you have specific fears there

In your own home – particularly if you have agoraphobia or OCD involving a specific fear of items at home

Your CBT therapist can be any healthcare professional who has been specially trained in CBT, such as a psychiatrist, psychologist, mental health nurse or GP.

First sessions

The first few sessions will be spent making sure CBT is the right therapy for you, and that you're comfortable with the process. The therapist will ask questions about your life and background.

If you're anxious or depressed, the therapist will ask whether it interferes with your family, work and social life. They'll also ask about events that may be related to your problems, treatments you've had, and what you would like to achieve through therapy.

If CBT seems appropriate, the therapist will let you know what to expect from a course of treatment. If it's not appropriate, or you don't feel comfortable with it, they can recommend alternative treatments.

Further sessions

After the initial assessment period, you'll start working with your therapist to break down problems into their separate parts. To help with this, your therapist may ask you to keep a diary or write down your thought and behaviour patterns.

You and your therapist will analyse your thoughts, feelings and behaviours to work out if they're unrealistic or unhelpful and to determine the effect they have on each other and on you. Your therapist will be able to help you work out how to change unhelpful thoughts and behaviours.

After working out what you can change, your therapist will ask you to practise these changes in your daily life.

This may involve:

Questioning upsetting thoughts and replacing them with more helpful ones

Recognizing when you're going to do something that will make you feel worse and instead doing something more helpful

You may be asked to do some "homework" between sessions to help with this process.

At each session, you'll discuss with your therapist how you've got on with putting the changes into practice and what it felt like. Your therapist will be able to make other suggestions to help you.

Confronting fears and anxieties can be very difficult. Your therapist won't ask you to do things you don't want to do and will only work at a pace you're comfortable with. During your sessions, your therapist will check you're comfortable with the progress you're making.

One of the biggest benefits of CBT is that after your course has finished, you can continue to apply the principles learned to your daily life. This should make it less likely that your symptoms will return.

CHAPTER THREE

HOW TO DEFINE A SPECIFIC GOAL TO WORK TOWARD OVER THE COURSE OF 6 WEEKS

Because of CBT's success, some of its tenants have become well-known. You might already have heard, for example, that thoughts affect feelings, or that behavioural change can affect negative thoughts.

But what other Cognitive Behavioral Therapy techniques and tools are there, and how do they help you? How are these CBT techniques used in a session?

AGENDA SETTING IN CBT

This is a collaborative process between your therapist and you to determine how to best make use of each session. At the start of each appointment both you and your therapist suggest items you'd like to discuss. A decision is then made on the order the points will be discussed, and how much time each one needs.

The point of agenda setting is to make sure that the session is well spent, and that the hour isn't lost to something that isn't of itself productive, like simply rehashing the events of the week. It is always a good idea to be thinking before your session about what you want to put on the agenda, so you don't walk away feeling something important was missed.

In the first few sessions your therapist will model for you how to set agendas. So you don't have to instantly feel comfortable enough to add items to the agenda yourself, but can learn over time. This is itself a valuable process, helping you take charge of your problems and their solutions.

GOAL-SETTING IN CBT

Again, this is a collaborative process designed to maintain structure and focus. The point is to make the goals for your therapy those that are relevant to you, with input from your therapist to make sure they are clear and are what you actually want as opposed to what you think you should want. Goal-setting makes CBT productive by highlighting the possibility of change, making insurmountable problems appear more manageable, and increasing your hope of overcoming them.

While there are many different approaches to goal setting, one of the more common techniques used by CBT therapists is the SMART way.

SMART goal setting creates a clear and vivid picture of your goal and helps you maintain your motivation for achieving it.

This is what the acronym stands for :

Specific: Avoid generalisation. Be clear and focused on

exactly what you want. A specific goal has a much greater chance of being accomplished than a general goal.

Measurable: Establish concrete criteria for measuring progress toward the attainment of each goal you set. Ask yourself questions such as, "How much?" and "How many?" "How will I know when I have met my goal?"

Achievable: Make your goals attainable and feasible! How are you going to make this goal a reality? What can you do to make it more achievable?

Realistic: Is your goal realistic given your skills, time frame, etc? While setting high goals can be a great way of increasing motivation, it can also be disheartening when they are so high that you cannot reach them. This can leave you feeling like a failure.

Timely: Set realistic time-frames to avoid procrastination or giving up on your goal.

In pursuing your goals, if you find that that you are not able to complete a particular step along the path to your goal, take a closer look at it. It is possible that the step was too big, so do not be afraid to break it down further and go from there. It could also be that the step was not SMART from the start. See if you can rework it to make it one you can tackle.

Learning goal setting skills takes practice, but can be

invaluable in helping you do those things you have been avoiding or "just don't seem to get to" and feel a sense of accomplishment. Consider consulting with a CBT therapist if you think therapy may be helpful for you in reaching your goals.

Understanding the importance of Goal setting

A lot a people who come for therapy it is usually because their relationships are suffering, and so they are suffering. It could be a teenaged boy whose severe social anxiety prevents him from spending time with his friends, a woman with depression that makes it hard to be the partner she wants to be, a father whose expressions of anger have put distance between him and his kids, or the college student whose alcohol-fueled behavior has alienated her friends. It's hard for our relationships to thrive when we're hurting.

Effective therapy can improve our relationships, whether or not those relationships are the specific target of the treatment. A relatively brief course of cognitive behavioral therapy (CBT)—which has been tested more than any other treatment—can lead to marked benefits not only for the person in therapy but for those close to that person. Some of the major relationship benefits of CBT include:

1. Greater presence. It's hard to overstate the importance of our presence in a relationship, since we can't truly "relate" to someone who's not there. One of

the biggest complaints about partners that I hear in my practice is that "s/he isn't there for me". Sometimes the person means quite literally that their partner is absent—always traveling for work, for example. Just as often the problem is that even when the person is there in body, his or her mind is elsewhere.

Mindfulness-based CBT can address both of these issues; for example, training in mindfulness has been shown in multiple studies to increase one's ability to attend to the person we're with. A CBT framework can help translate one's intention to be present into a plan of action to make it happen.

Try it: The next time your partner talks with you about something, bring your full attention to what they're saying. Practice seeing the person as though for the first time, really focusing on them and what they're saying.

2. Less anxiety. When we're overwhelmed by anxiety, we're not our best selves. It's no surprise that untreated anxiety disorders take a toll on our closest relationships. For example, the need for a "safety companion" in panic disorder and agoraphobia can lead to strain as the supporting partner has to adjust his or her schedule to accommodate the other person's travels. Similarly the chronic worry in generalized anxiety disorder frequently leads to tension and irritability, causing conflict between partners.

For any anxiety diagnosis, the treatments with the most evidence for their effectiveness come from CBT. The relief a person feels from a marked reduction in anxiety extends to greater harmony in the relationship.

Try it: If you've struggled with uncontrollable anxiety, consider looking into the best treatments for your condition on the website for Division 12 of the American Psychological Association. You can also search the therapist directory of PsychologyToday.com for a therapist who provides the treatment you're looking for. If a suitable therapist is not available, you might pursue self-guided CBT (such as with this book), which has been shown to be effective.

3. Improved mood. As with anxiety, untreated depression wears on couples. It's a struggle to be the partner we're capable of being when we have no energy, little enthusiasm even for activities we would normally enjoy, and no sex drive, among other symptoms. After a typical course of CBT for depression—12 to 16 weeks—the average person will not only feel substantially better but will be able to function much more effectively and happier individuals make happier couples.

Try it: As with anxiety, you can search for a CBT therapist through the PsychologyToday.com therapist directory. There is also evidence that self-guided CBT can be effective for treating depression (e.g., CBT in 7

Weeks or Cognitive Behavioural Therapy), so CBT is available even when a therapist is not. You can even do Internet-based CBT (Be always careful for the Internet-based information)

4. Better sleep. As many as 23% of adults in the US suffered from bad sleep in the past month. When we're not sleeping well we tend to be cranky and impatient—not a recipe for the best interactions with the people who love us. Furthermore, insomnia can turn the bed into a place of worry and stress, which interferes with a cozy night's sleep beside our partner. CBT for insomnia (CBT-I) is typically 4 to 6 sessions and is the treatment of choice for insomnia. It helps a person fall asleep faster and sleep more soundly, and restores a strong association between the bed and sleep. And better sleep helps with pretty much everything.

Try it: If you've struggled with sleep, consult these guidelines for healthy sleep habits. The National Sleep Foundation has suggestions for finding a CBT-I therapist. CBT-I is also available through self-guided books (e.g., End the Insomnia Struggle) and apps.

5. Healthier relationship with alcohol. Problematic drinking can kill a relationship. Alcohol use disorder is tied to higher divorce rates, greater intimate partner violence, lower relationship satisfaction, and a host of other problems. CBT can effectively target the thoughts and behaviors that maintain problems with alcohol, and

replace drinking with healthier ways of coping. Interestingly, the treatment with the strongest research evidence is Behavioral Couples Therapy, with both the patient and his or her partner actively involved in the treatment.

For many individuals with an alcohol use disorder, lifelong abstinence is necessary. However, there is modest support for a treatment program that includes the possibility of moderate alcohol consumption for some people.

Try it: If you're interested in learning more about the Moderate Drinking program, some information are in this book (but not all the necessary ones so look for something more specific). You can also consult the PsychologyToday.com directory to find a therapist who provides Behavioral Couples Therapy for alcohol use disorders.

6. Happier kids. When a child is struggling with intense fears (e.g., phobias, obsessive-compulsive disorder), it can lead to tremendous stress for the family. Parents inevitably feel the strain when a child is refusing to go to school, struggling socially, or having problems at bedtime. As the saying goes, "You're only as happy as your least happy child."

Furthermore, most couples have somewhat different parenting styles, with one partner more lenient and the other more of the disciplinarian. A child's intense struggles will tend to amplify these differences, leading to conflict between the parents. At the end of the night when the kids are finally in bed and both parents just want to unwind, they may instead find themselves arguing about how best to help their child. Thus they may feel like their reserves are exhausted, with little left to give their child or each other.

The American Academy of Child and Adolescent Psychiatry recommends CBT as a first-line approach for treating many childhood conditions, including anxiety and OCD. Similarly, the American Academy of Sleep Medicine recommends behavioral treatments for sleep problems in infants and children, which can help both the child and the parents sleep through the night.

Try it: There are books available that detail how to apply the techniques of CBT to help your child with anxiety (e.g., Helping Your Anxious Child) or OCD (e.g., What to Do When Your Brain Gets Stuck). There are also many CBT-focused web resources available, such as from the International OCD Foundation and the Society of Clinical Child and Adolescent Psychology.

7. Healthier Thought Patterns. Even if we're not dealing with a diagnosable condition like anxiety, depression, insomnia, or a substance use disorder, the tools of CBT can have powerful effects on our relationships. CBT is based on an understanding of the connections among thoughts, feelings, and behaviors. When our thought patterns are aligned with reality, they generally lead to positive feelings and behaviors. However, when our

thoughts become distorted in some way, they start to work against us, including in our relationships.

For example, we might notice that our partner left his clothes on the floor and think, "He expects me to pick up after him. He thinks I'm his maid." The result might include a fight driven by resentment and defensiveness. Or we could think that our partner seems distant and tell ourselves, "She's unhappy with me and our relationship," leading us to withdraw in turn.

The cognitive part of CBT encourages us first of all to notice the thoughts we're telling ourselves; oftentimes they happen so quickly and automatically that we don't even recognize the story our mind is creating. Once we've identified the thoughts we can test them out to see if they're accurate. Maybe our partner's clothes on the floor say nothing about his view of us, or expectations that we clean up his mess. And perhaps our partner's preoccupation has nothing to do with our relationship and everything to do with her worries about her ailing mother. With practice we can replace distorted and destructive thoughts with more accurate and constructive ones.

(Importantly, cognitive techniques are not about fooling ourselves or pretending things are better than they are. It would be important to know if our thoughts are actually valid so we can deal with the situation directly.)

Try it: The next time you're upset with your partner, write down the thoughts you notice and the emotions you feel. Then ask yourself the following questions (adapted from Retrain Your Brain: Cognitive Behavioral Therapy in 7 Weeks):

What is the evidence for my thought?

Is there evidence that contradicts my thought?

Based on the evidence, how accurate is the thought?

How could I modify this thought to make it fit better with reality?

8. Greater enactment of our intentions. All of us want to be the best significant other we can be. We want to be attentive, supportive, generous, patient. And like anything else, the road to impoverished relationships is paved with the best of intentions. If we're not deliberate about living out our values, we risk leaving them in the abstract—vague platitudes without substance.

For example, we might tell ourselves, "My family matters to me more than anything," and then live as though family is our last priority. We might idealize presence in our relationship yet attend more to our phone than to those around us.

The tools of CBT can help even when there is no "disorder"—when we simply want to commit to sustained action that supports our deepest values. It starts with taking an inventory of our relationship, and setting clearly defined goals based on what we find—for example, To listen when my spouse talks to me. It includes identifying specific behaviors we want to practice that will move us toward our goals.

We might plan, for instance, to turn off our phone during dinner and focus on our conversation. The goals and activities can be anything that's important to us in our relationship—we get to decide. It can be very beneficial to collaborate with our partner in the process by asking what they need more of from us.

A CBT approach also includes planning activities as specifically as possible so they stay on our radar, like putting "Come home early to make dinner" in our calendar, and protecting the time. Through daily practice of our intentions, we give our relationship the nourishment it needs not only to last but to be extraordinary.

CHAPTER FOUR

CBT FAQS

Answers to frequently asked questions about CBT, such as how to find a therapist and what to expect in treatment, are outlined below.

How will I know if CBT is for me?

Although many people can benefit from CBT, not everyone finds it helpful. You might find that it just doesn't suit you, or doesn't meet your needs.

I think it can go either way. I've been through a long course of CBT a few years ago, and for some people it helped, whereas for others it didn't.

Before deciding to have CBT, it might be helpful to think about the following:

Is short-term therapy right for me? If you have severe or complex problems, you may find a short-term therapy like CBT is less helpful. Sometimes, therapy may need to go on for longer to cover fully the number of problems you have, and the length of time they've been around.

Am I comfortable thinking about my feelings? CBT can involve becoming aware of your anxieties and emotions. Initially, you may find this process uncomfortable or distressing.

How much time do I want to spend? CBT can involve exercises for you to do outside of your sessions with a therapist. You may find this means you need to commit your own time to complete the work over the course of treatment, and afterwards.

Do I have a clear problem to solve? You may find CBT is less suitable if you feel generally unhappy or unfulfilled, but don't have troubling symptoms or a particular aspect of your life you want to work on.

Most people know within the first few sessions if they are comfortable with CBT and whether it is meeting their treatment needs. The therapist will also check to see that CBT is the right "fit" for you. When the fit is not quite right, the therapist may adjust the treatment or suggest other treatment options. However, in general, CBT may be a good therapy option for you if:

You are interested in learning practical skills to manage your present, day-to-day life and associated emotional difficulties.

You are willing and interested in practising change strategies ("homework") between sessions to consolidate improvement.

CBT may not be for you if you want to focus exclusively on past issues, if you want supportive counselling, or if you are not willing to do homework between sessions.

How can I find a qualified CBT therapist in my area?

It is most probably wise when seeking a therapist who provides CBT to try and assess which of the above-mentioned categories they may fall into. Many therapists will report that they use CBT, but few have actually had specific supervised training in the model and many do not provide cutting-edge treatments for specific disorders.

In addition, it would also be important to check whether or not the therapist has specific experience in your area of concern. For instance, an individual may have plenty of experience in working with anxiety or depression, but little experience or expertise in treating tic disorders, insomnia or psychosis, for example. Below is a list of reasonable questions that one could ask a therapist prior to making an appointment or during an initial appointment aimed at assessing their experience with CBT.

Have you received any training in CBT?

Training could vary from an introduction during a masters programme to an internationally-certified qualification.

Did your training include individual supervision of case material from an experienced or internationally-certified CBT therapist?

It is important to distinguish between theoretical training and practical, supervised training that includes individual supervision in the use of CBT in working with clients.

Does your CBT training include international certification from an international training standards committee?

Typical international certification is from the Beck Institute or the Albert Ellis Institute. Other training centres in the USA and the UK also exist.

How many years' experience do you have in practising CBT?

We all start with little experience and build our knowledge base. It would be wise not to doubt a well-trained and supervised CBT therapist with one or two years' experience. It, however, goes without saying that those therapists with greater practical experience bring the expertise accumulated from this experience to helping you.

In what way do you use CBT in your practice?

Many people will tell you that they integrate CBT in to their practice. This typically would entail using skills or techniques from more than one theoretical orientation at the same time. This approach is known as eclecticism. This is not unethical nor an unacceptable practice. Should you look for a CBT therapist specifically, this is obviously not the type of service provided by a therapist with an eclectic approach. Therapists will also tell you that they use different theoretical approaches to treat different clients and problems. This is also an acceptable approach. It would, however, be important to determine if the therapist is sufficiently trained in CBT and if the therapist would suggest CBT for your specific problem.

Ask if the therapist has training in the CBT treatment of your specific disorder.

It important to know that the therapist has disorder-specific training in the condition that you require help with.

To find the contact information for certified CBT therapists in Canada and the United States, consult the following resources:

Academy of Cognitive Therapies www.academyofct.org

Association for Behaviour and Cognitive Therapies www.abct.org

What can I expect on my first visit with a CBT therapist?

You will meet your therapist and they will introduce themselves, ask for your preferred name and help you to feel at ease. They may also introduce a little bit about what CBT is and the way that the sessions will be. You do not need to know anything about CBT before you begin your therapy and your therapist should explain it in an easy-to-understand way.

Your therapist will talk to you about confidentiality, the number of sessions you may work towards, how often your sessions will be, how long they will last, how to cancel appointments and what happens if you miss an appointment.

Your therapist will usually have the information you gave at your initial screening appointment but may ask you a little more about the main problem you would like some help with and about you and your circumstances. This is not to get you to 'tell your story all over again', but to help you and your therapist reach an understanding of how you will work together and what you will focus on within the sessions.

Your therapist may also ask you to think of some positive goals so that you have something you are working towards. This can help you to connect with something important to you or to work towards something you would like to do if you no longer had the problem.

Your therapist may talk to you about 'homework'. Homework is an integral part of CBT and after each session you will think with your therapist about how you can apply the things you have done in the session to your day-to-day life. After your first appointment, you may be asked to keep a monitoring diary or to read some information/handouts relevant to your problem.

You will do the same questionnaires you completed at your first appointment. These will be asked at every appointment to help you and your therapist keep track of your progress. You may sometimes be asked to do an additional questionnaire more specific to your problem, however, this will vary from client to client.

Your therapist will check with you if you are at any risk to yourself or from anyone else. This is something we ask every client so that we can help you to stay safe.

You will make your next appointment with your therapist.

Your therapist will go at a pace that suits you and the above points are a guide only. You may do more or less than this in your first appointment and that is OK. You can also ask questions and express any concerns about therapy at any time in your appointment. Your therapist wants to work with you as a together to help with your recovery. While your therapist can offer ideas about what has helped others with similar problems in the past, they also know that you are the expert in your problem and how it affects you, and you should both be playing an active role in therapy together.

What happens in a CBT session?

CBT sessions can be given to clients individually or in groups. Both formats follow the same predictable structure, as follows:

Mood check: The therapist asks about your mood since the previous session. This may include the use of scales to assess depression, anxiety or other emotional problems. The purpose of the mood check is to see if your mood improves from session to session.

Bridge: The focus of the previous session is reviewed to create a bridge to the current session.

Agenda: The therapist and client identify issues to address in the current session that will act as the agenda.

Homework review: Homework from the previous session is reviewed to note progress and troubleshoot any difficulties that may have emerged.

Agenda items: Agenda issues are addressed using cognitive and behavioural strategies.

New homework: Exercises and tasks for the upcoming week are assigned.

Summary and client feedback: Wrap up of the session.

How can I get the most out of CBT between sessions?

CBT is a treatment approach that teaches you skills to become your own therapist over time. You learn new skills in the therapy sessions, but ultimately much of the change occurs between therapy sessions when practising the skills in your own environment as part of homework. Early in treatment, the CBT therapist will suggest homework, such as monitoring thoughts and behaviours, taking steps to reduce avoidance behaviour, conducting experiments to test out predictions and completing worksheets to challenge negative thoughts or beliefs. As treatment progresses, you will learn to set your own homework between sessions to help you accomplish your treatment goals. Research demonstrates that the more you successfully practise the skills of CBT in your homework, the better the treatment outcome.

How frequent are the sessions?

CBT usually starts out with weekly sessions. As treatment progresses, sessions may be spaced further apart, such as every two weeks or month. Once people have finished a course of CBT, it is common for them to return for occasional "booster" sessions to keep up their progress, deal with any setbacks and prevent relapse of problems. Again, hospital-based programs are typically pre-set (e.g., a group meeting weekly at the same time for 12 weeks) and are less flexible in terms of scheduling and spacing sessions than community-based CBT therapists.

Do I need to prepare for CBT sessions?

Preparing to discuss a specific problem at each session helps you to get the most out of CBT. Coming prepared helps to keep you focused on your goals for therapy. It also helps to build a therapeutic relationship between you and your therapist and to communicate well throughout the session.

Will the CBT therapist be able to understand and appreciate my own unique background?

Research on CBT demonstrates that it is an effective treatment regardless of gender, race, ethnicity, culture, sexual orientation or social economic status. CBT therapists are trained to recognize the importance of cultural values and to adapt their treatments to meet culturally unique needs. They are trained, for example, to:

Be aware of their own personal values and biases and how these may influence their relationship with the client.

Use skills and intervention strategies that are culturally appropriate for the person being seen.

Be aware of how certain cultural processes may influence the relationship between the therapist and client.

As a client in CBT you should feel that you can openly discuss aspects of your culture or sexual orientation, for example, and that your treatment will be delivered in a manner that is consistent with these values.

Is CBT an effective treatment for children and adolescents?

CBT has been adapted for use with children and has been shown in research to be an effective intervention for a variety of clinical problems that can emerge in childhood, including anxiety and depression. The content and pacing of the therapy is adjusted to be appropriate for the child's level of development. Often, the CBT therapist will work with the parent and child— the younger the child, the more involved the parent will be in learning and delivering CBT strategies for their child's problem.

What are the common barriers that come up in CBT?

Barriers to treatment can include:

- Perceived stigma associated with mental health treatment

- Difficulty identifying and distinguishing emotions and their intensity

- Difficulty in reflecting on thoughts

- Difficulty tolerating heightened emotions

- Not completing homework

- Financial constraints

- Chronic conditions and multiple difficulties

- Low optimism toward improving

- Avoiding treatment sessions.

The therapist will work with you to reduce these barriers and will also offer strategies that you can use to overcome barriers.

Should I start treatment with medications or CBT or both in combination?

Many people who seek treatment for emotional difficulties in Canada are first treated by their family doctor with one or more medications (e.g., antidepressants) before CBT is considered. Not much research has been done to show whether it is best to start treatment with medication or CBT or both. However, research has shown that CBT, with or without certain types of medications, is equally effective for the treatment of anxiety problems, and that CBT and medications together are best for treating severe depression and psychosis. Importantly, taking these kinds of medications has not been shown to interfere with CBT, and in some instances may help people to get more out of the therapy.

There is, however, one class of medication commonly prescribed to people with anxiety problems, known as benzodiazepines, which can potentially limit the benefits of CBT. Medications in this class include clonazepam (Rivotril), alprazolam (Xanax) and lorazepam (Ativan). While these medications can rapidly relieve and control anxiety in the short term, they can also make it harder to learn new things, which is essential to benefit from CBT and reduce anxiety in the long run. If you are taking these medications and are about to start CBT, your CBT therapist will want to review the advantages and disadvantages of continuing with these medications during CBT treatment.

When considering or starting CBT, discuss all of your questions or concerns about your medications with your CBT therapist and/ or your prescribing medical doctor. Medications can be monitored and discussed throughout treatment and adjusted depending on your progress in CBT. Note that recommendations or changes to your medication can only be made by your prescribing doctor. If your CBT therapist is not a doctor, he or she can—with your permission—communicate with your doctor to help ensure that you receive the optimal combination of treatments.

How can I stay well after finishing CBT?

A major goal of CBT is for you to become your own therapist and to continue to practise CBT skills even after you are feeling better. You may also wish to return for follow-up or "booster" sessions from time to time. A key component of CBT treatment is teaching relapse prevention strategies. This includes helping you learn to identify the triggers and early signs of relapse and to develop an action plan to prevent downward spirals of negative emotions.

CHAPTER FIVE

ALTERNATIVE COGNITIVE BEHAVIOURAL APPROACHES

Of the hundreds of psychological treatments available, several are closely related to CBT, but have distinct approaches. Although the effectiveness of these alternative CBT approaches is not as well proven as the mainstream approach described so far in this guide, the four introduced on the following pages have been found to be effective in helping people with certain types of problems. Overall, they all share a common goal of helping people learn how to "let go" of focusing on and reacting to their thoughts.

Mindfulness therapy and mindfulness based cognitive therapy

Mindfulness techniques can be used to help people distance themselves from their negative thinking and recognize that thoughts do not have to determine behaviours. Mindfulness is a state of awareness, openness and receptiveness that allows people to engage fully in what they are doing at any given moment. Mindfulness skills are mainly taught through meditation; however, other experiential exercises (e.g., walking or eating with awareness) can also be used to teach these skills.

A middle aged woman is feeling overwhelmed, anxious, depressed, hopeless and depleted of all of her energy. She explains to her doctor that she has been having feelings of self doubt and is desperate to turn back the clock to a time in her twenties and thirties when she knew she was "beautiful", "thin", and "revered". She has tried everything from Pilates, energy healing, life coaching, herbal remedies, hypnotherapy, Reiki, and has visited an array of holistic spas and retreats.

Yet she continues to fee chronic emptiness and impending doom. It is as if she is suffering from a should sickness. Not doubt the alternative treatments were effective, at least initially. But the days of long-lost youth and feelings of worthlessness returned. When her psychotherapist recommends learning mindfulness meditations, she agrees in her desperation.

Psychotherapy and pharmacological solutions are some of the common treatment options for patients with mental disorders. But, alternative treatments for psychiatric conditions are increasingly becoming popular. Lately, doctors have been advising alternative treatments, like meditation and yoga, for mental issues, particularly for anxiety disorders and depression.

According to a recent study published in the Journal of Child and Adolescent Psychopharmacology, significant changes were evident in the brain regions that control emotional processing of youths who were given mindfulness-based therapies.

Though anxiety disorders are common among children and adolescents, antidepressants administered to treat the condition are many a times not tolerated well by children who are at a high risk of developing bipolar disorder.

So, the researchers at the University of Cincinnati (UC) have now found out how cognitive therapy that utilizes mindfulness techniques, such as meditation, quiet reflection, and facilitator-led discussion, may help as an adjunct to pharmacological interventions. The study was part of a larger investigation to understand the effectiveness of mindfulness-based therapy.

The respondents were chosen from a group of youths who had anxiety disorders (generalized, social and/or separation anxiety) and who have a parent with bipolar disorder. The study, published in the Journal of Child and Adolescent Psychopharmacology in July 2016, tried to evaluate neurophysiology of mindfulness-based cognitive therapy in children who had higher risks of developing bipolar disorder.

Mindfulness therapy increases activity in brain

The nine participants aged 9-16 years were made to undergo functional magnetic resonance imaging (fMRI) while they were involved in a continuous performance of tasks with emotional and neutral distractors prior to and following 12 weeks of mindfulness-based cognitive therapy.

"Our preliminary observation that the mindfulness therapy increases activity in the part of the brain known as the cingulate, which processes cognitive and emotional information, is noteworthy," said co-principal researcher of the study Jeffrey Strawn, M.D., an associate professor in the Department of Psychiatry and Behavioral Neuroscience, and director of the Anxiety Disorders Research Program.

"This study, taken together with previous research, raises the possibility that treatment-related increases in brain activity (of the anterior cingulate cortex) during emotional processing may improve emotional processing in anxious youth who are at risk for developing bipolar disorder," he added.

Speaking about the effectiveness of mindfulness techniques, co-author of the study Sian Cotton, Ph.D., an associate professor of family and community medicine at UC, said, "Mindfulness-based therapeutic interventions promote the use of meditative practices to increase present-moment awareness of conscious thoughts, feelings and body sensations in an effort to manage negative experiences more effectively." These alternative approaches augment traditional treatments offering new strategies for coping with psychological problems, he said.

Recovery roadmap

The researchers noted that increases in mindfulness were associated with decreases in anxiety in the participants.

However, the researchers called for further studies into this for more clarity. "The path from an initial understanding of the effects of psychotherapy on brain activity to the identification of markers of treatment response is a challenging one, and will require additional studies of specific aspects of emotional processing circuits," Strawn said.

For any mental health condition, be it anxiety disorder or depression, early intervention is the key. Hence, if a loved one is exhibiting any psychiatric symptom, seek the advice of a doctor immediately.

Mindfulness skills can be broken down into three categories:

Defusion: distancing oneself from and letting go of unhelpful thoughts, beliefs and memories.

Acceptance: accepting thoughts and feelings without judgment, simply allowing them to come and go rather than trying to push them out of awareness or make sense of them.

Contact in the present moment: engaging fully in the here-and-now with an attitude of openness and curiosity.

Mindfulness skills promote freedom from the tendency to get drawn into automatic negative reactions to thoughts and feelings.

Mindfulness techniques have been used in the treatment of chronic pain, hypertension, heart disease, cancer, gastrointestinal disorders, eating disorders, anxiety disorders and substance use disorders. Mindfulness-based cognitive therapy has been found to be effective in reducing relapse to depression.

Acceptance and commitment therapy

While some therapies attempt to change upsetting thoughts and feelings, acceptance and commitment therapy (act) helps people to simply notice and accept thoughts and feelings in the present moment.

ACT views psychological suffering as being caused by avoiding or evaluating thoughts and feelings, which in turn can lead to ways of thinking that interfere with our ability to act consistently with important personal values. The focus of act is on helping people accept what is out of their personal control while committing to doing what is within their control to improve their quality of life.

ACT aims to help people handle the pain and stress that life inevitably brings and to create a rich, full and meaningful life. People learn how to deal with painful thoughts and feelings in ways that have less impact and influence over their lives. For example, they learn to:

- Distance themselves from upsetting thoughts (cognitive defusion)

- Accept experiences in the present moment

- Discover important and meaningful personal values

- Set goals consistent with these values

- Commit to take action

ACT has been found to be effective in treating depression, anxiety, stress, chronic pain and substance use disorders.

Dialectical behavioural therapy

Dialectical behavioural therapy (dbt) is an effective treatment for people with excessive mood swings, self-harming behaviour and other interpersonal problems related to the expression of anger.

DBT has an individual and a group component. In individual therapy, the therapist and client follow a treatment target hierarchy to guide their discussion of issues that come up between weekly sessions. First priority is given to self-harming and suicidal behaviours, then to behaviours that interfere with therapy, and next to improving the client's quality of life. The quality-of-life improvement part of the therapy involves identifying skills that the person has but is not using to full advantage, to teaching new skills, and to discussing obstacles for using those skills. Weekly group therapy focuses on acquiring new skills.

Clients keep diary cards to help monitor their use of the skills and have access to 24-hour phone consultation with their therapist.

The four modules of dbt are core mindfulness, emotion regulation (e.g., identifying and labelling emotions and reducing vulnerability to negative emotions), interpersonal effectiveness (e.g., assertiveness skills) and distress tolerance skills (e.g., crisis survival skills such as distracting, self-soothing and improving the moment).

Meta-cognitive therapy

Metacognitive therapy is sometimes described as a type of therapy that involves changing how people think rather than what they are thinking about. In this way, metacognitive therapy is distinct from cognitive behavioral therapy, which focuses more on the content of people's thoughts.

Two psychologists, Dr. Adrian Wells of the University of Manchester and Dr. Gerald Matthews of the University of Cincinnati, developed the theory underlying metacognitive therapy in the early 1990s. Initially intended only for patients with generalized anxiety disorder, metacognitive therapy has since been adapted for use in treating a variety of mental health problems.

According to metacognitive theory, maladaptive thinking that occurs in various psychiatric disorders tends to take on a life of its own, growing from thoughts about a specific situation to a more global world view. For example, people who are anxious may initially worry about external situations, such as missing a train. With time, however, they may begin to develop a second type of worry, focused on their own thought processes. In essence, according to this theory, they begin to worry about being worried.

In people with attention deficit hyperactivity disorder (ADHD), problems with metacognition more often encompass difficulty in planning or executing tasks. The goal of metacognitive therapy in ADHD is to improve organization skills, planning, and time management.

Most of the research evaluating metacognitive therapy has focused on anxiety disorders such as social phobia, post-traumatic stress disorder, and generalized anxiety disorder. Only a few studies have evaluated its use in helping adults with ADHD (none have been conducted in children). The research is therefore preliminary, but so far promising.

In one study, researchers at the Mount Sinai School of Medicine recruited 88 adult participants with ADHD, diagnosed using a structured interview based on criteria in the Diagnostic and Statistical Manual of Mental Disorders, Fourth Edition (DSM-IV). The group was carefully selected; few had substance abuse or other types of coexisting psychiatric disorders, which is more the norm in the community. The researchers randomly assigned half of the participants to metacognitive therapy and the others to supportive therapy, both offered in group formats consisting of 12 weekly sessions.

Those assigned to metacognitive therapy underwent a sequence of sessions designed to begin with learning specific skill sets (such as using a daily planner) and then progressing to broader abilities (organizing and executing a complex project). Those assigned to supportive therapy received encouragement and reinforcement of productive behaviors.

Some participants improved after both interventions, but those assigned to metacognitive therapy showed a greater degree of improvement on both objectively rated and self-perceived measures of organization, ability to complete tasks, and other practical components of attention skill. A greater proportion of people assigned to metacognitive therapy responded to therapy, defined as at least a 30% improvement in ADHD symptoms. In all, 19 of 41 (42%) of participants who completed metacognitive therapy responded, compared with five of 40 (12%) of those who completed supportive therapy.

This suggests that metacognitive therapy may indeed help some adult patients with ADHD. But before your husband tries it, just be aware that there are no long-term data about whether the potential benefits are retained over time. Your husband may also find it helpful to investigate other options to improve organization skills, such as cognitive behavioral therapy or coaching.

Meta-cognitive therapy (mct) was first developed to treat generalized anxiety disorder and is now also used to treat other anxiety disorders and depression.

Metacognition is the aspect of cognition that controls mental processes and thinking. Most people have some direct conscious experience of metacognition. For example, when a name is on the "tip of your tongue," metacognition is working to inform you that the information is somewhere in memory, even though you are unable to remember it.

People with depression or anxiety often feel as though they have lost control over their thoughts and behaviours. Their thinking and attention become fixed in patterns of brooding and dwelling on themselves and on threatening information. They develop coping behaviours that they believe are helpful, but that can actually worsen and prolong emotional distress. This pattern of thinking is called cognitive-attentional syndrome (cas).

In mct, people learn to reduce the cas by developing new ways of controlling their thinking and attention and of relating to depressive or anxious thoughts and beliefs. They also learn to modify the beliefs that give rise to the cas.

CHAPTER 6

APPLYING COGNITIVE BEHAVIORAL THERAPY (CBT) TO OVER-THINK NEGATIVE PATTERNS

Negative thinking can slow down the recovery of depression, and the reason is clear: If you think negative thoughts, you are more likely to remain depressed. But the way people with depression deal with positive emotions is less obvious. Researchers made a surprising observation: People with depression don't lack positive emotions, they just can't feel them. This cognitive style is called "dampening," it involves suppressing positive emotions with thoughts such as "I don't deserve to be happy" or "This good feeling won't last." For example, a new mother with postpartum depression may say she doesn't deserve to recover because she's a bad mother because she's depressed. Why do depressed people think so? We refers to this negative voice as a defensive pessimism-protection against high hopes. "you don't want to be foolish, so you use positive thoughts to protect yourself from possible disappointment."

How CBT can help with negative depression

Depression therapy has been found to be significantly helpful in treating depression. In CBT, you work together with your therapist to agree on behavior patterns that need to be changed. The objective is to recalibrate the part of your brain that holds happy thoughts so tightly.

"The root of the dampening effect could be an unexpected reaction to a major life event" through CBT, you and your therapist address it and work to put it into perspective." Regular CBT sessions and work you do on your own outside of therapy can help strengthen the new patterns: "It can be very liberating to be able to recognize these negative thoughts and leave them behind,"

CBT Techniques to Counteract the Negative Thinking of Depression

It was discovered that people with depression rarely respond well to self-study by CBT techniques to counteract negative thinking about depression. For this reason, we recommend that at least six weeks be committed to CBT. Your therapist will teach you CBT strategies to counteract depression-related negative thinking. She or he can also help you keep track of the techniques. You may end up working on five CBT strategies with your therapist:

Locate the problem and brainstorm solutions.

Journaling with your therapist and talking can help you discover the root of your depression. Once you have an idea, write down exactly what disturbs you in a simple phrase and think about ways to improve the problem. A hallmark of depression is despair-an unbelief that things can ever get better. Writing a list of things you can do to improve a situation can help ease the feelings of depression. If you are fighting for loneliness, for example, action steps to try may include joining a local club based on your interests or signing up for online dating. Write self-declarations to counter negative thoughts. After finding your depression's root problems, think about the negative thoughts you use to dampen positive thoughts.

Write a self-declaration to counteract any negative thinking.

Remember your self-statements and repeat them to yourself when you see the little voice creeping in your head to snuff out a positive thought. You will create new associations in time to replace negative thoughts with positive ones.

The self-declaration should not be too far from negative thinking, or the mind may not accept it. For example, if the negative thought is, "I'm so depressed right now," instead of saying, "I'm really happy now," it could be better to say, "Every life has ups and downs, and mine also has ups and downs." At the same time, your mind applauds the fact that joy is kept in check to protect against disappointment. "Recognizing that part of you is trying to do something healthy is okay."

Self-reporting is sometimes too routine and needs to be refreshed. We recommend that you translate your self-declarations into other languages you can speak or rephrase, possibly even bumping up your joyful feelings. "For example, the self-statement" it's okay to explore my ups" may turn out to be "it's okay to have a super "up" day."

Find new opportunities to think positive thoughts.

People who enter a room and immediately think, "I hate the color of the wall," could instead train to locate five things in the room they feel positive as quickly as possible. Set your phone to remind you of something positive three times a day. It recommends that someone else work on the same technique should "buddy up." You and your friend can be excited to share positive thoughts and experiences throughout the day.

Complete every day by visualizing the best parts.

At the end of each day, write down the things you're most grateful for in your life or type them into an online journal. The recording of positive thoughts and even sharing them online can help you form new associations in your mind or create new paths. Someone who created a new way of thinking could wake up in the morning and think, "Ugh, another working day "to "What a beautiful day it is."

Learn to accept disappointment as a normal part of life.

Deceptive situations are part of life and your response can affect how fast you can move forward. Someone who goes through a breakup may blame him or herself or even gain weight, saying, "What's the point of looking good? I'll never meet anyone else. "Maybe a better approach is to be disappointed and remember that some things are out of your control. Work on what is in your control: Write down what happened, what you learned from the experience and what you can do next time differently, taking care of overly negative thoughts. This can help you to move forward and feel better about your future.

Cognitive behavioral therapy Effective tips

Research has shown that we can have better control of thoughts and feelings by identifying our distorted thoughts and beliefs. Having distorted thoughts or beliefs doesn't mean we're wrong. At different times in our lives, we have all distorted thoughts and beliefs. Examples of distorted thoughts:

Over-generalization

Sometimes we can see things as everything or nothing. If one thing goes wrong with a project, for example, we may think the whole project is a failure. Or, if there's one thing that upsets us about a person, we can decide that we don't care about him.

Mind Reading

We assume we know what someone thinks. We can say that someone thinks we're "stupid "or doesn't like us, even if there's no evidence to support this thought. That's called reading the mind. We exaggerate how "abhorrent "something is or imagine the worst outcome possible. Maybe our boss wants to talk to us and we're disastrous to be fired. Or, it's raining on one of the holidays and we think "this is the worst thing that could have happened."

Fortune Telling

We think we surely know what will happen. We say, for example, "I know I won't get this promotion "or "I won't be able to handle this task." Specific behaviors or skills, including social skills, assertiveness, organizational skills and relaxation techniques, are also taught. During and between sessions, these are taught. Below, there are seven pearls I will share with you that I have found useful in my practice over the years:

Discuss treatment goals

During the initial evaluation phase, it is important to work together on treatment goals. This helps to maintain focused and productive treatment. Therapy can end up focusing on any problem that arises this week without objectives and can interfere with the progress of the original problems presented. Sometimes the patient may not be able to describe a goal specifically except for a vague "I want to be less anxious "or "I want to be happier." It's okay at the start. However, you should return to this discussion about goals in the first couple of months to see if they can be described in more specific terms. For example, if someone has depression, the goals may include: Finding a fuller job, going back to college, exercising three times a week, making two new friends and stopping marijuana use.

Each session with an agenda

Each session should begin with a collaborative agenda between the therapist and the patient. Again, this helps to focus and make the session more efficient. The agenda should include follow-up on previous session homework, check-in on mood and week, bridging or reviewing the topics and progress from the previous session, and topics related to the current session, which are related to a specific objective.

Discuss where to address the issue

Most therapeutic objectives will have several components, including distorted thoughts, beliefs or behaviours. Therefore, during the session, decide collaboratively on which level to meet the objectives. If you work on distorted thoughts, it is important to determine which thoughts or images lead to distress, such as anxiety, low mood or a certain behavior. If you work on certain behaviors such as social skills or relationship problems, it is important to discuss when the skills are used and how likely they are used. Another useful technique for addressing behaviors is the play of roles and visualization that helps to practice skills and address any behavioral blocks or anxieties.

Use Flashcards

Flashcards can be used to remember the session's key points or a mantra that can help with certain thoughts or feelings. If I work with a patient who is struggling with depression, I will name the flashcard something like "Survival Kit "and it will include strategies to cope with depression, such as reaching a friend, leaving the house, reaching me or taking care of a small chore.

Stay focused

At the start of treatment, therapeutic objectives are discussed. The therapy session can sometimes go in a direction unrelated to any of the treatment goals. This is appropriate at certain times, but if this happens every session and for the whole duration, the progress of therapy may be limited. In CBT, structure is important, but flexibility is also important. This would be a time to work together to discuss whether to continue with the current diversion or issue being discussed or to return to what has been discussed in the agenda.

Assign homework

A collaborative discussion on homework or "action tasks "takes place between sessions towards the end of each session. If one of the problems is time management or the recording of thoughts and images that occur during stressful periods in a notebook to discuss and address at the following session, an action task may be to buy a calendar. Always ensure that the homework or action task is monitored at the next session, or it creates the impression that working on problems or objectives between sessions is not a crucial part of improving.

Ask for feedback

At the end of the session, ask what was going well during the session, what could have gone better and what are the main messages to take away. This helps build the alliance, improve sessions in the future and maximize progress.

Cognitive behavioral therapy is a highly effective form of therapy with or without medicines and an excellent way to practice psychiatry.

Cognitive behavioral therapy at home Tips that can help ease your anxieties

CBT is based on the idea that our thoughts, emotions and behaviors are interconnected and that one can change the other. This may sound trendy, but it is also effective and has been studied rigorously. CBT varies from anxiety to depression to schizophrenia to substance use disorders for all types of mental health problems.

The goal is to learn skills to address real-life problems outside the therapist's office, Lindgren says. The more you practice, the more a habit will become of CBT skills.

"If you're someone who has good intentions but needs someone to be accountable, I'd meet a therapist" but if you know you're a good self-taught person, it's reasonable to think about doing it on your own."

Here are her tips for practicing at home (or wherever you are).

Change your perspective

You can modify problem thoughts by using a technique called cognitive restructuring, which can help you change your behaviour. The next time you notice that you are anxious or depressed, ask yourself: What do I think about or what emotions do I struggle to make me feel like this? Notice if certain thoughts or memories cause distressing physical symptoms; you can even list them. This will help you understand how your emotions and thoughts are connected and what is triggering you.

Balance your thoughts

Many struggles in mental health involve thoughts or predictions that influence behavior that are distressing but inherently faulty. For example, if you're anxious when you're in crowds and actively avoid them, you might be told that if you tried to go to a crowded place-like a sports game or concert-you'd panic, do something to embarrass yourself, and you wouldn't enjoy it. This belief then strengthens your avoidance. Notice how your brain makes decisions based on fear or avoidance and then ask yourself: What is the evidence for this thought? Are there any cold, hard facts that things are going to go wrong, or do I just speculate? Consider if you could have other thoughts that would be more balanced or helpful. If you changed your thinking a little bit to be less frightening or negative, what new emotions could arise? If you work to balance your thoughts, your emotions and behaviors will probably follow.

Be patient with yourself

Change won't happen overnight, so don't expect it if you try CBT alone (or even with a therapist to guide you). Instead, your goal should be to develop your skills so that you feel better equipped to deal with any challenges your mental health wants to take. Focus on getting ready for small victories, then build up your goals slowly over time. Be proud of any positive change, however small it may seem. Recognize that progress is not linear; it will be easier for some weeks, harder for others, and that's normal.

Be kind to yourself

Without even realizing it, it's easy to get caught up in negative self-talk. But getting constantly on yourself won't inspire the confidence you need to make you feel better. When you notice negative thoughts-things like "Why can't I get it together?" or "other people have no problem "-replace them with something nicer. Ask yourself if your friends will ever tell you the things you say to yourself. No, no? So don't let yourself tell them either. This doesn't mean you should apologize for yourself if you made a mistake or did something wrong, but instead encourage you to cut the slack you usually reserve for others.

Do what you love

Anxiety, depression and other mental health struggles can remove the activities that matter to you in life, either because you are afraid of them or because you have no motivation to pursue them once. Maybe you liked reading, but now you're tired. Or you may have liked to go out with your friends, but now you're afraid to be away at night. Take the time to do one or two things regularly that always brought you joy and did your best to be present instead of being distracted or worried about the past. Then ask yourself how you feel you've done it. Did you feel better?

Be Self-aware

Maybe when you try to fall asleep or beat yourself over something you told a friend when you should finish an important work project, you're ruminating about work problems; either way, you're not focused on the moment. Instead, try switching your thoughts whenever they're not in line with what's going on right now. Ask yourself: Do my emotions reflect what's happening right now? If not, concentrate on the senses. What are you seeing and hearing? What's happening around you in the world? Instead of what happened in the past or what you're afraid will happen in the future, try to be aware of what's right before you.

A bright future

In the end, one of CBT's most powerful things is that it can give you hope.

"Inherently, it's optimistic. It teaches you to believe that change is possible and that you can change your life."

CHAPTER 7

MOST COMMON ERRORS MADE IN COGNITIVE-BEHAVIORAL THERAPY

In the course of my clinical practice, I have found a number of common errors that can prevent cognitive-behavioral therapy (CBT) from being as effective as it could be. The following describes these errors and how to correct them.

ERROR 1: Not Understanding the Necessity of Repetition for Change

A few years back when I was lecturing a group of psychiatric residents (future psychiatrists) about using CBT with sexually traumatized clients, one of the doctors stated "I tried that cognitive therapy with my patients and it doesn't work at all!" As I explored with her the specifics of what she had tried with her patients, I ascertained that, basically, she had told them how they should think and then expected them to change their thinking.

When I asked her what method she used to help them practice and repeat the new ways of thinking in daily life, she was speechless. I then explained that the key to successful cognitive therapy was repetition of the statements that challenge the irrational thinking and that the therapist must use a method to help clients do that.

People don't change their thinking just because they are told to think differently. If that was the case, most people wouldn't need CBT because someone else has probably already told them how they should think. The difference with CBT is that a variety of methods have been developed to provide the steps to change thinking.

The importance of repetition as a key component of CBT can't be emphasized enough. This is true of any new skill. When I was training for my black belt in Kenpo karate my instructor told me "When you have done this self-defense move 6,000 times, it will be automatic." And he was right! At first, I was awkward and slow in executing the movements. I had to think about every aspect of each move. I thought initially that it would never be automatic. However, I continued to practice. One day (after years of training) when I was teaching one of the brown belts, I realized that I was able to automatically respond to a wrist grab and put him on the ground without even thinking about it.

Changing your thinking is learning a new skill in the same way you learn a physical skill. You don't expect to be a proficient golfer without swinging the club a few thousand times. In fact, in the book "Outliers" by Malcolm Gladwell, he sets the magic number for success at 10,000 hours. According to Gladwell, when we examine the lives of the most successful people in any sport or profession, we typically find that they have spent at least 10,000 hours honing their craft.

Certainly, that doesn't mean that it will take 10,000 hours to change your thinking and to have a positive impact on your life. In fact, with frequent repetition of the rational challenging thoughts you should notice changes in four to eight weeks. However, you will need more repetition than that for the new way of thinking to become automatic.

Think of it this way. How many hours have you spent in your lifetime repeating the detrimental irrational self-talk? You likely have become very automatic in that way of thinking so now you need to re-train your brain to think in a different way. To do that you need to identify specific thoughts that are beneficial and to deliberately think those thoughts repeatedly.

Sometimes it is difficult to achieve the necessary repetition especially when you are first learning. That is why reading articles about CBT or motivational thinking can be helpful. The more you read, the more repetition you obtain. Also, that is why I have created some audios that focus on changing thinking. The audios provide repetition without a great deal of effort.

ERROR 2: Making Assumptions about CBT Based on Social Comparision.

Many times when I first explain cognitive therapy to clients and we examine their irrational thinking and explain why it is irrational, they exclaim "That makes so much sense! I've never thought about it that way before!"

However, for some people, once they understand the process of using irrational thought challenges, they believe that that they should just be able to think that way without having to examine their thinking and deliberately change it. They make the mistake of using social comparison assumptions. In particular, they might state "I should be able to just think this way. Everyone else doesn't have to do this (referring to the CBT methods)."

What they don't realize is their assumptions about others not using CBT techniques is inaccurate. Just about anyone who is successful in life is using these techniques! However, they may not have been taught the techniques of CBT specifically and they may not know the terms such as "mind-reading" or "generalizing" but they are still using the methods.

I tend to think that CBT is just a compendium of methods that have helped people achieve success for thousands of years. For instance, if you read the "Tao te Ching" examining it for cognitive concepts, you will find that it contains all the same challenges to irrational thinking and methods of successful living that you will find in any book by Aaron Beck, Albert Ellis, or David Burns.

If you listen closely to people, you will begin to recognize how they apply these methods in their lives. For instance, I frequently hear people (outside of the office) say when describing a difficult event, "...but then I told myself..." In other words, they were using self-talk to cope with a situation. I've also heard people say things such as "Then I took a deep breath and..." describing how they calmed themselves before tackling a problem.

So don't assume that because you are having to learn these methods and deliberately apply them that you are doing something others don't have to do. The only difference is that you may not have learned the methods naturally while growing up and you are learning them now. You may not have had the role models or opportunities to learn these methods when you were young.

People aren't naturally successful. Anyone who is successful, whether in life, sports, career, or relationships, has learned these methods at some point in their lives and are applying them routinely.

ERROR 3: Not Making CBT Methods a Lifestyle Change

Many people don't realize that CBT is training the brain to react differently to situations. As a result, they often mistakenly believe that recognizing the error in thinking and correcting it a few times will impact a change in their life. After they have some initial benefit they may believe that it isn't necessary to continue practicing the methods.

However, cognitive-behavioral changes need to be thought of as lifestyle changes just as exercise or an effective diet is a lifestyle change. You wouldn't expect to exercise for a few months, tone your muscles, stop exercising and expect your muscles to remain toned. Nor, is it reasonable to expect to lose weight by restricting your calories but not expect to gain weight when you return to eating everything you want.

A lifestyle change refers to any activity or behavior in which we engage regularly to maintain our health. In the case of the CBT methods, we make a change to improve our emotional fitness. But we can't expect that fitness or change to remain intact if we don't devote attention to practice.

People have come to realize that the body needs maintenance to retain fitness and optimum health. Too often, however, people think that the brain does not require maintenance. Therefore, many people obtain initial benefits from CBT but will revert to prior thinking patterns and behaviors due to the lack of attention to the CBT methods.

A good example of what may occur is the use of relaxation methods during a time of stress. The regular use of relaxation reduces the degree of stress experienced. However, many people are likely to think "I feel good. I don't need to do this relaxation anymore." However, stopping the relaxation practice may result in a return of the symptoms associated with stress.

Unfortunately, when this occurs some people may conclude "That relaxation stuff really doesn't work!" However, that is like saying exercise doesn't work because when you stop exercise you lose muscle strength.

ERROR 4: Not Using Relaxation Regularly

A closely associated error is that many people believe they should obtain benefits from relaxation even though they use it infrequently. I can't tell you how often clients report being stressed or anxious, yet when I ask them how often they engaged in relaxation, they respond "once" or "not at all." The same clients, however, may report a very positive response from the relaxation when they use it.

Again, the regular practice of relaxation trains the brain and the body to respond differently. This practice can create a very powerful response. You may be familiar with strong automatic negative responses. For instance, if you have been very stressed at work, you may notice your body reacting with symptoms when you drive by you place of employment on your day off. Our bodies can become conditioned to stress responses and associate the stress response with a place, person, or thing.

However, our bodies can also become conditioned to the relaxation response. I had an experience once that illustrated to me just how powerful the relaxation response can be. Years ago I listened to a particular tape (before CDs and MP3s) whenever I had a stress headache. One day, years later, while I was driving and listening to the radio, my entire body suddenly relaxed. I felt an incredible, soothing peacefulness. Wondering why I suddenly felt so relaxed, I realized that one of the songs that I used to listen to was playing on the radio. My body had become conditioned to relax to that music.

To be able to experience the powerful benefits of relaxation, however, it is necessary to practice regularly.

ERROR 5: Expecting Results Without Practice.

Very closely related to the importance of using the methods regularly, is the expectation many people have that using the methods one time should be effective. In the course of my practice, I have frequently heard a client say, "I tried breathing when I was anxious and it didn't work." When I asked them how much they had practiced prior to using it for the anxiety, they have told me not at all or very little.

If you were playing baseball, would you expect to hit the ball during a game if you had never tried hitting a ball before? Of course not! However, people often believe that the techniques of CBT should be effective when they have never practiced them. I think this may be due to the techniques being very similar to other normal daily behaviors so people think that they should just be able to do it without an previous training or practice.

For example, they might think that since breathing is something they have done every day of their lives, they should be able to just slow it down at will. However, the fallacy here is that although they have been breathing their entire lives, they have not been regulating their breathing at will. These are two different things.

To put this in perspective, if I asked you to lower your body temperature (without any artificial means such as ice) you might tell me I'm crazy, that it can't be done.

But your brain has regulated your body temperature all your life just as it has regulated your breathing. So why do you believe that you can't lower your body temperature? Probably because you are not as aware of it as you are of your breathing. However, it is possible to change our physiological responses such as body temperature or blood pressure but it requires advanced practice.

The point is that practice is necessary to achieve the ability to change our physiological responses. We can't expect to be proficient at calming ourselves if we never practice the techniques. In CBT, homework is everything! (I know I repeated this concept several times but it's really important!)

ERROR 6: Believing CBT is the Same as Positive Thinking.

Another common error that people make about CBT is believing that it is all about positive thinking. I have frequently heard the remark, "I've tried that positive thinking—it doesn't work." However, CBT is not about positive thinking at all. In fact, positive thinking can be just as irrational and problematic as negative thinking.

For example, if someone believes "Everything will be okay. I don't need to worry" when a catastrophe is occurring, they may not take the necessary steps to control the situation which allows it to become worse.

There are times when we need to be concerned so that we can take appropriate action.

However, cognitive therapy approaches this in a realistic manner. If we are worrying about something that is not likely to occur, then we are making ourselves feel bad about something for little reason. Therefore, CBT is practical and realistic. It is about assessing our thinking so that we can take the most reasonable approach.

ERROR 7: Believing That Emotions Are Always Irrational.

Sometimes people take CBT too far and believe "If I'm completely rational, I won't feel anything." In fact, I heard Albert Ellis, one of the founding fathers of cognitive therapy, state this idea at a seminar. He said that if we are always rational, we would never be angry.

I hope I misunderstood his statement because I disagree with this concept. We are emotional beings. Emotions are an important part of our information processing system. Emotions allow us to be aware of problems that need to be addressed. So I neither believe that normal human beings can be completely free of emotions nor do I believe that it is healthy for us to not have emotions. Without emotions we can miss very important information in our environment.

For example, if you are threatened on a dark street late at night, what do you think reacts first? Do you think your emotions react first warning you of danger? Or do you intellectually assess the situation first? The initial emotional reaction prepares us to flee or to fight. The intellectual response is to determine what might be the better decision.

Certainly, our emotions can cause us to over-react. For instance, on that dark street you might feel threatened when you really aren't. And that is where CBT can help. It helps us to learn to keep our emotions in perspective and to recognize when we may be over-reacting. However, it should not be used to prevent emotions completely.

Many CBT therapists are finding standard CBT too limiting in this regard and there has been much movement to mindfulness-based CBT, often referred to as MBCT. MBCT focuses more on learning to tolerate the various emotional states through mindfulness approaches rather than trying to eliminate them. The intellectualized approach in standard CBT can be problematic for people who already have a more analytical style with avoidance of emotions.

ERROR 8: Placing Demands on Rationality

As people learn about CBT, sometimes they come to believe that if being rational is good and benefits their life, they might place a demand on themselves: "I SHOULD be completely rational all of the time."

Now, if you know anything about cognitive therapy, you know that this statement is irrational in itself for several reasons. One, is that it is a perfectionistic demand. Such demands are impossible to achieve which then causes additional distress and dysfunction. Cognitive therapy is about decreasing stress by being realistic in our expectations of ourselves.

Another reason this statement is irrational is because it is black-and-white reasoning which is the idea that if something is bad, the opposite should be good. But this isn't the case either. CBT is about finding balance whereas black-and-white thinking is about extremes. Even CBT when done to the extreme can be unhealthy.

I have often had this issue with my anxious clients. When we work on exposures to anxiety-provoking situations so that they can desensitize to the situation, they may come to believe that it is always good to challenge anxiety. In other words, if you are afraid of something, you need to face it. But that is not true because sometimes challenging a fear unnecessarily can cause more harm than good.

In particular, this attitude can cause unnecessary stress which may interfere with someone challenging the fears that are important to face. A person needs to evaluate a fear, determine in what way and how much it affects satisfaction in life, and then decide whether it needs to be dealt with. If I have a fear of snakes that doesn't really affect my life much, why should I face it? However, if it prevents me from doing something that is very important to me such as riding my bike on a wooded path, then I might choose to face it.

ERROR 9: Using CBT to Justify Not Being Responsible for Change.

Another area where people need to be cautious with CBT is using it as a justification to not change or try. Although CBT teaches a person to appreciate all aspects of themselves, it is meant to be used for building a foundation that provides a stable base from which a person can make changes.

Practitioners of CBT believe that if you feel good about yourself, you will have greater confidence to try new things and to make improvements. You are more able to acknowledge your flaws or areas in need of improvement without that acknowledgment causing you to feel bad. So we teach acceptance of yourself.

However, some people may use this concept as justification for not taking responsibility to make changes: "I am fine just the way I am." Or, they may focus on only a very specific aspect of a cognitive belief without considering the complexity of the situation. For instance, if I tell a woman "Certainly, you have the right to expect your husband to help with half the housework, but all rights come with consequences and you also need to consider the consequences of that demand and determine how it affects your marriage" I might soon hear from her husband saying that his wife told him that he should help with half the housework! She ignored the rest of the challenge to her thinking.

My point here is that CBT shouldn't be used as a justification for behavior that is unhealthy or inappropriate. It is meant to help a person examine thoughts and choices so as to improve satisfaction with life and with relationships. It is not meant to help a person to continue problematic behaviors. So even if the words are the same, it may not always mean the same thing. You need to look at the underlying meaning as well. In other words, a "should" is not always a "should." And to paraphrase Freud, "Sometimes a should is just a should (and nothing else)."

ERROR 10: Placing Demands on Mindfulness

Another frequent error is the tendency to place expectations or demands on the practice of mindfulness. The problem with this is that demands prevent the experience of mindfulness so the more we try to be mindful the less we are able to be mindful.

I experienced this years ago as a college student. During a womens' retreat, we were instructed to listen to some music to allow us to experience imagery to develop personal understanding. As I am lying on the mat and trying to allow the music to create images, I became very frustrated. I thought "I'm not having any images! Nothing is occurring! Everyone else is going to experience something and share what they are experiencing. And I have nothing! How embarrassing! This is a waste of time."

As you can see, I was not mindful at all. Of course no images occurred. I was so caught up in my (irrational) thinking that I couldn't be mindful. Finally, in frustration, I gave up. I said to myself "I don't care! I'm just going to listen to the music and not worry about trying to have any images."

As I continued to listen to the music and let all my thoughts drift away, I suddenly had one of the most powerful images that has guided my life to this day. More importantly, I learned the critical concept of not trying to be mindful. Instead of trying to be mindful, learn to allow yourself to be mindful. The more you remove the demand of mindfulness, the more you will achieve it.

Things You Should Know About Cognitive Behavioral Therapy

You've probably heard about cognitive behavioral therapy (CBT), a method of treatment based on evidence focused on changing negative thoughts and behaviours. Almost every self-help article online seems to mention it: Sleep problems? Try CBT. Trauma from childhood? Maybe CBT can help. Anxiety, depression, low self-esteem, flying fear, hangnails? CBT is your answer.

Basically, you have a good chance of receiving CBT or knowing someone you have. So what's it about? Is it really relieving psychological distress, and if so, how? How much does it cost, and can you use the techniques alone? Such details can be a mystery to the public at large. Fortunately, I'm a clinical psychologist who uses CBT in my practice, so I should be able to answer most of your questions. Now seeing the most common questions, we will do a repetition of what we have seen throughout the whole book. Let's see if you remember all the topics

1. First, what's the CBT heck?

CBT is one of a number of psychotherapy treatment methods. It is based on the assumption that many of the problems in life stem from faulty thoughts and behaviors (from which "cognitive "comes). We can alleviate distress by deliberately shifting them towards healthier, more productive goals. In practice, cognitive behavioral therapy usually involves identifying and replacing problem thoughts and behaviors with healthier responses. For example, in social situations, Jane Doe is anxious and has begun to avoid gatherings in favor of isolating evenings at home. A CBT therapist can teach her about the irrationally triggered fear response, teach her how to shift her thoughts and relax her body, and develop an action plan to help her stay calm while participating in this weekend's party. They will evaluate what worked and what didn't work next week and tweak their methods until Jane can socialize comfortably.

2. What kind of problems can CBT help and how do I know if it's right for me?

CBT is used for everything from phobia, anxiety, depression, trauma, self-esteem and ADHD to relationship problems such as poor communication or your partner's unrealistic expectations. In essence, if it's a problem involving thoughts and behaviors (which covers a lot of ground), CBT has a treatment approach. Is it okay for you? That's a hard question. Do your problems have to do with how you think and act? Do you ruminate about a previous breakup, for example, or do you find yourself mindlessly shopping online? If so, yes, you might benefit from CBT. If you are more concerned about your purpose or meaning in life, or what moments of your past color you are today, there may be other approaches that are better suited to you (and we will get to that in question #9).

3. What is the popularity of CBT?

One of the reasons why CBT is so well known and widely used is that it has been so extensively studied. Studying is a good way because it emphasizes short, direct, solution-oriented interventions. In other words, the objective is to bring about clear, measurable changes in thinking and behaviour, which is a gold mine for researchers. It also means that you can see quick results. Since a high percentage of people in our practice deal with some form of anxiety (social anxiety, anxiety about health or disease, OCD, panic, etc.), it is a central part of the work to be able to gently challenge people to confront their fears and develop new ways of relating to their own thoughts " CBT provides us with the tools to encourage people to do something very unpleasant: confront the things they avoided"

4. What's going on in a CBT session?

CBT is a form of psychotherapy, so you can expect the early sessions to be what you would see in any initial therapy sessions: Discussing payment information and cancelation policy, your therapy goals, your history and your problems review. After that, you'll talk about your struggles and try to formulate together the most effective response. In essence, the customer brings the problems they want to overcome or the situations they find stressful, and the therapist and client work together to create an action plan. An action plan means identifying problem thoughts or behaviours, finding a way to change them and developing a strategy for this change in the coming week. There's "homework "here.

5. How are CBT homework?

CBT focuses on providing rapid (8 to 12 sessions, which are rapid according to therapeutic standards) and effective symptom reduction, which is best done throughout the week, not just during the therapy session. Typical homework may include relaxation exercises, keeping a journal of thoughts and emotions throughout the week, using worksheets that target a particular area of growth, reading a book that addresses your problems, or looking for situations to apply your new approach. For example, Jane may want to keep an eye on meet-up events that challenge her to overcome her fears while applying her new techniques for relaxation. Another example: Let's say that his negative internal self-talk is a major factor in John Doe 's depression-he constantly lowers himself on a loop. John and his CBT therapist can talk about a technique called "stop thinking, "in which he abruptly disrupts the flow of negative thoughts by yelling (in his mind) "stop! " as he turns his thoughts to something more positive, such as an affirmation or a meditation app. Homework can involve at least once every day practicing this technique until the next session. In the next session, John and his therapist will debrief, assess what worked and what didn't work, and tweak the process for the next week.

6. How long does CBT usually last?

One of CBT 's highlights is that it focuses on eliminating symptoms as quickly as possible, usually in a couple of weeks or months. Of course, people rarely have only one problem to work on in therapy, so this length depends on the number and severity of the problems, but briefness is essential for this approach. This leads to one of the main differences between CBT and many other forms of treatment. One of CBT 's founders, Donald Meichenbaum, says, "[We ask] what questions and how. While other treatment approaches spend a lot of time digging deeply and asking why you feel depressed, anxious or low self-esteem, CBT adheres to current thoughts and behaviors. CBT focuses on helping you reduce your fear rather than examining why you are afraid of snakes. While some people are happy to reduce their symptoms, others want to know why they first exist. Deeper approaches such as psychodynamic therapy may be more satisfactory for them.

7. Can people use CBT techniques outside of actual therapy sessions?

Did you ever keep a journal of gratitude? What about your donut intake monitoring? Did you track your daily steps or check your sleep? Then you're using some of CBT 's principles in your daily life. Many others CBT techniques can be found in books such as David Burns ' Feeling Good or Edmund Bourne 's Anxiety and Phobia Workbook, online, or in popular applications such as Headspace and Happify. But a period of time in structured therapy is still the best approach for a CBT course tailored to you and your problems.

8. How much does CBT cost and is it covered by insurance?

CBT is psychotherapy, so if your insurance covers psychotherapy or behavioral medicine, most, if not all, of your CBT treatment should be covered. If you pay out of the pocket, the cost of CBT ranges from free or sliding in some community clinics to $200 + per session in a private practice. Once again, the time someone spends on treatment is usually less than other treatment approaches, so it can be cheaper in the long run. On a therapist finder website such as Psychology Today or Good Therapy, you can search for a therapist who practices CBT and fits your budget.

9. Are there any sides to choose CBT compared to another type of treatment?

Some clients may feel that therapy is a place where they come and process their experiences with their therapist's gentle facilitation. Their main objective may not be to deal with a particular symptom or problem habit, but rather with general growth and a long-term relationship with a therapist. They may want to explore their memories, dreams and early relationships with their therapist's guidance. Since CBT can be a more direct and practical therapy style, it may not be helpful for someone who is looking for this kind of profound, relationship work. However, many qualified CBT therapists are very flexible in their approach and can adapt to the needs of a variety of clients. As Dr. Hsia admits, CBT is not without its criticisms. " CBT 's fair criticism highlights its assumptions about what helps people get better, "he says. Again, CBT focuses on symptoms rather than the deeper roots of these symptoms, and some psychologists who feel that the deeper roots are essential would consider CBT to be short-sighted. In the end, you have to find out what works best for you, which may take some trial and mistake. It may be helpful to talk to your therapist (or potential therapist) about what you are looking for and ask them how they approach the treatment. Whether you are receiving CBT treatment or another method, the most important thing is that you feel a safe, confident relationship with your therapist and that the treatment makes sense for you.

Pros & Cons of CBT Therapy

There is always a risk that bad feelings will return, but it should be easier for you to control them with your CBT skills. This is why it is important to continue to practice your CBT skills even after you feel better and have completed your sessions. CBT may not, however, be successful or appropriate for everyone.

Below are some of the advantages and disadvantages of the approach.

The benefits of CBT

In cases where the patient does not see an improvement with medication alone, cognitive behavioral therapy is effective. It does not take as long as other types of treatment. Cognitive behavioral therapy is also structured in such a way that it can be offered in different formats, including group therapy, self-help books and online programmes. Most people receive cognitive behavioral treatment because it teaches them practical strategies that can be applied to everyday life. It offers patients solutions to improve their minds every day.

Below are some specific benefits of CBT;

• can be as effective as medication in the treatment of certain mental health disorders and

• can be helpful in cases where medication alone has not worked. Compared to other speech therapies, it can be completed in a relatively short time.

• Focus on retraining your thoughts and changing behaviors to change your feelings. CBT 's highly structured nature means that it can be provided in various formats, including in groups, self-help books and computer programs.

• The skills you learn in CBT are useful, practical and helpful strategies that can be incorporated into everyday life to help you better cope with future stresses and difficulties even after treatment is complete.

CBT 's disadvantages

First of all, a high level of commitment is required for cognitive behavioral therapy. If you don't cooperate, your therapist can't help you. If you have a busy lifestyle, the frequency of cognitive behavioral therapy sessions may be a challenge. In addition, it may not be a good choice for people with complex mental problems or learning difficulties due to the highly structured nature of cognitive behavioral therapy. Many people fear cognitive behavioral treatment because it forces them to face their root of anxiety. You should be prepared for an initial period of fear and discomfort if you choose this type of therapy. Another significant disadvantage is that cognitive behavioral therapy does not address other problems, such as families and social factors, that can have a significant impact on the patient. It is not suitable for everyone, however effective cognitive behavioral therapy is. Although it can work wonderful things for your friends, you may not benefit from it. In addition, cognitive behavioral therapy tends to focus instead of the cause on the specific problem. The therapy focuses on the identification of current problems rather than past problems. Someone with a mental condition resulting from childhood trauma, for example, may not see much improvement in cognitive behavioral therapy.

Below are some specific disadvantages of CBT;

• To take advantage of CBT, you must commit to the process. A therapist can help and advise you, but without your cooperation, you can't get rid of your problems.

• It can take a lot of your time to attend regular CBT sessions and perform any additional work between sessions.

• It may not be appropriate for people with more complex mental health needs or learning difficulties due to the structured nature of CBT.

• Since CBT can confront your emotions and anxieties, you may experience initial periods of anxiety or emotional discomfort.

• Some critics argue that CBT does not address the possible underlying causes of mental health conditions, such as an unhappy childhood, because it only addresses current problems and focuses on specific issues.

• CBT focuses on the ability of the individual to change himself (his thoughts, feelings and behaviors) and does not address broader problems in systems or families that often have a significant impact on the health and well-being of an individual.